— FATHERS WHO FAIL —

— FATHERS WHO FAIL —
Shame and Psychopathology in the Family System

Melvin R. Lansky

Routledge
Taylor & Francis Group
New York   London

Routledge is an imprint of the
Taylor & Francis Group, an informa business

Published by The Analytic Press, Inc.
365 Broadway, Hillsdale, NJ 07642

Reprinted 2009 by Routledge

Earlier versions of chapters 2–15 are reprinted here, in revised form, by permission of their
copyright owners: chs. 2 & 15—*Fathers and Their Families,* ed. S. Cath, A. Gurwitt & L.
Gunsberg (1989, The Analytic Press); ch. 3—*The Borderline Patient,* Vol. 2, ed. J. Grotstein, M.
Solomon & J. Lang (1987, The Analytic Press); ch. 4—*International Journal of Psychoanalytic
Psychotherapy* (1980, 8:429–456); ch. 5—*International Journal of Psychoanalytic Psychotherapy* (1985, 11:409–425); ch. 6—*British Journal of Psychotherapy* (1989, 6:10–25); ch. 7—
Psychoanalytic Inquiry (1987, 7:77–98); ch. 8—*International Journal of Family Psychiatry*
(1984, 5:151–168); ch. 9—*International Journal of Family Psychiatry* (1984, 5:21–40); *ch.
10—The Many Faces of Shame,* ed. D. Nathanson (1987, Guilford Press); ch. 11—*International
Journal of Family Psychiatry* (1989, 10:159–178); ch. 12—*British Journal of Psychotherapy*
(1991, 7:230–242); ch. 13—*Family Systems Medicine* (1990, 8:231–240); ch. 14—*Hillside
Journal of Clinical Psychiatry* (1989, 11:169–183).

Library of Congress Cataloging in Publication Data

Lansky, Melvin R.
   Fathers who fail : shame and psychopathology in the family system
   / by Melvin R. Lansky.
      p.   cm.
   Includes bibliographical references and index.
   ISBN 0-88163-105-1
   1. Mentally ill fathers. 2. Mentally ill fathers—Family
relationships. 3. Problem families. 4. Shame. I. Title.
RC451.4.F38L35   1992
616.89—dc20   92-18664
                                                        CIP

Printed in the United States of America
10 9 8 7 6 5 4 3 2 1

For Karen, Madeleine, and Joshua

.

Contents

IV. Shame and Symptom Formation

V. Treatment Difficulties

Preface

This collection of essays is assembled from writings published separately over a period of 15 years. The reader perusing the book as a whole will notice both differences in focus from the point of view of psychoanalysis to that of family therapy to that of general psychiatry and differences in emphasis because the papers, even though updated for this volume, were written in very different stages of what has been a continually evolving perspective on the spectrum of psychopathological predicaments found in the psychiatrically impaired father. What is more, the papers vary in the extent to which they concern fathers specifically or psychopathology commonly found in impaired fathers in a more general light. The book as a whole, then, has discontinuous and overlapping areas, redundancies, and omissions. It is nonetheless a complete work, not a motley — one which attempts an approach to the psychiatrically impaired father through an explication of the intrapsychic and intrafamilial context of paternal failure that is due to severe psychopathology.

Part I, an introductory essay, deals with the themes that comprise the rest of the book. Part II wrestles with the topic of what constitutes data about fathering, considered both from the point of view of the external observer and from that of the person recalling experiences with his or her own father. Part III (Chapters 3 to 7) concerns the intrafamilial defenses against shame. I have emphasized overt conflict or blame, pathological preoccupation, and impulsive action. Part IV moves to the arena of conflict escalation to the point of symptoms, and points to the role of shame in symptom formation in domestic violence, suicide, organic brain disorders, and the sequelae of trauma. Part V consists of a single, final chapter dealing with treatment difficulties.

The book, then, presents a progression from personality considered psychoanalytically to family systems to symptoms to treatment difficulties. Symptomatology that is among the most serious faced by general psychiatry is discussed in the context of the family and seen in terms of the escalation of conflict that results from unacknowledged shame. Finally, I consider treatment difficulties in treating the psychiatrically impaired father when that father is outside of and rejected by his family system.

Drawing as I have from psychoanalysis, systems theory, and general psychiatry to formulate an overall dynamic understanding of the psychiatrically impaired father, I have attempted an integration that leaves out many other aspects of paternity. Many of these have been dealt with in the recent and excellent contributions to the study of fatherhood in collections edited by Cath and his collaborators and by Lamb.

I owe many debts of thanks to colleagues who have expanded my knowledge and supported my efforts in the study of psychoanalysis, of family systems, of dynamic general psychiatry, and of the study of fathers. To name a few: Leon Wurmser, Thomas Scheff, Suzanne Retzinger, Jack Katz, Benjamin Kilborne, and Andrew Morrison have expanded my grasp of shame in the interpersonal and intrafamilial context. My colleagues on the Family Treatment Program at the Brentwood Division of the West Los Angeles V.A. Medical Center have worked with me for many years, struggling with these problems in a setting where they were vital day-to-day treatment issues: Carol Bley and Geneva McVey have been my comrades in arms and treatment collaborators for almost two decades. Several years of intensive work from 1983 to 1986 with Ellen Simenstad resulted in an in-depth study of over 100 psychiatrically hospitalized fathers admitted to the Family Treatment Program for clinical problems that covered the entire gamut of psychopathology. Supportive leadership at the Brentwood Division of the West Los Angeles V.A. Medical Center and the UCLA Department of Psychiatry has allowed my work to evolve and continue. I am grateful to Drs. L.J. West, Max Unger, Manuel Straker, Milton Greenblatt, Fritz Redlich, Norman Brill, the late Ransom Arthur, Mark Mills, Don Flinn, Gary Tischler, Cyril Barnert, and Spencer Eth for the continued understanding and help that I have received from them over the years.

From my colleagues in the Issues in Paternity discussion group of the American Psychoanalytic Association meetings, I owe much for their help in my development of a psychoanalytic focus on fathers: Drs. Stanley Cath, Alan Gurwitt, John Munder Ross, Linda Gunsberg, Richard Atkins, and others have provided me with stimulation, insight, and encouragement over the last twelve years.

I am grateful also to The Analytic Press and especially to Dr. Paul Stepansky and Eleanor Starke Kobrin for their help, patience, and encouragement in allowing this book to emerge in its present form.

— I —

Introduction

The concept of a perspicuous
representation is of fundamental
significance to us. It earmarks the
form of account we give, the way
we look at things.

Wittgenstein
Philosophical Investigations, I, 122

1

Symptom, System, and Personality in Fathers Who Fail

This is a book on psychopathology in the family system applied to the special predicament of the psychiatrically impaired father. The essays that make up this volume should not be thought of as a work on development. Their central concern is neither the role of the father in development nor fatherhood as a developmental phase. I have not attempted to add to the recently burgeoning appearance of literature on the father considered developmentally, but rather to assemble in one volume a collection of preliminary attempts to understand the psychiatrically impaired father in a truly dynamic way. The contributions concern psychopathology with special emphasis on characterologic adaptation to narcissistic pathology, that is, of proneness to shame and fragmentation proneness within the family system. These papers, therefore, deal with family dynamics in general and the specific dynamics of handling shame in particular.

The dynamically informed literature—that is—the literature drawing from psychoanalysis and informed by a knowledge of family systems—that concerns impaired fathers is so scant as to be almost nonexistent. Even the recent explosion of interest in the father in child development and fatherhood as a developmental stage (Abelin, 1971, 1975; Lamb, 1976, 1981, 1986; Cath, Gurwitt, and Ross, 1982; Cath, Gurwitt, and Gunsberg, 1989) has contributed very little to the understanding of the psychiatrically impaired father.

Until the early 1970s, there was a surprising dearth of work on the role of father in development. In view of the early and one-sided psychoanalytic view of the father as a figure of central importance, such neglect is

3

surprising and somewhat counterintuitive. Early formulations, centering as they did on the castration complex in both sexes, were phallocentric and seemingly patrocentric. They emphasized males almost entirely to the neglect of issues and conflicts of nurturance and mothering.

The evolution of psychoanalysis to include what has come to be called object relations theories, along with an increased psychoanalytic understanding of nurturance within the mother-child dyad, brought with it a new-found interest in child development, in mothers, and in the "mammocentric" conflicts that had to do with symbiosis, separation, and the need for nurturance. This expanded perspective, together with the direct observation of child development that flourished after World War II, resulted in the acquisition of a substantial body of knowledge about development and a heightened awareness of the mother-child dyad rather than an exclusive focus on the individual child. This line of thinking is epitomized by Winnicott's pronouncement, "There is no such thing as a baby." That is, there is no such thing as a baby outside the context of the baby's relationship to the human environment, especially to the mother. Developmental observations, for reasons of conceptualization and clear-cut data collection, have often been confined to the dyad. In this context, the study of the mother-child bond and of mothering as a developmental phase emerged and became an object for independent study.

Only secondarily, and after decades of study of child development, of the mother-child unit, and of motherhood as a developmental phase, did awareness of fatherhood, fathering, the father-child bond, and the relation of father to the family as a whole become evident. It then became clear that the original psychoanalytic patrocentric, phallocentric point of view was based on fantasies about father and about the phallus, not on observations about actual fathers and actual men in relation to their children and their families. Only when knowledge of development expanded to include family systems (that is, at least three people) and began to conceptualize extra dyadic data, did such a literature emerge (Abelin, 1971, 1975; Cath et al., 1982, 1989; Lamb, 1976, 1981, 1986).

The reasons for this neglect of the study of the father are complex. They have to do in part with the fact that mothering and fathering are not exactly symmetrical concepts. In common usage, mothering and the wish for a mother are felt to be dyadic and more or less observable. One can imagine where the cameraman, so to speak, would stand to film data associated in the common consciousness with the experience-close, dyadic caretaking connoted by the word, "mothering." But "fathering" itself is more context- and system-dependent. In the common conscious and perhaps in unconscious fantasy, "I want my father" has much more to do with a wish to master the world and to face challenges than it does with the more regressive wish to be cared for and exempted from responsibility that is connected with a wish for mothering. These are, of course, over-simplifications, but they point to the methodological and conceptual difficulty in specifying what observational data constitute "fathering." It is not always easy to say where the cameraman would stand to photograph the activities that constitute fathering. Are these the data of providing for the family? protecting? counseling? Or are the data details of the one-to-one relationship between father and child? Or are they, in fact, what the mother tells the child about father and the implications of that information for the kind and quality of fathering that is taking place? All of these and other sources of data about the nature of fathering merge and coalesce in the mind of the developing child and of the adult so that, clinically as well as observationally, it becomes very difficult to ascertain what the data are that underlie the individual's notion about his or her own fathering and his or her relationship with father.

Among the reasons for the neglect of the psychiatrically impaired father are all the problems of conceptualizing and studying fatherhood and fathering. But paramount among them is the reluctance of those fathers to acknowledge and discuss what is one of the most mortifying of human predicaments: the awareness of failure in the parental role. Only with the advent of renewed and sophisticated attention to the dynamics of shame (Kohut, 1971, Lewis, 1971) could this silence—in the literature and in fathers themselves—be better understood. Shame has been called the veiled companion of narcissism. It is certainly the veiled and silent companion of the narcissistic injury of men who see themselves as having failed in the paternal role.

This book is not intended to be a balanced discussion of psychopathology in fathers. It is a very specific book, not a general one. What strength it has derives from the concrete circumstances under which the clinical observations put forward were made. My clinical experience over the last two decades has been divided between the office practice of psychoanalysis, psychoanalytic psychotherapy, and family therapy, and my academic post as founder and director of a family-oriented inpatient service at the Brentwood Division of the West Los Angeles V.A. Medical Center. Those two settings, however much they enrich each other and however much each provides counterpoint to the perspective offered by the other, provide a limited part of the full spectrum of psychopathology in fathers. I have resolved nonetheless not to stray beyond that which was in the purview of my personal, in-depth, clinical experience, and the limitations of this collection of papers reflect the limitations of that experience.

The theoretical underpinnings of these essays are intimately tied to my evolving appreciation of shame, of narcissistic vulnerability and proneness to humiliation, and of regulation or failure of the regulation of narcissistic equilibrium in the family. The failure of the fathers reflects the cost to offspring of both the regulation and the effects of disregulation of narcissistic equilibrium in the family. The papers deal, then, with the relation of symptoms (not always in the impaired father himself) to the family system and to the personality.

The two largest sections of the book, Parts III and IV, concern respectively the regulation of narcissistic equilibrium in families and the symptomatic disequilibrium due to the shame that results from the escalation of conflict. It is my hope that a perspicuous view of the underlying sources of paternal dysfunction will enable the understanding of the cost to family members, the father included, of these familial defensive processes and regulatory mechanisms.

The essays in Part III explore regulatory mechanisms that deal, at however great a cost, with minimizing shame and preserving the narcissistic equilibrium in the family. Even a defense that is successful in terms of the father's emotional safety and narcissistic equilibrium may be fearfully costly to others in the family. Pathological preoccupation (chapter 5), for example, characterized by emotional absence while the father is physically present, often has devastating effects on the well-being of others in the family and provokes or precipitates more visible, overt conflict, blaming, depression, or symptomatic impulsive action in others.

Symptomatic impulsive action (chapter 6) is the central psychopathological concept that unifies Parts III and IV. Impulsive symptomatology seen in the context of narcissistic breakdown, dissociation, and attempted restitution foreshadows the discussions in chapters 8 through 14, which cover specific symptoms. Symptoms are seen in the light of the escalation of conflict and the failure of intrafamilial defenses to contain shame. What we see clinically as symptoms are chaotic attempts to repair fragmented and dissociative states that result from personality breakdown. In Part IV, symptoms are discussed under the topics of domestic violence, suicidality, catastrophic reactions in organic brain syndrome, and the effects of adult trauma on young adults with preexisting and predisposing childhood trauma.

The role of shame in these varied clinical situations has came to be understood only recently. My evolving understanding of the role of shame owes much to two great books on the subject, which both appeared in 1971: Heinz Kohut's *Analysis of the Self* and Helen Block Lewis's *Shame and Guilt in Neurosis*. Kohut's understanding of the relation of shame to fragmentation or disorganization of the personality, and Lewis's brilliant and unequivocal demonstration of the progression of unacknowledged shame into rage are pivotal to an understanding of the all-too-rarely studied phenomenon of conflict escalation. For brilliant insights into the topic of conflict escalation and its relation to shame and threats to the social bond, I am indebted to the writings of and numerous personal discussions with Professor Thomas Scheff (1987, 1990) and Dr. Suzanne Retzinger (1987, 1991). Symptoms that result from the escalation of conflict are best seen in the light of a family system that fails to provide defenses sufficient to contain shame; lacks capacities for acknowledgment, deference, or empathy sufficient to dissipate shame; and hence fails to prevent unmanageable shame from arising and conflict from escalating.

My clinical interest in fathers arose both from psychoanalytic sources and from the study of defensive processes in family systems in a population of adult hospital patients, predominantly males. These investigations were given impetus by my involvement in "Issues in Paternity" discussion groups at meetings of the American Psychoanalytic Association for a period of over more than a decade. I am indebted to the writings of and my discussions with Drs. Stanley Cath, Allen Gurwitt, John Munder Ross, Ernst Abelin, Linda Gunsberg, and Richard Atkins, to name only a few of the many creative and stimulating colleagues who have pioneered the psychoanalytic study of the father.

This psychoanalytic interest evolved *pari passu* with the sustained study of hospitalized fathers on the Family Treatment Program at the West Los Angeles Veterans Administration Medical Center, especially from 1983 to 1986, when my colleagues and I studied intensively every father admitted to our unit (Lansky, 1984a). My colleagues, Carol Bley, Geneva McVey, and especially Ellen Simenstad, who was my major collaborator on the fathers study, spent those years systematically exploring the experience of impaired fathers hospitalized for a variety of diagnoses and predicaments: schizophrenia, bipolar illness, chemical dependency, domestic violence, suicidality, organic brain syndrome, posttraumatic stress disorders, and manifestations of character pathology.

We were privy to the agony of many of these fathers at revealing the devastating absence of satisfactory experiences with their own fathers. We could appreciate the insurmountable residual deficits that they felt had left them chronically ashamed and unprepared for adulthood generally and fatherhood in particular. We heard horrible invectives against wives, who were often blamed for isolating the father from the family and alienating his children from him. No matter what the father's role in bringing such ostracism upon himself, the suffering, alienation, and sense of betrayal and failure were horrible to hear. Most overwhelming of all was the fathers' admission of failure with their own sons and daughters and the sense of shame, defeat, and worthlessness that followed in the wake of that failure. These fathers, many of whom had been embittered by poor relationships with their own fathers, realized that they had failed utterly in the paternal role. They had gained power by rage and intimidation rather than by generativity and guidance. Uncontrollable rage or florid chemical dependency had rendered them feared, loathed, and held in contempt by their offspring as well as their wives. The deficits posed by severe psychiatric illness had left them unprepared and unequipped to father their children. The residua of combat experience, withdrawal due to psychiatric illness, the vulnerability to narcissistic wounds in deep character pathology had left them self-absorbed, unstable, unable to tolerate closeness from the children they also idealized and adored. Most horrible and shameful of all was the realization that they had given no better than they had received from their own fathers. These experiences of failure were among the most humiliating and tragic we have ever encountered.

Years of clinical experience with a wide range of psychiatrically impaired fathers have convinced me that these men will talk about almost anything rather than admit these failures at fathering. They complain of "voices" or of suicidality. They admit to substance abuse, domestic violence, even homicide. They acknowledge failures on jobs, in marriages, and in relation to their families of origin. But they will do almost anything rather than face their failures as fathers. They will even absent themselves from broken families and from children for decades or permanently to avoid the horrible self-confrontation with these failures and the confirmation of the fact that their children are truly ashamed of them.

When faced with their failures, often when encounters with offspring or acknowledgment of failure is forced upon them by circumstances, psychiatrically impaired fathers experience a narcissistic mortification that is one of the most devastating spectacles that I have ever witnessed. When circumstances or family members confront the father with his failure and the consequences of that failure—often failure that the father sees in the light of his own highly idealized aspirations of what a father should be providing for his children—the usual result is a state of shameful futility that is like no other anguish imaginable. That anguish is often unbearable to witness even by seasoned professionals who work year in and year out with psychotic decompensation, crushing depression, and suicidal despair.

A family systems perspective is the key to tying these observations together. What developmentally oriented psychoanalysis ever-so-slowly acknowledged only in the 1970s the family therapy movement put forward from the start: that the individual and the dyad, even the mother-child dyad, are powerfully under the sway of the entire family system, not only fathers, siblings, and extended family currently in relational equilibrium with each other, but also the family over generations. The intergenerational family therapists, such as Lidz, Fleck, Bowen, Framo and Nagy, have had an enormous influence on my conceptualizations and investigations.

To their ideas I have attempted to add the understanding of collusion in transpersonal defense, especially defense against shame. I have been greatly influenced by Melanie Klein's (1946) concept of projective identification, the bridge between individual and systems thinking, and the unconscious underpinning of collusion in intimate relationships. I part with the Kleinian school, however, in seeing aggression and envy not as primary but as secondary to unacknowledged shame. Here the influence of Kohut, Lewis, Scheff, and Retzinger has been great.

The sources of shame include developmental arrests that leave one with a sense of dirtiness, emptiness, and unloveability. I have come to appreciate, in addition to these, the sense of shame posed by the fragmentation proneness of the incohesive self and its shame-producing reliance on selfobjects (Kohut, 1971), as well as the shame prompting the struggle against identification (Greenson, 1954), especially with a same-sex parent who was held in contempt.

Realizing that shame, from whatever source, underlies the manifestation of envy has enabled me to bridge some central and profound Kleinian notions with a nuanced understanding of shame and its sources and the effects of unacknowledged shame.

My thinking about self, object, and affect, paralleling that in psychoanalysis generally, has evolved considerably. It began with relatively static notions of a more or less stable self in relation to more or less stable others and regulated by affects, especially fear and guilt, and defenses against them. This basic, albeit inaccurate, model has become progressively modified by the implications of the insights known long ago to the philosophers (Hegel, 1807; Sartre, 1945) that a Self is only a self in relation to the Other that defines it. I have drawn from the works not only of Hegel and Sartre but also of 20th-century sociologists (Goffman, 1959; Scheff. 1987, 1990; Retzinger, 1987, 1991; Katz, 1988) a deep understanding of the tentativeness of the sense of self and the social bond that unites it to others. I have come to appreciate the centrality of shame as the regulatory emotion of that sense of self in relation to the other (Scheff, 1990) and of the contingency of the experience of self on recognition (Hegel), affirmation, or, as Goffman (1959) put it, deference from the other. Failure to attain that recognition, deference, or, as therapists might prefer, empathy constitutes a danger to the standing of the self among others—a weakening of the social bond itself. The master regulatory emotion signaling threat to that bonding to others, which empowers the sense of self, is shame. Shame is either a signal of danger to the bond or the end-stage affect signaling loss of the bond. Shame may denote either the affect itself or the social comportment aimed at avoiding the threat to the bond; that is, it is the defense against shame (Schneider, 1977). The French words *honte* and *pudeur* well convey the distinction between the affect and the defense.

The writings of Heinz Kohut (1971, 1972, 1977) of course have added a psychoanalytic, especially an object relations, dimension to these observations. Kohut, whose emphasis was on fragmentation of the personality, loss of the sense of self, and the use of the object specifically to ensure cohesion of the self, drew attention not only to the ubiquity of the need for what he called selfobject functioning, but also the centrality of shame, rather than guilt or fear, as a regulatory emotion ensuring continuity of the self. The personality, with its varying needs for buttressing self-experience by recognition, deference, empathy, that is to say, by *selfobject functioning*, is always in a steady state with the social surround and always vulnerable to embarrassment and narcissistic injury, or shame and fragmentation.

As much as I owe to Kohut, my own point of view differs significantly from his in several important respects. First, I see his central insights as expanding, not narrowing, the scope of intrapsychic conflict. To see narcissistic disturbance simply as a deficit or a developmental arrest due to a lack of satisfactory mirroring or idealizing experience is, as I see it, naive and outright incorrect. The central Kohutian vision of the ubiquity of selfobject needs and the fixation of the personality to selfobject relations in narcissistically vulnerable persons increases the scope of conflict dramatically. That an empathic break, a narcissistic wound, the change in distance from a selfobject, or the failure of a close person to provide selfobject functioning threatens the immediate integrity of the self does not at all imply that deficit supersedes conflict. It adds to the magnitude of conflicts and compounds them immeasurably.

The exacerbation of conflict and shame by the presence of severe selfobject fixations becomes the more dramatic outside of the psychoanalytic situation when one considers the networks of intimate relationships in which *each* member both is desperately needy of selfobject functioning and also serves such selfobject functioning for others. Seen from the perspective of a psychotherapeutic or psychoanalytic dyad, the desperate struggle for autonomy and integrity and the intimate struggle *not to be a selfobject* for the other—that is, *not to be reified as a simple function*—become more dramatic. In many dysfunctional families in which there is a life-and-death struggle to avoid psychic annihilation, to provide rather than receive empathy, *it is the loser who becomes the selfobject*. The possibilities for shame expand exponentially when one considers not simply the dyad (or half-dyad, as in a psychoanalytic situation, where the analyst's needs are never really in focus), but systems in which one may be ashamed both of one's need for the Other. Secondarily the same person may feel guilty about being ashamed of the needed person and guilty about his or her resentful or envious attacks on the person for whom one has a disowned need as a selfobject. Many dysfunctional families have networks of conflicts centering on shame about basic neediness of the other but also secondarily involving guilt and fear.

A second difference with Kohut and with most of the self psychology school concerns the role of aggression. While I agree with Kohut and his followers that fragmentation and shame are more basic and fundamental than aggression, and I certainly disagree with formulations based on a primary aggressive drive, I do not believe that Kohut or his proponents fully appreciate the intimate connection between shame and rage. Kohut (1972) did take up the subject of narcissistic rage but, in my opinion, not in great enough depth to develop an adequate psychology of human affect and interaction that can be applied to dysfunctional families and symptomatic individuals in the family context. Here I draw on the seminal work of Helen Block Lewis, never sufficiently recognized in psychoanalytic circles, and of her colleagues, Thomas Scheff and Suzanne Retzinger. Lewis (1971), in her monumental *Shame and Guilt in Neurosis*, pointed to the unequivocal relationship between unacknowledged shame and rage. Nuanced studies by Scheff and Retzinger have developed this connection further. Put psychoanalytically, these observations point to the fact that *we have grossly underestimated the ubiquity of the transformation of shame into narcissistic rage in social relations generally* (Morrison, 1989). Scheff (1990) has developed these ideas brilliantly from a sociological point of view.

This book is an attempt to integrate them further into psychoanalytic and family systems thinking. If the ramifications of this integration are fully understood, one begins to see the intimate relation of *shame*, the master emotion regulating threat to the social bond, and *envy*, which is so destructive to that bond. Envy underlies a vast array of clinical phenomenology that includes hostile dependency, domestic violence, and a whole array of manifestations of destructive ambivalence in human relations generally. Shame and envy are both *self-conscious emotions* that result from seeing oneself through the eyes of another in such a way that a prideful bonding to others is threatened. My own clinical and theoretical contributions have been unified by the realization that Lewis' central insight—that unacknowledged shame is transformed into rage—essentially links narcissistic rage and envy to unacknowledged shame.

This central insight, the relation of unacknowledged shame to envy, sets the stage for consideration of another major pathological feature linking symptom, system, and personality, that is, the *escalation of conflict* (Retzinger, 1987, 1991). That two or more vulnerable, fragmentation-prone personalities become bonded to each other with day-to-day requirements for recognition, deference, empathy, that is to say, selfobject functioning; that these needs are experienced as shameful; and that those very needs often preclude one's providing them for another, is the central theoretical formulation underlying the understanding of conflict escalation and uniting the conceptualizations of symptom, system, and personality that form the basis for this collection of clinical papers.

These essays are based on articles and book chapters written over a period of 15 years. All have been edited and updated. Some, especially chapter 4, have undergone major revisions to bring them into line with my current thinking on narcissistic vulnerability in the family system.

Part II contains a single entry, "The Paternal Imago," which is aimed at conveying the complexity of data concerning fathers and the difficulties concerned with the conceptualization of the father and of the experience of fathering—difficulties that arise both with clinical attention to what patients say is their experience with their fathers and with observational investigations and the data they choose to include.

Part III concerns defenses against shame, or regulatory mechanisms that deal with narcissistic equilibrium in the family, over conflict (blame), rationalized emotional absence that has a powerful effect on intimates (pathologic preoccupation), and symptomatic impulsive action.

Understanding of the natural history common to various types of impulsive action is the conceptual bridge to the discussion of symptoms taken up in the chapters in Part IV. That section attempts to focus on symptoms as reactions to disturbances in narcissistic equilibrium that threaten social bondings and, in some sense, however destructive, that are attempts aimed at restitutive repairing of those bonds. In providing this focus, I hope to help the reader achieve a perspective on the sources of symptoms—not simply the individual manifesting them, but the disturbance in the entire family system.

The emphasis in this book is much more on clinical understanding of fathers who fail than on treatment. At this early stage of our understanding, a broad perspective of pathological processes is far more useful than the glib or formulaic precepts that inevitably take the place of an in-depth understanding of very complex phenomena underlying problems that do not have simple solutions. Part V consists of a single chapter on conflict and resistance, emphasizing unconscious obstacles to treatment both in impaired fathers and in therapists—obstacles that threaten to impede or undermine any treatment focus and strategy.

These chapters sketch the progression of vulnerability and turbulence from the personality to the family system to the symptom. Proneness to fragmentation and shame necessitate a certain type of transpersonal defense in relationships to protect against personality disorganization, modulate outbursts of narcissistic rage, and regulate excessive needs to keep intimates at optimal distance. By optimal distance, I mean the emotional distance that is the most comfortable compromise in minimizing fear of intimacy, exposure, or impingement if the Other is too close and fear of abandonment if the Other is too far away. The failure of such regulation produces symptoms, breakdown products of narcissistic vulnerability in the personality that either are not contained or are provoked by the family system of vulnerable persons.

Although treatment per se is beyond the scope of this book, a discerning view of the pathology involved has far-reaching implications for treatment strategies of many types. Treatment of these difficulties often must move in the reverse direction from the origin of the problems. We start with symptoms—especially if they are destructive—and proceed only later to the system that binds, but that also may enable, the symptoms; and, still later, to the vulnerable personality system that takes refuge in a pathological family system or disorganizes into impulsive symptomatology.

I view treatment, not from the vantage point of the psychoanalyst or of the family therapist, but from that of the dynamically oriented general psychiatrist who draws from psychoanalysis and from family systems theory to implement treatment strategies of all kinds. Whereas some of the clinical situations discussed in Part III may respond to a single modality—psychotherapy or family therapy, and, in some cases, unmodified psychoanalysis—the more serious symptomatic predicaments discussed in Part IV more often than not require multimodal responses—not only individual and family psychotherapies, but also hospitalization, psychotropic medication, 12-step programs, and, at times, others. The principles underlying the integration of such treatment modalities would require a separate volume of at least this size. Suffice it to say that this book will have been successful if it provides a wide-ranging view of the pathological predicaments such modalities would be assembled to address.

— II —

General

The Emperor of Russia was my father.
O that he were alive, and here beholding
His daughter's trial! That he did but see
The flatness of my misery, yet with eyes
Of pity, not revenge.

Shakespeare
The Winter's Tale, III, ii, 119-123

2

The Paternal Imago

THE CONCEPT

Laplanche and Pontalis (1973) defined the concept of "imago" as follows: "Unconscious prototypical figure which orientates the subject's way of apprehending others; it is built up on the basis of the first real and fantasied relationships within the family environment" (p. 211). They warned against simplifying this definition into something that would make "imago" closer in meaning to "image," that is, a distillate of real memories of the person in question. Nonetheless, imago has commonly been felt to be a prototypic imaginary construct, a fantasied photograph, as it were, codifying the relationship with the other. It would be, of course, naive to assume that such a memory is undistorted. Memories or reactivations of attitudes toward persons resembling the prototype in some way are distorted by the defensive needs of the subject.

Common psychoanalytic usage places the paternal imago as one of many object representations colored by defensive needs but, like the maternal imago or other images, substantially derived from real experiences with that object. The common connotation of the paternal imago, therefore, is that of a defensively modified residue of the subject's relationship with father that serves as a template for reactions to those who, in some important way, signify father in later life. Data concerning the paternal imago are inferred from the patient's associations or responses to people in similar roles. Distortions woven into the (inferred) imago are unraveled *pari passu* with the unfolding and resolution of the transference

17

neurosis. The transference neurosis provides insight into distortions based on provocation, hostility, devaluation, and other defensive operations that color, both positively and negatively, the subject's view of father.

I maintain that such a notion of the paternal imago, however straightforward it may appear, is oversimplified and, further, that this oversimplification may hold us captive, much to the detriment of theory, clinical practice, and the relationship between theory and practice. There is a superficial plausibility in conceptualizing the paternal imago as a buildup of associations, expectations, and reactions derived from actual transactions with father himself. But such a view, with its assumptions that data derive from the dyad, may arrange our receptivity to clinical data so as to close out an appreciation of the significance of the full scenario that is the basis for the patient's associations. In the clinical situation in which the paternal imago is the focus, the analyst's comprehension of what it is that the patient is associating to may be unnecessarily constricted by explicit or implicit theories about the paternal imago. Are the patient's thoughts associations to the paternal object representation? To aspects of the self-representation? To the maternal representation? Or to the entire family constellation composed of not only object representations but also their relations to each other?

A constricted and reified set of preconceptions forecloses an appreciation of the way in which the paternal imago illuminates a great deal about self-representation and other (especially maternal) object representations and about internalizations derived from the parental marriage or the family as a whole. Oversimplified views of the paternal imago, then, widen the split between theory and practice, supporting either a rigidified theoretical view of internal representation that is of no clinical use, or, alternatively, a somewhat nihilistic view of the imago as no more than another type of ideational material for analysis and without further theoretical significance. The purpose of this chapter is to work toward a clearer view of the paternal imago, one that puts theory and practice in a reciprocally enriching relation to each other, clarifies our theoretical notions, and enhances clinical understanding of the concept.

Scrutiny of the evidence that is the basis for inferences about the paternal imago reveals more complexity to the subject than might at first blush be imagined. *Observational data* that contribute to an understanding of fathering are more enigmatic than those which aid in the understanding of mothering. Mothering is often thought of as feeding, cleaning, nurturing, cuddling, all experience-near and dyadic—that is, activities administering to regressed, somewhat childish needs if they take place in a clinical setting and behaviors that can be defined and studied largely by observation of the mother-child dyad.

Fathering, however, is not an entirely analogous concept. Such functions as providing, protecting, guiding, and leading—those felt not only in common parlance, but also in conscious and unconscious fantasy, to be father's role—often extend beyond the dyad and lie beyond immediate observation. Father's interactions with the child are both important and specific (Lamb, 1976; Tyson, 1982; Yogman, 1982), but they may be only a small part of the relevant data. Father may be represented as heroic and valiant, Olympian in power and discernment, by a mother who creates and sustains the illusion of such a father. Or a man with the attributes and behaviors of a very strong father may be represented in a light that emphasizes his undependability, his letting mother down, his self-centeredness, his absence, his arrogance, his lack of success or sexual prowess, or any other shortcomings. Mother's contribution may so powerfully affect the child's appreciation of comparatively sparse data from interactions with father himself as to constitute the greater portion of what makes up the child's experience of fathering. A mother inclined to integrate the family and promote a positive experience may cover over and compensate for shortcomings and convey an experience of marvelous fathering where, in fact, very little has transpired. The subject's experience of father may have to do with extended family, with sibling systems, and with others in a much more complicated fashion than the experience of mother usually does.

In *conscious fantasy*, the maternal and paternal object representations are, again, not symmetrical. The fantasy "I want my mother" is generally regressive and concrete, a wish for soothing, feeding, exemption from responsibility, harbor from hurt, and something dominated by the pleasure principle. It is a wish for somebody to soothe one and free one from unpleasure. The fantasy "I want my father," on the contrary, is more dominated by the reality principle, a wish for help, power, mastery, justice while one faces the world (as opposed to a regressive retreat from the world).

Our *theoretical understanding* of the paternal imago, then, is not based on the same dyadic relationship as is the experience of mother. Atkins (1982, 1984) has argued that the maternal contribution may form a large part of what the child feels to be experiences of father. Attitudes, moods, and occasional statements like "Wait till I tell Daddy" and "Won't Daddy be proud," "Won't Daddy be surprised!" may convey the sense of father's imminent presence, even throughout long absences or when father's actual contribution is, in fact, minimal. Likewise, even the best-intentioned father may be represented as a pompous, irresponsible, brutal, insensitive lout during his absence, and the child may pick up complaints that externalize blame from a mother who is depressed, upset, divisive, and discontent. The child's experience of the memory may be as something about father, rather than something about mother or family as a whole.

CLINICAL ILLUSTRATIONS

Example 1. An unmarried attorney in his late 20s with difficulties in close relationships began analysis at a time when his girlfriend had gone on an extended trip. She complained that he was overly dependent on her. Early in the analysis, he described his immigrant family in idealized terms as closeknit, educationally aspiring, sacrificing, and dedicated to professional excellence. As the analysis began to unfold, a more complex picture of the family developed. His recollections of his father were, at first, of a very rough, punitive man. Remembering a state of extreme anxiety at the age of four, he recalled that he used to cry at night, luring mother from the parental bedroom to soothe him. He recalled that on one occasion he had cried, expecting his mother, but was surprised that father was the one who burst in, angry, furious, and blustering. The patient was convinced that he had, at those times when he was three or four, interrupted sexual activities between his parents. This recollection came when the transference was replete with ambivalence toward me and provocation on the patient's part. He devalued me as overweight, not stylishly dressed, and probably not very successful—reproaches he also leveled at his father. Attention to the hostility and resultant anxiety in the context of the transference reduced his anxiety level and evoked more memories of father. A mild-mannered, nurturing, companionable aspect of father emerged in his memories of that time. Father assumed a warm, even protective, role with his business subordinates. He had sheltered the patient from competitive sports and had arranged vacation activities so that the patient would not be exposed to the athletic competition and peer harassment that he had always found difficult.

Later in the analysis, when the patient was at the point of breaking up with his girlfriend, who by then had become more committed to him and was pressing for marriage, some of his anxieties about women became increasingly clear. His associations went to his mother, a strong, educationally ambitious woman, talking of father and telling the patient in secret of father's potency difficulties after a prostate operation. These secret conversations took place at a point in mother's career when she wished to move from the small northwestern town in which they lived to a big city. She told the patient that his father's attachment to his own job and to his family showed how weak he was, how tied he was to his parents, and how unable he was to make progress in the world. She saw men as being basically weak, dependent, unadventurous, and contemptible. As the analysis progressed, the patient became aware of his own mixed reactions to these conversations with his mother. He was thrilled by the intimacies, by being given special status as his mother's confidant; at the same time, he was filled with anxiety. He was aware that there was something wrong with his relationship with his mother, and there seemed to be something deeply upsetting about the way women regarded men. This confusion was conveyed in his reports of his dialogues with his mother.

Only after many years of analysis did the patient realize that he had recalled *talks with his mother* rather than actual *transactions with his father*. As the analysis continued to unfold, the mother's castrativeness, seductiveness, and contemptuousness became increasingly evident not only in his memories of her but also in his experiences with the strikingly similar women whom he selected as sexual partners. These relationships tended to confirm an inner world in which men were held in contempt; they shed light on why he was both attracted to and frightened by serious attachments to such women. In retrospect, the dialogues with mother could be understood as divisive and seductive, binding him in a gossipy, hostile relationship that devalued father sexually and otherwise. Mother's complaining aggravated antagonism between the patient and his father and at the same time offered him a specialness so seductive that it did not seem to him an act of divisiveness at the time; nor did it until relatively late in his analysis.

Example 2. A man in his late 40s came for analysis after years of difficult relationships with women in which he had felt trapped and alienated. He came with criticisms of his third wife, whom he wanted to leave after many years of marriage. Early in the analysis he discussed his lifelong difficult relationships with women. As he recalled his family of origin, his associations went to his experiences with his father, a rough, punitive man who belittled him. The patient had been an overprotected youngster, whose home was an apartment in back of the father's business. He recalled daydreaming in his room, starting school late, being frequently absent from school because he was sick, hearing his father do business in the store, and being very frightened of his father. As the analysis continued, the scenes in which father blustered and yelled at him unfolded as ones in which father had felt that mother overprotected him and exempted him from responsibilities. He frequently stayed home from school and was pampered and cuddled by a very vulnerable mother, who had, for a short time after his birth, been unable to care for him. She had gone away for what had been called a "rest period," perhaps suffering a postpartum psychosis, for several months before he was a year old.

Somewhat later in the analysis, he recalled that his family situation had changed dramatically when he was in early adolescence. Father had made enough money to sell his business and retire to managing his property. The patient recalled his father as weak, servile, soft, even effeminate, lavishing praise on him and staying with the mother despite her disagreeableness and open contemptuousness. He wished that his father had either stood up to his mother or left her. He recalled a conversation with mother, who had taken him aside and complained bitterly about his father, saying, "All I need is a real man," (meaning sexually). "That's all that's wrong with me." This intimacy in the conversation with the mother left the patient thrilled, but upset and confused. His attention was riveted on his father when he discussed these memories. Why had father endured such indignities? Why hadn't he put her in her place? Why hadn't he left? What had happened to his manliness?

These preoccupations led straightaway to an analytic focus on the patient's seeing himself *as his father* in his many unsatisfactory relationships with women. He had picked extremely dependent, often dysfunctional partners in the hope that he would prove to be the strong one in the relationship and not, like his father, an object of contempt. Analytic attention to these fears led him back to more recollections of his conversations with his mother in which she talked contemptuously of his father. These recollections occurred when his difficulties with his wife had escalated in response to his threats to leave her. The current situation was in resonance with memories of his mother's debunking conversations with him about his father, and, for the first time, he was able to focus specifically on his fears of contempt and devaluation by women and to link these with his mother's discourse rather than with his actual experience with his father alone. It had taken him many years and several attempts at treatment to unravel the significance of her divisiveness and binding to him by an angry method of complaining that devalued, castrated, and belittled his father.

Example 3. A married woman in her early 40s entered psychotherapy complaining of difficulties with her second husband, a priggish, controlling man with whom she quarrelled constantly. She had a low-key clinical depression. The marriage had been a verbal battleground from the outset. The patient complained of her husband's withholding, controlling, and stinginess; he (according to her) complained of her irresponsibility, wastefulness, and disorganization. Therapy intensified, and the patient began analysis. She talked in a warm, apparently unambivalent way to me but spent many hours complaining. Analytic focus on the complaining illuminated her relationship to her mother, to whom she regularly complained about her husband.

She was the eldest child and only daughter of elderly parents, who lived nearby. The parents' marriage had been difficult, a difficulty attributed by her mother to her father's gambling, drinking, and business failures, all sources of shame and embarrassment to the entire family. The patient had been her mother's confidante for the mother's marital difficulties. In adolescence the patient did not bring friends home for fear that her father's behavior would embarrass her.

Her own difficult marriage was a focus of continued commentary from her mother. While she appeared to show sympathy and understanding for her daughter's plight, the patient's mother also bombarded her with admonitions to remain in the marriage and to lavish on her husband caretaking that seemed excessive and unnecessary. She was advised not to take short trips or even to have evenings out with friends, lest her husband's meals not be prepared or his laundry done. Her efforts to deal with her husband straightforwardly were discouraged. Her only protests were ineffective, angry outbursts or episodes of financial irresponsibility that invited more discrediting of her and more control and more withdrawal on his part. A similar provocativeness emerged in the transference; she had so arranged submission of insurance claims that she fell seriously behind in the payment of analytic fees. Interpretive attention focused not only on the provocatively late payment, but also on the genetic (infantile) and current (marital) parallels to what was transpiring in the analysis. These included her fears of closeness to the analyst/(father, husband), which seemed to her to forebode either desertion or outright attack from her mother. Just as she was gaining insight into the significance of these struggles, she impulsively lost a large sum of money on a foolish investment and decided to discontinue treatment for several months.

She resumed with a clear awareness of the self-sabotage that had threatened the treatment and a fearful eagerness about exploring her tendency to undermine herself. She bewailed her lack of accomplishment in life, her lifelong pattern of obsequiousness peppered with angry outbursts, and the type of provocativeness typified by her financial bunglings in the analysis and in the marriage that sabotaged what seemed to be her own projects and her own credibility. She increasingly saw herself as the author of her own unhappy marital destiny and a person shockingly like her own mother, whom she saw as contemptible because she complained about her marriage but did not manage either to deal with the marriage or to leave it.

She agonized about her similarity to her mother and began to give thought to her mother's expectations that she would complain about her marriage continually but never change it. The undermining effect of her emotional reliance on her mother became the central focus of treatment for a long time.

In the meantime, self-sabotage both in the marriage and in the analysis began to abate. She began to stand up to her husband, and she insisted on changes, which were not undercut by irresponsibility on her part that allowed the husband to discredit her. She began to distance herself from her mother, whom she saw for only the time necessary for her to manage some of her parents' affairs and arrange for needed medical treatment. She neither complained nor tolerated complaining, and she became circumspect with her mother about her marital difficulties.

In the course of a long and largely successful treatment, this woman's views of her husband and of her father changed very little. Her father seemed to her as he always had: weak, overly dependent, ineffectual, uninterested in anything but his own comfort. What had changed was her ability to modify factors amplifying her shame about her mother and about herself. This shame had been split off from her self- and maternal object representations and were experienced as embarrassment about her father. Her husband remained portrayed as constricted, rigid, and unsatisfying, but the marriage improved and became a source of support for her young children. She no longer cited her husband's shortcomings to justify her regressive attachment to her mother. She had used the attachment to me in the way she could never use the relationship with her father. She was able to separate from the regressive dyad with her mother, which was organized around self-sabotage and complaining. She became aware of her own provocation and irresponsibility, which confirmed her sense of identification with her mother. And she became able to assume leadership in her marriage and make it into a functional (if somewhat unsatisfying) union on which she and her children could rely.

Example 4.   An advertising executive in his mid-30s entered analysis to deal with recurrent episodes of carelessness and self-sabotage that had ruined his career by plummeting him into personal and financial difficulties repeatedly when he was at the point of success. In the midst of one of these bouts, his wife had made an offhand remark about his lack of success in his corporate career. She was then convalescing from surgery for a bowel obstruction. He flew into a rage and left her for some months. Before he turned to analysis, he sought first brief psychotherapy and then pharmacologic help for his sprees of overactivity.

He represented his father as a cruel, competitive man who came home and singled him out for bullying and debunking. The patient himself had been a gifted youngster and described repeated encounters in which his attempts to impress father were met with ridicule. The patient's father, an attorney, worked excessively long hours, feared his partners greatly, and never allowed himself vacations. The patient's mother, a near-psychotic eccentric, had taken to her sickbed, kept unusual hours, and never seemed to interact with her husband or nurture the children.

The patient maintained a warm, subordinate, but always collegial and friendly stance toward me. In the early years of the analysis, there seemed to be no trace in the transference of the relationship he had described with his father. He did, however, treat his two eldest sons in ways that were clearly derived from his view of that relationship. The elder son he treated as an inept, presumptuous, bungling, irresponsible upstart; his rantings against this child were reminiscent of the patient's recollections of his own father. (The patient, too, had been an eldest son.) The younger son, on the other hand, was treated as the child the patient himself would like to have been. He was loved, physically cuddled, praised, and cherished.

The patient's external circumstances took a marked turn when a close female associate became ill and unable to function. He became upset, sleepless, overtly terrified of the world, and furious at a host of female employees and at his wife again. He viewed himself as a bluffer, a fake, a failure in the world of aggressive men, one who hung around with women and depended on them for support because he could not exert his power in the world of men. Those issues reached the point of crisis when he decided that he was financially unable to continue in his current business situation and began to inquire about other firms. Only when a surprisingly good offer was made to him from a prestigious and cordial firm could his anxieties and sleeplessness be seen in relation to me. He wondered what would happen if he took the job. He would earn more than I. I would resent it and think of him as an upstart. Manifest anxiety became clearly associated, for the first time, to his fear of reprisal from me. Interpretive attention to this transference anxiety led to his feeling much better and taking appropriate steps to establish himself in his new firm.

Further associations went to his provocations of his father, which were designed for him to obtain nurturance and care when he was fearful of dealing with the world and could not get soothing from his mother. Behind the fear of retaliation, then, was the *wish* that he could be in a helpless, childlike state so that father would care for him, cater to his regressive needs, and provide soothing, nurturance, and support. Embedded in the positive oedipal struggle, then, were his fearful identifications with his dysfunctional mother and his wishes to escape the masculine role, with its risks and dangers, and obtain from his father what he had not gotten from his mother.

Both parents had left this patient with a sense of terror at what he saw as the male role. He viewed his father as ruthless, debunking, competitive, yet at the same time fearful of dealing with colleagues and clients in the business world and emotionally deserted by a wife who took to her bed for years. His mother was seen as regressed, self-centered, divisive, incapable of nurturance or support, and barely able to escape from her own tensions. It was the failure of complementary and mutual support between his parents, combined with the terror of the competitive outside world, that so shockingly split this man's inner world into a rough, competitive, retaliatory, masculine world and a self-centered, incompetent, regressed, feminine one. His fears of women, precipitated by his wife's and colleague's illness, had to be analyzed before his view of the male world (i.e., his paternal imago) could be modified by analysis.

SCREENS OF FAMILIAL DYSFUNCTION

The patients just described reported difficulties with their fathers in two ways. In Examples 1, 2, and 4, the early memories, negatively tinged, were of interactions with father himself and portrayed defensive reactions on father's part. He was gruff, rough, punitive—angry defenses that patients often are not aware that they have provoked. Often such provocation involves a regressive coalition with mother. Other experiences of father, however, were reported (unbeknown to the patient) as dialogues with mother about father (Examples 1, 2, and 3) and showed mother's omnipotent defenses. These dialogues left the patient with a sense that the memory is entirely about father, whereas the actual material reveals a discontented mother, bonding in a devious manner with her child and portraying father in a way that is divisive, devaluing, and contemptuous. In Example 4, the mother's failure to nurture figured powerfully in the patient's view of the terrors of the male role and his attempts to avoid it.

Each of these examples conveys a drama with a father who is prominently onstage and a divisive mother who is not only also an actor, but also producer, director, narrator, and even writer of the script. This particular group of analysands had mothers in whom divisiveness, splitting, seductiveness, and absence of what Atkins (1984) termed "transitive vitalization"—mother's capacity to allow the child to make attachments to the world and develop outside of the mother-child dyad—are strongly evident in the case material. Abelin (1971) drew attention to the father's role in the child's successfully traversing the separation-individuation process. The father is the "other-other," the one who joins with the child to offset the tie to mother, which would otherwise become regressive, unmanageably ambivalent, and fraught with dangers of excessive closeness on one hand and terrifying abandonment on the other. The clinical examples point to divisiveness and a lack of bonding within the parental marriage that foreclose the possibility of a stabilizing relationship for the child, not just in infancy but lifelong. In each case, the memories that provided data for inferences about the paternal imago contained a dialogue with a mother who employed a divisive kind of dyadic binding with the child instead of an integrative type of familial leadership. Devalued aspects of the paternal imago are conveyed in the narrative of a mother portrayed as complaining, disappointed, devious, and castrating, one whose pairings-off, rather than integration within the family, and whose omnipotent defenses are represented in the dialogue about the father.

This supradyadic focus has major implications for our understanding of the specifics of the process of splitting and of internalization. If, for the male, the view of father is compounded by the recollection of mother's attitudes toward father as weak, impotent, and contemptible, such a model for introjection (exaggerated by the youngster's oedipal rivalry) is internalized as a damaged introject and powerfully affects the patient's sense of self. For women, the same binding with mother, portrayed in memories of mother's complaining about father, is taken in as a message whose manifest content concerns men, but whose latent content activates the fear of attack or abandonment by an envious and competitive mother if the young girl were to bind herself in a secure way to her father. The split representation is based on an internalization of a felt split within the family, not simply of the child's dyadic ambivalence toward father. That is, the paternal representation is split into a strong, primitive aspect (that often records father's phallic narcissistic defenses when provoked) and a devalued, contemptible aspect (that reveals mother's omnipotent defenses through a dialogue between mother and child about father). The split paternal imago, then, codifies not only the child's phase-appropriate ambivalence exerting a self-fulfilling force on the family, but also a divided family that powerfully and destructively reinforces the child's ambivalence at the expense of his or her development. Difficulties in that development are encoded in the self- and maternal representations, both of which are screened by the paternal representation.

IMPLICATIONS FOR THEORY AND PRACTICE

Clearly, what we call, for theoretical and clinical convenience, the paternal imago might be called a screen representation, or at least one that has a screening function, both revealing and masking sources beyond the specific father-child dyad and powerfully mediated by the patient's impression of the mother and her attitudes toward, and relations with, the father. Hence, the paternal representation is not simple ideation, in the sense that a photograph is a record of the scene it captures, or even a composite version of that notion. Rather the "representation" is a set of recollections or views of the paternal object that serves important defensive and screening functions for self- representation and other object representations considered in isolation and for the family as a whole.

The notions of self- and object representations might well undergo the same scrutiny as did the notion of memory in Freud's 1899 paper, "Screen Memories." That work modified the very earliest theory, that of the early 1890s. There was a simple elegance to the earliest theory: all its major precepts centered on clearcut notions of "ideas." Pathogenesis was accounted for by a traumatic event, represented by something like a picture of it—a memory, a photo, so to speak, of an occurrence that had a charge or a quota of affect attached to it. Symptoms, insofar as the patient had a *psycho*neurosis and not an *aktual*neurosis, were also representable by ideas—of a feared object in the phobias, of a dysfunctional part of the body in the conversions, of a forbidden impulse in the obsessions, and of a persecutor in paranoia. The method was, as it remains today, the association of ideas, and interpretation made the patient aware of complexes of ideas that elucidated unconscious significance. Cure was a discharge of affect by abreaction and a return of the walled-off memories to the mainstream of associative connections. Assumed here was that one event, especially a sexual one, can cause pathology. Hence the importance of memory, which was a record of that event. Symptoms were understood by analysis of the ideas involved in phobias, conversions, obsessions, and delusions. The association of ideas led to certain interpretations by way of understanding complexes. The energy necessary to keep the memory out of awareness was thus liberated, and the mnemic ideas became free to enter the associative stream of ideas.

Freud's work deepened, and as he began to expand past an oversimplified seduction hypothesis to appreciate the workings of fantasy and the role of infantile sexuality, he began to put less theoretical emphasis on what actually happened and how it was represented. The memory, therefore, became less central. This deemphasis continued as the structure of the psyche and the structural aspects of psychopathology became more and more understood. But before these changes took place, Freud (1899) wrote "Screen Memories," a work that, in my opinion, is not taken seriously enough even now, although it should be at the very foundation of psychoanalytic work. Our current conception of screen memories goes far beyond Freud's illustrative case, in which the memory was vivid, intense, but innocuous in content.

Every memory can be viewed as an ideational product, woven afresh and concealing as well as revealing. A memory, like a dream, has both manifest and latent content. Memory has come to be seen as more like a dream than like a photo of an event. A memory, like the manifest content of a dream, is reworked and woven afresh for defensive purposes, or (if I may reify the way Freud did at that time) one memory defends against another. The level of the complexity of the 1899 paper is significant because it grants full importance to trauma, fantasy, and defense, that is, to both internal and external reality. It presumes that trauma and its reconstruction are important but also shows awareness of the fresh weavings of the mental product, the memory. Ideas that are memories, like those that are symptoms, or dreams, may be formed afresh. After the publication of *Three Essays on Sexuality* in 1905, emphasis came to center much more on the internal world and on infantile sexuality, so much so that interest in what actually happened tended to be neglected, especially theoretically. As a result, the theory of memory and of screen memories had less centrality than it had had in the days when an actual traumatic event was presumed to be a sufficient explanation for a psychoneurosis.

I dwell on these points because I think the same issues appeared after the more or less Aristotelian turn in psychoanalysis that followed the advent of the structural theory in 1923, with subsequent emphasis on direct observation of the development of ego, id, and superego in the child and of the development of early object relationships. The introduction of concepts that are abstract distillates of anamnestic data moved away from an exclusive reliance on *the idea* and emphasized a concept of structure that was not as clearly related to discrete units of ideation (e.g., dream, joke, slip, symptom) than it had been in the heyday of the earlier topographic theory. There has, of course, been continued recognition that in the early lives of neurotic patients something did happen—not trauma as the result of one sexual event, but cumulative traumata not necessarily capable of mental registration as a single event. Relating such cumulative traumata to the patient's actual ideation about early familial relationships has nowhere near the theoretical tightness it had in the times preceding awareness of psychic structure in the development. But *the "idea"* does persist in Hartmann's (Hartmann and Loewenstein, 1962) and Jacobson's (1964) writings, as self- and object representations.

I cannot, within the scope of the present discussion, deal with the many advantages, nor the theoretical problems, that go with the usage of these terms. Self- and object representations, or images, are similar terms for the "idea" that one has about one's own or another's person. They are inferred by the analyst from affect-laden memories or from actions, cumulative or isolated, integrated or not. Frequently they are evoked in discussions of unintegrated or split-off parts of the personality. Questions arise regarding the concept of representations that are similar to those raised by the concept of memories in the heyday of the seduction hypothesis, namely, whether or not they correspond to some pathogenic event that actually occurred. In the case of object representations, the ideational content is that of a relationship rather than that of an isolated trauma. Thus, the same type of psychoanalytic complexity applies to object representation as to dream or memory, and the same analytic penetration is required for the representation as for other mental products that are analyzed. That is, one may imagine screen representations or imagos along the same line of thinking by which one conceptualizes screen memories.

The paternal object representation is colored by the emotional climates supplied by the mother (another object representation or imago) and by that which is disowned or repressed as an attribute of self-representation and often is detectable in the transference. Thus, the paternal imago may serve as a screen memory, as it were, for views of the mother or of the family or of the self, especially if, as we see so commonly in clinical practice, something about the self is in relation to that imago either repressed or not representable in any simple way.

The maternal object representation, then, can be split and displaced onto the paternal object representation. We see in many clinical presentations what might be called screen paternal representations in the associations of patients of both sexes. Very real difficulties that a patient has with men (repetition of what is presumed to be a relationship embodied in the paternal object representation) are embedded in the paternal imago in ways that also screen difficulties of the mother in her relationship to the father and deemphasize loyalty conflicts within the family that threaten to overwhelm the patient with anxiety.

Psychoanalysis showed, from its beginnings, an awareness of conflictual oedipal predicaments, phallocentric, and organized around the father and only later evolved an understanding of what was preoedipal, mammocentric, and organized around the mother. In our current, more sophisticated return to interest in the father, we are faced with the need to refine theoretical constructs from the psychoanalytic situation itself to allow for integration of purely psychoanalytic data with the results of direct observation of development. The predicament is similar to the one Freud was in when he developed the idea of screen memories. We will need much philosophical and theoretical clarity before our terms can be used in ways that do not prejudge the world on matters of fact. And we need to realize that what appear to be representations of one object, perhaps father especially, may derive from the relation of father with mother or with siblings for that matter, or from relationships and loyalties that can be understood only from observations of the whole family. Much clarifying work will have to be done to integrate material from direct observation into psychoanalytic theory and even to permit consistent usage of our terms.

What patients in the analytic situation recollect of their fathers often does reflect in part their experiences with their fathers. Memories often reflect a father's defenses aroused when he was provoked by the patient, provocations that become evident as the transference unfolds and is worked through. When consistent transference interpretation has resulted in working through (as in Examples 1, 4), such memories commonly are supplemented by others that are more pleasant and mellow and portray satisfying or even terrifyingly intimate aspects of the relationship with father.

The paternal representation codifies a great deal about the self-representation and, in men, about identification with a damaged or devalued paternal introject and a struggle against that identification

(Greenson, 1954). The young male sees himself *as understudy to a male—* his father—*in relation to a female—*his mother. Father's value, or lack of value, as a model is defined for the youngster much more by dialogue and experience within the home than in other areas. The paternal imago, then, contains a record of the patient's model for identification and an entire set of attitudes toward this model. Examination of devalued, or damaged, introjects and of the struggles against them or, alternatively, exploration of brutal and persecutory introjects and provocations of them forms a large part of the work of analysis.

The paternal imago also encapsulates a great deal of information about how mother is seen and about the patient's fears and desires relating to her. The maternal imago in Examples 1, 2, and 3 was split, and projected bad parts were experienced by both patient and mother as *belonging* to father. Mother's defensive activities (that is, to protect her self-representation) so dovetailed with the patient's defensive workings (which protect the self- and maternal object representation) that both mother and child took defensive opportunities to split off unacceptable parts of mother and experience them as either due to father or residing in father. Hence, father absorbed a great deal of ambivalence in the mother-child dyad. This displacement or screening function is reflected in the paternal imago.

What is internalized is not to be confused with self-representation or maternal, paternal, or other object representations. Rather, a sense of self comes from internalization of the family, it is a self as defined by father in relation to mother and to other children in the family. Split representations are reflective of splits in the family, which, in turn, induce or amplify serious splits in the ego that (as a manifestation of the compulsion to repeat) show up in later object choices that will preserve the same constellation of difficulties.

It is uncommon, in my experience, for patients in psychoanalysis or in psychoanalytic psychotherapy to have a strong and useful relationship with their fathers. Those paternal relationships that are hailed initially as good usually unfold in the patient's expanding perspective as seductive and divisive. In the rare instance where a very caring, supportive father appears to have been in a close relationship with the patient, the mother is often found to have been highly dysfunctional or even psychotic. The paternal representation, negative as it so commonly is early in analytic work, provides us with a focus for analytic scrutiny not just of the relationship with father, but of mother's capacity to integrate and to allow meaningful attachments outside of the mother-child dyad. It allows us a window on her ability to tolerate otherness or even on her divisiveness or sabotaging of attempts at separation from her. People with a strong positive relation with their fathers usually have a strong relationship with both parents. They are not often seen in the consulting room. Their satisfying recollections point not only to positive aspects of the relationship with the father, but also to the presence of a mother who integrates, tolerates separation, and makes possible, even promotes, such a relationship with the father. The patient with poor paternal relations, on the other hand, usually proves to have not only a poor relationship with father, but almost always an intensely ambivalent relationship in the dyadic situation with mother, that is, with a mother who cannot tolerate separation, tends to be fixated to dyads, and sabotages any attachment outside of the mother-child dyad.

We also learn from the paternal imago much about the patient's self-representation. The paternal imago contains latent commentary about self in relation to father and mother. Behind a negatively portrayed paternal imago in the examples sketched earlier were the patients' divided selves, selves who sought out or were drawn into situations where the patient was a go-between and then experienced the same seductive binding to one person and hostility coming from another, who was excluded (Slipp, 1984). The paternal imago, of course, like the dream and the screen memory, is not the bedrock of analytic thinking, but a subject for further analytic work. What the paternal imago tells us about the relationship with father is like the manifest content of a dream or a memory. Useful information is often conveyed, but the significance of the manifest content must be seen in the light of latent content, which must be reached by further analysis. It is this process that makes for modifications of the self-representation, maternal representation, splits in the family, process of internalization, and the capacity to be freed from dyadic fixations within the family. The paternal imago, when it reflects disturbance, is indicative of disruption radiating outward from the self. Vulnerabilities to personality disorganization show up as clingingness and fixation on the mother-child dyad. When the mother-child dyad becomes too hotly ambivalent and risks eroding the relationship with mother, displacement from the analysand's maternal imago may dovetail with the mother's defensive needs (to protect her self-representation) so that mother and child act in collusion against father. This collusion is often combined with activities that provoke defensive reactions from father, which further confirm negative aspects of what is, in an oversimplified way, called the paternal imago.

These considerations set the stage for an analytic focus that gives us a good deal of feeling for the cohesiveness, sense of separateness, fixation to dyads, and methods of defense not only in the patient but in the family, and the processes of internalization against which these patients so frequently struggle.

The paternal imago is a powerful indicator of the patient's internalizations. It reveals much about the capacity for binding or for divisiveness in the narrative of the patient or of that of others in the family. The narrative of the mother, especially, points to the patient's experience of her effect on cohesion or disruption in the family: either to her binding, transitive vitalization, integration, capacity to tolerate depressive anxiety (that is, Eros); or to her divisiveness, unbinding, detachment, castrativeness, sabotaging, or a retreat to the paranoid-schizoid position (that is, Thanatos). But the data that constitute the paternal imago provide sources for analytic understanding that are fed by expressive and defensive resonances not only from the mother-child dyad and the patient's relationship to the parental marriage, but also from the very earliest father-child dyad and from the family as a whole.

— III —

Defenses Against Shame:
Narcissistic Equilibrium in the
Family System

Chorus	Now is the time for a man to muffle his head And over the land to urge his stealthy way, Or else, sitting the thwarts to row, To trust his life to a ship's swift course on this deep— Such are the threats that the sons of Atreus, two in power, Stir towards us. I am in dread to share With him the blows and hurt of the killing stone; For an awful thing to be near is the doom that holds him.
Tecmessa	No longer so. After the lightning Flash and leap of the storm wind, He is calm. But now, being in clear mind, He is freshly miserable. It is a painful thing To look at your own trouble and know That you yourself and no one else has made it.
Chorus	But still, if his fit is past, I should think he was lucky; A seizure, once done with, matters less.
Tecmessa	If someone posed the question, which would you choose: To grieve your friends while feeling low yourself, Or to be wretched with them, shares alike?
Chorus	The last, lady, is twice as bad a thing.
Tecmessa	We are ill no longer now, but merely ruined.
Chorus	What do you mean? I cannot understand you.
Tecmessa	Ajax, so long as the mad fit was on him, Himself felt joy at his wretchedness, Though we, his sane companions, grieved indeed. But now that he's recovered and breathes clear,

His own anguish totally masters him.
While we are no less wretched than before.
Is this not a redoubling of our grief.

Chorus   You are quite right. Lady, I wonder
If a tearful blow of God's anger may have hit him.
It is strange that he feels no happier sane than raving.

Tecmessa   Strange perhaps. But the facts are as they are.

Sophocles
Ajax (247-281)

3

Shame in the Family Relationships of Borderline Patients

Compared with the more easily conceptualized emotions of anxiety, guilt, and depression, shame, for complex and far-reaching reasons, has been bypassed in our theorizing. The result of this oversight is a failure to integrate aspects of our understanding of affect and defense in severe character pathology, especially its interpersonal manifestations. The neglect of shame and the difficulty conceptualizing it have resulted in models that lend themselves better to more mechanically derived notions based on guilt, ones that give us an incomplete and misleading view of the patient in intimate personal relationships.

This tendency to bypass explanations involving shame is of special importance in the understanding and treatment of the severe character pathology designated by the unfortunate term "borderline." There is increasing evidence that significant family psychopathology permeates in the family of origin of borderline patients and that it is impossible to appreciate their pathology without a clear grasp of the dynamics of shame and modes of handling it. Borderline patients endure continuing disturbances in all interpersonal relationships, disturbances that can only be understood with the dynamics of shame in mind. Most of the defensive operations of borderline patients are reactions to their shameful self-consciousness among others. Borderline patients are exquisitely humiliation prone. They have a pronounced tendency to experience others as deliberately inflicting shame on them. This presents technical difficulties in their treatment and that of their families, especially because similar personality organizations and defensive needs, organized by collusive defenses, tend to be found in the same families.

For these reasons I attempt here to reintegrate the consideration of shame into the thinking about the borderline patient. I shall begin with a discussion of how shame originally occupied a prominent place in psychoanalytic thinking about affects and then disappeared in analytic thinking for several decades. The reasons for this are complex and significant enough to warrant some detailed discussion. I shall briefly cover some aspects of shame that illuminate defining characteristics of the borderline patient and then turn specifically to the topic of shame in the family relations of borderline patients. I shall describe three transpersonal modes of handling shame in a more or less covert fashion. These are often, but not invariably, found in the same family: blaming, impulsive action, and pathological preoccupation. Overt shaming in the family is often accompanied by violence.

SHAME

Shame is fundamentally and irreducibly a human phenomenon. Nietzsche, in fact, defined man as "the animal with the red cheeks." Charles Darwin (1872), discussing blushing, the observable expression of shame, called it the most peculiar and most human of expressions and noted that the common denominator is attention to self. In view of its obviously central and even overriding importance, it is curious that shame should have been so neglected. Indeed, in the earliest psychoanalytic writings, avoidance of shame is seen as a major motive in defense. In *Studies on Hysteria* (Breuer and Freud, 1893-1895), Freud wrote:

> [B]y means of my psychical work I have had to overcome a psychical force in the patients which was opposed to the pathogenic ideas becoming conscious [being remembered]. From these I recognized the universal characteristic of such ideas. They were all of a distressing nature calculated to arouse the affects of shame, of self-reproach and of psychical pain and the feeling of being harmed; they were all of a kind that one would prefer not to have experienced, that one would rather forget. From all this there arose, as it were, automatically the thought of *defence* . . . . The patient's ego had been approached by an idea which proved to be incompatible, which provoked on the part of the ego a rebelling force of which the purpose was defense against this incompatible idea [pp. 268-269].

Later in *Three Essays on Sexuality*, Freud (1905a) noted:

> Our study of the perversions has shown us that the sexual instinct has to struggle against certain mental forces which act as resistance and of which

shame and disgust are the most prominent. It is permissible to suppose that these forces play a part in restraining that instinct within the limits that are regarded as normal, and if they develop in the individual before the sexual instinct has reached its full strength, it is no doubt that they will determine the course of its development [p. 162].

Shame, being intimately connected with self-consciousness, cannot be mechanized. Because inferences about self-consciousness cannot be made in other species, there are no animal analogs to shame. Anxiety, guilt, and some sorts of depression have observable analogs and are even producible in nonhuman species under controlled circumstances. This is, perhaps, one reason why the other passions have gotten so much attention. Aspects of them are compatible with more mechanistic theories that were felt to be explainable in more comprehensible ways. Anxiety, for example—first as an accumulation of unpleasure in the nervous system that had to be discharged and later as a signal of danger to the ego—had two forms of rather mechanistic explanation. Guilt was seen as fear of the superego or internalized control of external punishment and could be understood with similar simplicity. Depression, seen as involving anger at internalized objects that regulate self-regard, could to some extent be understood mechanically. None of these explanations was, of course, complete, but each held out the promise of a certain grasp of the topics that could not be extended to the understanding of shame. The need for a mechanistic explanation has in general caused neglect of phenomena associated with self-consciousness, and indeed most studies of the superego ignore the dynamics of *being seen as a self in the eyes of others* in favor of some mechanical attempt to describe the process of internalization.

Freud's (1894) earliest thinking allowed for a central role for shame. In the initial theory, pathology was conceptualized in terms of ideas that were repressed, that is, dynamically kept away from awareness because they presented a view of the self that was incompatible with the view the patient wanted to maintain. Built into early topographic theory, with its emphasis on awareness of ideas, is a notion of consciousness of self as one would like to be or as one would not like to be. Although the method of free association is still prominent in the psychoanalytic method, psychopathology is no longer regarded as a simple repression of ideas (memories) from consciousness. As this intimate connection of defense and awareness waned, so did a model focusing on self-consciousness and defense as defense against awareness of ideas about self, rather than as defense against drive or affect. This turn away from a model emphasizing self-consciousness also heightened the emphasis on anxiety and guilt rather than shame, and defense in terms of *mechanisms* rather than *the avoidance of shameful consciousness itself.* As psychoanalysis moved away theoretically from an exclusive focus on the phenomenology and explication of ideas, the disturbing theoretical and practical problems connected with understanding shame were replaced by explanations in terms of anxiety and guilt.

Another reason for the neglect of shame has to do with the conceptualization of the mechanism of action of psychotherapy. It is easier and less disturbing to conceptualize the psychoanalytic process as dealing fundamentally with the patient's distortions, errors, ignorance, or fantasy that does *not* correspond to the patient's immediate reality than it is to partake of that person's sense of deficit, dirtiness, and emptiness. With the discovery of infantile sexuality and the role played by unconscious fantasy, it became possible to formulate a paradigm for psychoanalysis based on instinct and on unconscious fantasies that are by and large false when compared with the patient's current reality and especially with the relationship with the therapist. It is convenient also for the therapist to imagine that the patient's disturbing affects have to do with something that is basically false rather than basically true. If, for example, the patient suffers from oedipal fantasies or those of control, domination, and sexual or aggressive transgression and forthcoming retaliation, then the problem can be seen as irrational, and it disappears in principle, at least, under analytic scrutiny. But such a conceptualization tends to obscure parts of the process that have to do with shame in the presence of the therapist, that is, the actual experience of being seen as defective in the relationship, revealing oneself to a therapist who does not reveal himself or herself, seeking help from one who does not present himself or herself as needing help; and so forth. Erikson (1950) wrote:

> Shame supposes that one is completely exposed and conscious of being looked at, in one word, self-conscious. One is visible and not ready to be visible which is why we dream of shame as a situation in which we are stared at in a condition of incomplete dress . . . . Shame is early expressed in impulse to bury one's face or sink right then and there into the ground . . . . He who is ashamed would like to force the world not to look at him, not to notice his exposure. He would like to destroy the eyes of the world; instead, he must wish for his own invisibility [p. 252].

Shame before the therapist, then, stems not from an error but from self-consciousness. It is public, whereas guilt is private and often based on fantasy. Sartre (1945) wrote:

> Now shame as we noted is shame of *self*; it is the *recognition* of the fact that I *am* indeed that object which the Other is looking at and judging. I can be

ashamed only as my freedom escapes me in order to become an object . . .
beyond any knowledge which I can have, I am this self which another knows
[p. 350].

The "looking at" that Sartre described is very much amplified by the
features of the analytic situation. The analyst sees the patient, but the
patient does not see the analyst. The patient is revealed to the analyst, but
not the analyst to the patient. The patient's material becomes an object for
the analytic work, and so shame becomes a real, not an irrational, part of
the analytic situation.

This feature of analytic technique highlights and brings into focus the
sense of shame that is potentially present in all human relationships.
"Borderline" patients usually suffer self-consciousness and shame in intimate relationships. One frequently finds in the family of origin inconstant
caretakers or frequent changes of nurturance, involvement of the future
patient in an immature parental marriage by being parentified, scapegoated, or blamed, or sustained physical or sexual abuse (Lansky, 1980). These
factors, often in combination, favor self-consciousness, a desperate need to
control intimates, and an enduring sense of shame, both of self and of
family.

Shame also tends to be obscured by guilt. The defensive movement of
the patient in fantasy inevitably goes from shame-producing deficits and
inadequacies to fantasied transgressions (and often fears of retaliation).
These dynamics involving transgressions and guilt hide a pervasive sense
of shame. In unconscious fantasy, an event in which something simply
happened to the patient and left that person helpless tends to be transformed into something that the patient did in fantasy that controls the
situation, perhaps at the cost of inviting retaliation. Analytic work often
stops at fantasies of the transgression and control involving guilt without
progressing to the mortifying sense of absence, deficit, disorganization,
and shame such fantasies screen.

It has taken psychoanalysis a good many decades to develop a language
in which deficits registering as absences (and of which the patient is
ashamed) come into as much focus as fantasy transgressions (about which
the patient feels guilty). The incompleteness in the early notion of trauma
had to do mainly with trauma's being seen only as traumatic activity that
the patient did or suffered, not as traumatic absence resulting in deficits.
Shame was relegated either to anal erotic fantasies or to the component
instincts of seeing or being seen. A more sophisticated concept of trauma
includes traumatic absence that leaves deficits, and a consequent history of
attachments secured at the price of loss of self-respect, loss of self-control,
and a view of oneself as someone who is not in control. Before these

shame-producing deficits in self and family could be talked about and conceptualized, they remained opaque to analytic understanding of the patient's life and of the patient's relationship with the analyst.

"BORDERLINE" PATIENTS

There is a growing consensus that the borderline syndrome is a discrete entity. Dynamically, Kernberg (1975), continuing Melanie Klein's and Herbert Rosenfeld's emphasis on personality organization, has defined borderline personality organization in terms of splitting and the defenses reinforcing it: denial, projection, projective identification, devaluation, omnipotence and idealization. Descriptively, DSM-III (American Psychiatric Association, 1980) requires identification of five of eight criteria in long-term functioning for diagnosis: (1) impulsivity or unpredictability in two self-damaging areas such as spending, sex, gambling, substance abuse, shoplifting, overeating, physically self-damaging acts; (2) unstable and intense interpersonal relationships with shifts of attitude, including idealization, devaluation, and manipulation; (3) inappropriate and intense anger or lack of control of anger; (4) identity disturbance; (5) affective instability, with marked shifts from normal mood lasting hours to a few days; (6) intolerance of being alone; (7) physically self-damaging acts; and (8) chronic feeling of emptiness or boredom.

These are basically compatible ways of looking at the disturbance, one from the point of view of personality organization, the other from descriptively definable interview criteria. Both serve useful purposes but stop short of giving a complete enough view of the syndrome to locate the basic disturbance and the defensive response to the disturbance with enough perspicacity to distinguish the basic defect resulting in proneness to humiliation from defenses against shame (some of which actually amplify the overall sense of shame).

This incompleteness is of particular importance because dynamic views of splitting often emphasize defense, guilt, and the pain of depressive burdens. Explanations based on guilt dynamics are incomplete for reasons evident only after complex examination of the patterns of breakdown and defense in an individual and collusive defensive style among individuals so constituted that they cluster together in collusive defensive operations to ward off humiliation and shame.

The central difficulty of borderline personality organization is the patient's vulnerability to disorganization of the personality when optimal distance is not maintained in intimate relationships. Such vulnerability involves reactions of overwhelming humiliation, paranoid fear, and envy when intimates are too close, and fragmentation or separation anxiety that is disorganizing (often in a paranoid way) when those intimates are too far away. The awareness of self as so constituted that severe disorganization occurs is so humiliating that strong defensive operations invariably form to obliterate awareness of such fragility. These defenses consist of unconscious fantasies of control of the distance from intimate objects by incorporation (introjection) or expulsion (projection). These unconscious fantasies are accompanied by external activities that serve to regulate distance and control it. Because the activity and the fantasy both maintain internal and external control of distance to objects, therapist and patient may too soon agree that defense is aimed against activities of control and aggression. Controlling maneuvers are indeed present but not central and primary, as are the underlying propensities to disorganize. The shame-producing dynamics of disorganization may be defensively screened by the guilt-producing maneuvers that discharge aggression and secure collusive control.

The analyst, lacking a comprehensive view of the entire process, may not see manifestations of the need for control as deriving from the patient's sense of shame, which comes from an awareness of a lack of cohesion in his or her personality that requires intimates to be kept at a certain distance to hold the self together. When this distance is incorrect, one sees in the patient's activities maneuvers to readjust it: to bind by means of entitlement, manipulative self-destructive action, demandingness; or to detach by envious attack or paranoid outbursts. These behaviors may appear to be random and volatile if their distance-regulating function is not appreciated or if one does not realize how shameful they are to the person who becomes aware of them. Envy, anger, and the object-controlling part of projective identification involve control over distance. Omnipotence, devaluation, idealization all serve to blot out from awareness humiliating but cohesion-producing features of attachment. Projection and devaluation pass the shamefulness on to the other person in a collusive relationship.

Modes of regulating shame-producing awareness usually involve transpersonal defenses, that is, collusive activity by more than one person so that the experience of shameful mortification can be shared by two persons with similar defensive needs. Such collusive units, by virtue of their chaotic, changeable and unstable nature, may appear to be less organized than they actually are. Collusive operations do divert attention from the process of disorganization and restitutive pathologic distance regulation in each member. The shame and the loss of the sense of personal integrity in such persons are so mortifying that the awareness tends to find a mask, however costly, self-destructive, and painful. These prominent masks are often the criteria by which borderline personalities are diagnosed.

DEFENSIVE MODES

I shall discuss three main modes of defensive operation used to avoid the awareness of narcissistic vulnerability, and then overt shaming. These modes cannot be fully understood without an appreciation of the dynamics of shame involved.

Blaming[1]

Blaming is the most obviously conflictual and interpersonally based of defensive operation. Blaming transactions give the superficial appearance of disorganization and breaking apart over the specific issue around which blaming takes place, but actually they are general orienting maneuvers that bind a relationship of the blamer and the blamed and exclude others. Blaming often follows an invitation to blame by an impulsive actor or a preoccupied person. The sequence is more or less predictable: emptiness or a depressed mood or emotional withdrawal by the future blamer may trigger an invitation to blame in the form of impulsive action, which is followed by blaming activity in the person who originally felt empty, depressed, or withdrawn. For both there may be a loss of self when relationships become either emotionally distanced or too close. The act of blaming reestablishes a close bond, yet removes the blamer and the blamed from anxieties about intimacy too mutual to be comfortable. The activity of blame also restores emotional fullness and affect by the justifying self-righteous mode of relating of the blamer to the blamed.

The affective state of blaming, that is, the state of narcissistic rage, covers helplessness and shame, which are often strikingly revealed by a transcript of a vehement blaming transaction. The rage results from, but also covers over, the blamer's sense of shame, which was felt to be caused or amplified by the injustices of the blamed party. Emotional equilibrium is restored, at least while the act of blaming is in progress, and the blamer feels competent, masterful, in control—not helpless, empty, ashamed, and disorganized.

Blaming is distinguishable from other angry reactions to transgressions. In blaming states, incident after incident triggers the angry attack, and almost all such incidents involve change of distance from intimate persons—that is, they become too close or too independent or they withdraw attention from the blamer. A general sense of compensability or injustice is transmitted by the blamer, and it goes beyond the particular incident justifying blame. Devaluation and shamefulness are heaped on the person being blamed, often so much that the person and the entire relationship appear to have no value whatsoever. Blaming transactions exclude other

---

[1] See Chapter 4 of this volume.

persons from the immediate emotional field, but at the same time make them feel responsible for the conflict. This type of distance regulation has enormous impact on others in the family, particularly children. It makes them feel the need to control the situation and at the same time to feel helpless both about the parental marriage and about getting nurturance for themselves. The same may apply to the therapist when a family uses blaming to deal with its humiliation at being seen as disorganized and vulnerable.

Example 1.   A man in his late 40s screamed at his wife when she came 10 minutes late for a conjoint therapy session. He accused her of being unreliable, undependable, and irresponsible. The therapist, pointing to the discrepancy between the husband's vehemence and the issue at hand, was unsuccessful at getting the husband to reflect on the reasons behind such intense emotion. The wife responded to the attack in a rambling, placating way, which discredited her and indicated that she was available to be the target of such displays of rage. These blaming bouts continued session after session. The couple agreed that these attacks were typical of their 20 years of marriage. The husband had been orphaned early in life and passed from grandmother to several aunts, all of whom belittled males, dressed him in feminine attire, and considered him a burden. The wife, the youngest of several daughters, was the only child who stayed with the mother after divorce early in her life. The mother's alcoholism increased, and the young girl had to live with her father and older sisters. She invited and endured their criticism and harassment as a means of ensuring her acceptance.

Impulsive Action[2]

Impulsive symptomatic action—wrist slashing, overdosing, binge eating, binge drinking, impulsive sexuality, gambling, or suicidality—is a prime diagnostic feature of borderline pathology. It is usually seen as a symptom involving one person only. The distance-regulating effect, binding or unbinding, is often poorly understood because impulsive action arouses anxiety and anger and tends to be seen as "manipulative." Examination of impulsive acts often shows an obvious relation to a change in distance too close to or with too little control over an intimate person. The impulsive actor is at times conscious of disintegrating, paranoid, or depersonalized experiences followed by a need to do some impulsive act: drink, eat, slash, have sex, overdose. The act itself is often misunderstood and explained away as lack of will power, a need for gratification, or lack of discipline, or

---

[2] See Chapter 6 of this volume.

in terms of its effects on the control of people. These explanations in terms of transgressions, gratifications, and manipulations point toward guilt dynamics, which hide the essential features of disorganization and recovery by pathological distance regulation. These features are so shame-producing and mortifying that a powerful defensive movement is made to cover them up. Such disguise can be effected efficiently in a collusive relationship with a blamer, and it is common to have these two defensive modes combine collusively: the blamer, to objectify the unfairness and hurtfulness of a world that leaves him in a shameful state, attacks the impulsive actor, who invites the blamer's attention to transgression. Both conceal shame-producing propensities to disorganize.

Example 2. A father and son hospitalized on the same ward at the same time provided an opportunity to observe interlocking dynamics. Both men had problems with alcohol abuse, holding jobs, maintaining relationships, mood swings, and managing life in general. The son responded, at first, to support from the hospital environment. His mood improved, he abstained from alcohol, and he began seeking employment. He found a job and began to work. At about this time his father became apathetic, listless, and depressed and was frequently intoxicated. His change of mood was followed by a sudden and dramatic recurrence of binge drinking by the son and a consequent loss of his job. The father responded with self-righteous admonitions about lethargy, laziness, irresponsibility, and drinking. In the activity of blaming his son's impulsive action, the father's mood improved; he stopped drinking, but the son became impulsively intoxicated with great frequency, depressed, and petulant, and he finally took a near lethal overdose of antidepressant medication.

Preoccupation[3]

A subtle and more easily rationalized type of defensive mode may be used by persons who show caring and responsibility in relationships but who rationalize an emotional absence, often of schizoid proportions, by reference to some extrafamilial loyalty that draws them away from the process physically and emotionally. The schizoid propensities, which involve intense involvement but an inability to relate emotionally, are kept from shameful awareness in several ways: by being rationalized by loyalties outside the family (i.e., job, extended family, other pursuits of value to the family); by the value of the second loyalty (career or financial advancement, some promise of personal completeness or intactness, freedom from

---

[3] See Chapter 5 of this volume.

shame); and by the collusive attachment to family systems involving blame and impulsive action, which tend to perpetuate crises that utilize the reliability of the preoccupied person and divert attention from the inability to relate.

Example 3. An 18-year-old girl, the last of three siblings at home, was referred for treatment for suicidal thoughts, school underachievement, and promiscuity. Her mother berated her almost daily for her choice of boyfriends, spending hours on the phone, and failure to do homework. The mother accused her of taking lightly the many privileges she enjoyed as a member of a prosperous family. The father, a successful physician, had come from humble origins to establish a huge practice. Although close to retirement age, he left the dinner table each night to go to his study to do his book work. He was generous financially, physically present, and responsive to the material needs of his family. His emotional absence was felt to be justified by his duty to provide wealth and prestige for his family and the concomitant need for him to spend long hours attending to the business aspects of his practice. He responded to his wife's and daughter's constant upset states with vacations, trips, and expensive gifts, which justified more attention to money-making endeavors and even more absence.

Overt Shaming[4]

Blaming, impulsive action, and preoccupation may take fairly stable forms, allowing members of the same family to deal with a sense of shame in a way that, however painful, is not overtly and unremittingly humiliating for its members. In such cases, defensive emphasis is on evacuating the sense of personal inadequacy and disowning shameful parts of oneself. Only secondarily is it important to humiliate or mortify the other. Defensive maneuvers, however, may take a more volatile course if they deliberately and vengefully inflict shame on the other, often so that it is evident outside the family. Such situations may escalate into mutually torturing maneuvers, and violence is often the result.

Example 4. A 34-year-old man and his 46-year-old wife were seen in emergency consultation after he beat her. Both appeared panic stricken by the possibility of either hospitalization or outpatient treatment. In the emergency evaluation session, the husband emphasized his transgression, his power, his manliness, and his difficulty controlling his temper, both with his wife and with her son by a previous marriage. She spoke of her

---

[4] See Chapter 10 of this volume.

wish for a harmonious home and of her tribulations with such a volatile man. As the process evolved, they discussed recent events, including his driving around town with another woman in plain sight of his wife and her friends in a car that she had paid for. She talked in a humiliating and undercutting way about his inability to hold a job. She interrupted him constantly as he told the therapist about his difficulties with employers and his touchiness with people in authority. The process escalated into mutually deliberate shaming. The shame escalated when the husband requested hospitalization, was hospitalized, and was reported by his wife as the family defective.

TREATMENT IMPLICATIONS

It is not unusual to find a very vulnerable, fragmentation-prone family warding off shameful awareness of disorganizing propensities by the combined defensive modalities of an impulsive actor who invites blaming by a second family member and thus justifies protective "withdrawal" by a third, preoccupied member of the family. Families of borderlines are frequently composed of members who have a similar propensity for disorganization and have complementary defensive modalities for keeping such fragility from awareness. When overt shaming is part of the picture, violence is often in evidence.

Countertransference risks are great with this kind of patient. The therapist—unaware of, or uncomfortable dealing with, the patient's shame—risks responding to more prominent masking modalities involving anger, guilt, and control, without penetrating the essential core of the disturbance. The masks of collusive maneuvers usually appear quite clearly defensive. Nonetheless, the chaos and fluidity in borderline families may divert attention from the deep sense of shame that pervades every member. Defense is organized primarily around avoiding this kind of awareness. The therapist, by paying too much attention to transgression and control and not enough to disorganization and shame, risks interventions that are humiliating and "unempathic." Such unempathic interpretation is also incomplete for the same reasons. It involves a blamelike response to the patient's transgression, which misses the fact that the entire conflict also involves disorganization, shame, and the need for people to hold the personality together. At the other extreme, a response that fuses with the family system is sympathetic, not empathic, and risks fostering idealization and displacing negative aspects of the family's relationship with the therapist elsewhere. As protective, but emotionally absent, the therapist may unwittingly fit into a habitual defensive pattern that triggers exacerbation of symptoms. The same may be true if an overregulatory response to impulsive action increases the symptom.

Countertransference risks are many. A therapist, whether dealing with a borderline individual or a whole family, should be aware that familial transactions of blaming, impulsive action, preoccupation, and overt shaming figure powerfully in the patient's or family's relation to the therapist and exert powerful pressure on him or her to collude. Fragments of such relationships show up in the individual patient's anger, sense of entitlement, humiliation proneness, and need to control objects and at the same time deny their importance. With whole families, the therapist may miss the significance of blaming, preoccupation, impulsive action, and overt shaming as defenses against feeling shame before the therapist. Countertransferential overresponding to these defenses or joining them precludes dealing with them as usable resistances—defenses against shame before the therapist that may be utilized in treatment sometimes with decisive therapeutic gain.

The treatment implications are enormous. Experienced therapists always accommodate technique to the patient's or family's capacity to tolerate shame. The rationale for such an accommodation, however, becomes split off from our theories of pathological interaction and of technique by being referred to in terms of "timing, dosage, and tact" or subsumed by empathy. This unintegrated (and mostly oral) tradition of discussing techniques separately from theory underscores the ever-present risk of shaming in the therapeutic process. The cost of not recognizing shame theoretically is a failure to use humiliation proneness (so characteristic of borderline patients and their entire families) as a specific indicator of vulnerability and as a clue to assessing epigenetic and current life situations.

For some borderline patients and their families, direct strategies must be employed to keep the sense of humiliation from overwhelming the entire treatment situation and risking failure. A focus on shame, for example, may be useful, and specifically, on the paranoid form of shame, (i.e., humiliation proneness) may be helpful. Humiliation proneness is the tendency to impute to others, especially the therapist, the intent to inflict shame. For some patients, heavy emphasis on reconstructions may be necessary to help shed light on both the tendency to be ashamed and the specific things about which patients are ashamed. Those issues often have to do with attachments and detachments made without conscious choice or strong reaction when intimates get too close or too far away. Shedding light on early upbringing, often involving several generations, may help render such phenomena more understandable as processes and the patients as less shameful products than they seem to be without this understanding.

Treatment that ignores shame avoids the discomfort of dealing with it at the price of useful integration and involvement at optimal distance from the process. It is this integration that is so difficult for the borderline patient to meet in life. The therapist who shows toleration of discomfort, integration of complex reality, and involvement at optimal distance in the treatment process may impart these strengths to a patient or family that has hitherto been denied them.

4

Blame in the Marital Dyad

Progress in the conjoint psychotherapy of couples who engage in chronic verbal combat frequently comes to a standstill with accusatory episodes at the forefront of that couple's transactions. The unpleasantness of these episodes and the superficiality of the manifest issues being argued might suggest to the onlooker that the couple is dealing with issue at the point of crisis and is rapidly headed either toward resolution of the problem or toward dissolution of the marriage. But experience shows that blaming transactions often continue to be dominant not only in therapy, which may never progress beyond such flareups, but also throughout years and even decades of the couple's lives together as a chronic *modus operandi*. Blaming not only tends to preclude the resolution of the specific issues being contested, but also prevents the emergence of other issues in the therapy and affects other attachments in the couple's lives together. In the context of therapy this is a resistance; in the larger sense, it is a life style.

Couples do not usually enter treatment because of blaming. Blaming situations come to light in the midst of treatment for some other complaint, often one that arises from a change in equilibrium in the family system— troublesome conduct or underachievement by a child; depression, drinking, or work difficulties on the part of one spouse—so that the family homeostasis has been disrupted. Even severely dysfunctional blaming couples, however, especially if they are questioned while blaming be-

---

An earlier version of this chapter was the recipient of the Jacques Brien Award of the Los Angeles Psychiatric Society in 1978.

havior is observed during conjoint sessions, usually admit that blaming pervades their entire relationship but that bouts of blaming are not productive in resolving their difficulties. Nonetheless, it is extremely difficultfor a therapist to point effectively to the defensive nature of blaming. Therapeutic techniques that consider the contended issue at face value miss the deeper issues and the significance of the symptom. Those techniques that purport to go beneath the surface problem in an attempt to address underlying issues or mechanisms are opposed by the rather primitive defensive operations underlying such transactions. These are much more difficult to bring into useful therapeutic focus than are higher level, more neurotic mechanisms.

Both the distortion of issues and details and the vehemence of the primitive affects and defensive operations make it most difficult to secure a therapeutic alliance with the couple especially during the actual act of blaming. When one spouse is seen alone or at times when the blaming states are not present, the therapist gets the sense that an entirely different state of consciousness is in evidence and that neither the spouses nor the therapist is in touch with the states of mind present during the blaming situation. Blaming, at least the type of blaming that I am here describing, is a dissociative state, one that is split off from the mainstream of continuity of consciousness.

A fairly typical technical difficulty posed by the blaming couple is the collusive use of primitive defensive operations that renders reflection on the process while it is going on almost impossible and reflection on the process at some other time remote and ineffective.

Example 1.   Mrs. A, in conjoint treatment, proclaimed, "I'm a yeller. I get upset and yell. Then it's all over and I'm all right. I don't store it up. I just yell and get it over with. But if I don't, he walks all over me." This outburst took place early in her awareness that her ego states were not integrated with each other. In the angry blaming state she could vent anger and ward off domination vehemently but unthinkingly. In her more usual, calmer state, she was reflective and reasonable, but she felt prey to domination by her husband and powerless to ward off his influence. In this more relaxed usual state, she compared herself with her mother and sister, whom she saw as dominated by their husbands. Both states reflected her fear of domination and sense of powerlessness and inadequacy to manage her life effectively.

The phenomenon of blame, as such, has received very little attention. Although discussion of this kind of patient is not rare in the literature, blame per se is usually discussed as something else: as anger, as hostility, as narcissistic rage, as conflict, as marital disharmony, or in terms of a particular mechanism involved in the blaming, such as projection, sado-masochism, or projective identification. The clinical features seen in the blaming couple are commonly discussed as pathology of what has come to be called "borderline" phenomena: those defensive operations organized around the maintenance of splitting (as opposed to repression) and around the primacy of oral-aggressive rage. Such defensive operations derive primarily from dyadic, preoedipal disturbances and involve the mechanism of splitting and those mechanisms reinforcing splitting: idealization, devaluation, primitive forms of projecting, and projective identification in particular (Kernberg, 1967, 1975, 1976). Alternatively, they may be seen as manifestations of personality fragmentation or narcissistic breakdown (Kohut, 1971, 1977; Lansky, 1991), as expressions of narcissistic rage or as reactions to a disrupted selfobject bond.

Discussion of blaming phenomena subsumed simplistically under various intrapsychic mechanisms misses the richness of the clinical picture of the blaming couple. Such blaming situations have surprisingly stable structures that often endure for decades. The spouses may be chronically miserable, yet they stay together. Divorce is not nearly as common as might be expected given the evident and continual misery. Disputes do not resolve either cognitively or emotionally. One or both in the marriage may threaten divorce without making convincing moves either to get out of the marriage or to make the marriage better. It is the striking tenacity of such relationships in the presence of continued misery that makes necessary a full explanation of blame that goes beyond the surface experience, beyond a simple conflict model of verbal behavior called blaming, and beyond explanation entirely in terms of intrapsychic mechanisms.

In this chapter, the principal focus is on the therapeutic understanding of the transactional phenomenon of blame, on the significance of the blaming couple as a clinical syndrome. The difficulties of those who form blaming relationships can be seen as constitutional neediness and aggressiveness resulting from developmental failures, or from personality vulnerabilities predisposing to fragmentation, the emergence of shame, and consequent narcissistic rage. A spouse in such a relationship may have an affective disorder, a characterologic difficulty, a severe neurosis, or a narcissistic personality disturbance. Spouses may be treated separately or conjointly, with medication or without. Our present state of knowledge does not allow for definitive conclusions about etiology, diagnosis, or treatment. We can best proceed to deal with such difficulties only by trying to understand the significance of the blaming syndrome within a dyadic relationship.

The full richness of the blaming transaction is often missed when we are held captive by oversimplified models of blame, that is, when blaming is called something else. I shall, therefore, consider blame in terms of projection, sadomasochism, and projective identification only as a preliminary to a deeper understanding of the phenomenon. Early usages of these terms suggested mechanistic and entirely intrapsychic explanatory models. The connotations of each of these terms has, of course, evolved to a richer usage, one mindful of the adaptational and interactional significance of the processes involved. Because early and later usages are often confused, I will try to get beyond the conceptual entrapment that commonly accompanies the terminology by tracing the development of more sophisticated models from earlier ones. I will also attempt, in the discussion of the "mechanisms" underlying projection, sadomasochism, and projective identification, to push beyond the limited explanatory force of each of these terms. This will, I hope, allow for a fuller consideration of blame as a symptom, as a restitution, and in the therapeutic situation.

The clinical material on which this chapter is based is, for the most part, from the conjoint treatment of couples in many settings and with patients with varying levels of psychopathology. What is offered as evidence, therefore, is not the associations of individual patients, which depends on the sustained intrapsychic focus in one patient. Rather, the material deals with the phenomenology of the blaming situation from the perspective of the observation and treatment of the entire familial system of which blame in the marital dyad is the preeminent transaction.

INTRAPSYCHIC EXPLANATIONS: MECHANISMS OF BLAMING

Projection

I hold to the narrow sense of projection as a defense in which traits whose recognition in oneself would cause distress are disowned and attributed to others. To understand the role of projection in the blaming transaction, one must understand that the conscience of the blamer is a more primitive regulatory system than is the more mature conscience and, as Klein (1934) pointed out, much more savage. Disruptions in personal well-being are met with by savage attacks, whether those disruptions are an inner awareness of impulses, of shortcomings of the adaptive capacities, or of the avoidable or unavoidable failures in others with whom encompassing, symbiotic relationships serve to keep ego deficits, personality vulnerabilities, and uncontrolled drive manifestations from awareness. The experience of personality disorganization that results from exposure of the unacceptably needy, self-centered, or hostile behaviors or the inability to meet responsibilities or standards gives rise to a mortifying sense of humiliation that can be modified if, in fantasy at least, one disclaims responsibility and relocates unacceptable parts of oneself to another person. On such occasions when clear manifestations of primitive, humiliation-prone conscience are evident in treatment, the therapist usually senses an inescapable and mortifying sense of responsibility for defects. Spouses who may function at a reasonable level of responsibility outside the relationship may, nonetheless, require the blamed other spouse for the externalization of what are essentially self-reproaches. In the wake of the blaming process, there may be a therapeutic impasse because the blamer experiences even the most nonjudgmental of interpretations locating responsibility in himself or herself as a reversal of the projective process, as blame itself.

Example 2. Mrs. B, a woman in her late 40s, appeared reluctantly for a conjoint interview after her husband was told that treatment for his potency disorder would have to involve her. Her manner was angry and caustic. She spoke only of Mr. B's inadequacy and his inability to satisfy her sexually, his disgusting personal habits, his failure as a breadwinner, and his lack of respect for her relationship with her mother, which had dominated the household for decades of their married life. A tentative query from the therapist concerning her views on any part she might play in the unhappy marital situation was felt to be an accusation of the type that she leveled at her husband. She flew into a rage at the (felt) attack and left the first session, never to return.

Blaming, however, goes beyond self-exculpation and relocation of culpability in another person. Consider, for example, the three-party transaction, *gossip*, in which one party talks to another about the blame-worthy traits of a third. Within the phenomenon of gossip is not only blame of the third party but the strengthening of the bond between the two who gossip by virtue of sharing and reaffirming the standards by which the criticized trait is blameworthy. The disowned traits are envied ones at some level: aggressive behavior, competitiveness, exemption from re-sponsibility or punishment, or special status of some sort. That which is gossiped about is felt, by the parties who gossip, to be a danger to interpersonal bonds if applied to the gossips themselves. Disowning the threatening traits makes the bonds between gossipers stronger and the blame (and to some extent, the envy) is directed toward others outside of the gossiping dyad. Returning to the two-party blame system, one can see the same factors operative. Blaming is a phenomenon that goes beyond self-exculpation and relocation in the other of culpability. It constitutes, in some part, an attack on the activities which threaten the dyadic bond of a significant relationship. The blamed activities may be of obvious sexual, aggressive, or competitive significance or a simple increase of indepen-dence in which one spouse simply goes his or her way independently, thereby jeopardizing the restrictive dyadic relationship.

One can hear in the manifest reproaches of the accuser not only the projection of responsibility for the blamer's own unacceptable traits, but also the intense dependency and the blamer's need that the blamed other be free of those traits because of the type of bond between the blamer and the blamed.

*Example 3.*The following is from the transcript of the first few minutes of a taped session in which the wife, Mrs. C, was a few minutes late:

HUSBAND: But at three o'clock you should have been here.
WIFE: I got out of there about five minutes after three.
HUSBAND: (vehemently) You should have been done and at your car at three o'clock and all that other stuff should have been done and over with.
THERAPIST: I don't understand why you couldn't meet right in the office.
HUSBAND: Because she's afraid, I guess, of being by herself with some of the people around here, I guess. I don't know. She seems to be helpless sometimes and so able at other times.
THERAPIST: You're angry.
HUSBAND: (furious) I'm *goddamned* angry!
THERAPIST: What about?
HUSBAND: (screaming) At this unreliable . . . asshole . . . I come up here depending on her being here at a certain time and she ain't there. She's off doing her own thing . . . like this ain't the first time. It's the story of her life. I cannot depend on her to do a simple little function.

Example 3 points to the fear of either the dissolution of the relationship or the loss of the expected reliability and specialness that underlies the blaming episode. Although such a special bond can easily be inferred from a transcript of what is said, it is commonly overlooked because of the intense affect, self-righteousness, and attacking quality in the blamer. The surface issues are often not distorted so much as magnified in importance. The magnification bespeaks the attacker's dependency, fear of separation, and terrifying disorganization at the awareness of being let down.

Example 4.   A few moments later in the same session:

WIFE: Every time I make a mistake he blows it out of proportion.
HUSBAND: I don't. I get madder and madder and madder when you stand there and defend yourself when you're a hundred percent wrong. If you'd just said, "Honey, I'm sorry," I could forget

the whole thing, but you stand there like a fool and try to defend yourself.

WIFE: I guess maybe it's because you come at me and, well, as if I, and start fussing at me and jumping down my throat.

HUSBAND: Well, I have reason to . . .

WIFE: And, so . . .

HUSBAND: See, you're defending yourself some more. Goddammit, if you're in the wrong, can't you, haven't you got the guts to, to say, "Honey, I'm sorry."

THERAPIST: What should she have done?

HUSBAND: She should have either sat in her car from three o'clock on waiting for me to arrive.

WIFE: Most of the time when he says meet him some place, sometimes he hasn't thought it out exactly what he . . . uh . . . all the fine details evidently. Or he comes little bit earlier than what he . . . uh . . . should be coming. He shows up and then he decides that he can actually find me in a place. Well, he can't find me so he gets angry with the fact that he can't find me.

HUSBAND: Well, a 10-year-old girl, you would have to have to give Mommy or Daddy and lead them around by the nose for them to get someplace and I think that's just about where you're at because nobody else . . . I don't think . . . you have to tell that to. Anybody else would have enough sense to be able to figure, "Well, now, he's gonna come down here looking for me. I better make myself available."

In contrast to participants in blaming transactions, patients in psychotic paranoid states with fixed delusions may gain some measure of self-esteem by disowning traits, usually impulses, but no relations other than delusional ones are secured (Lansky, 1977b). Projection plays a prominent role in blaming transactions, but the phenomenon of the blaming couple cannot be explained by projection entirely. The concept fails to account for the collusive nature of the blaming transaction—why such relationships endure, why they do not correct themselves, why they are so prominent in binding couples together to the exclusion of other loyalties and attachments.

Sadomasochism

Blaming involves aggressiveness toward the blamed, and to the extent that punishment is inflicted or received in a repetitive fashion, one may be tempted to subsume blaming because of its presumed gratifications under the model of sadomasochistic relationships. Mutually accusatory relationships, however, fit such a model less aptly than relationships in which one person blames and the other willingly receives the blame; I shall confine my remarks to the latter sort of blaming relationship, where one party typically blames, accuses, bullies, or berates the other, who does not protest or does so only feebly.

In the dynamic sense, the term sadomasochism, as well as the terms sadism and masochism, have a history that renders their usage confusing if not incomprehensible. Prior to the consideration of aggression in Freud's (1920) *Beyond the Pleasure Principle*, sadism was regarded as an instinctual vicissitude, in particular, as erotism of the muscular apparatus, consisting in sexual excitation in the inflicting of punishment on another (Freud, 1905a, 1917). As a sexual perversion, sadism refers to sexual excitation enhanced by, or permissible only in the context of, inflicting punishment on another. Early theories of masochism saw it as the passive and complementary counterpart of sadism, the turning of sadism on oneself, i.e., sexual excitation at being the object of punishment, again a derivative of erotism of the muscular apparatus.

Since 1923 and the beginning of attention to the structural theory and to aggression, psychoanalytic theory has, of course, gone considerably beyond this explanatory mode (Brenner, 1959). As used today, the term, sadomasochism, has the disadvantage either of implying that actual sexual excitation accompanies the inflicting and receiving of punishment or of losing most of the explanatory advantages altogether. In the erotic lives of blaming couples both sexual excitation and intercourse are infrequent. Implied by the noninstinctual ego-psychological use of the term sadomasochism, however, is that there is some sort of sexual gratification underlying the apparent unpleasantness. The notion of collusion is implicit but is not spelled out. Out of adaptational context, the term sadomasochism provides no useful understanding of the blaming phenomenon.

Example 5.   Mr. C complained bitterly that his wife was unreceptive to his sexual needs and that he was chronically sexually frustrated. He voiced his sexual reproaches petulantly, belligerently, and reproachfully, and he complained that his wife was disloyal, unkempt, stupid, and undependable. While the aggressive attack served to express his feeling both sexually needy and sexually rejected, it also insured that sexual contact with his wife did not happen. The collusiveness in giving and receiving verbal punishment also served to avoid sexual contact.

Example 6.   Mrs. D continually berated her husband for drinking and being unemployed and often sided with her daughter from a previous marriage in contemptuous attacks on her husband. She protested that she was both needed and was eager for sexual contact but that her husband's resentment, drunkenness, depression, and frequent impotence made intercourse an infrequent occurrence. On one occasion, when she reported satisfying intercourse, her husband reported gratefully that he had "done his duty" for the first time in months.

Describing blaming relationships as sadomasochistic also fails to distinguish the *verbal act of blaming*—the inflicting of punishment by verbal assaults, accusations, criticism, contempt, or belittling remarks—from acts that inflict punishment in other ways: physical abuse, unconcealed infidelities, impulsive or addictive behavior, or openly hostile coalitions with children or in-laws. The essence of blame is that it is both verbal and dyadic.

The verbal behavior of blaming asserts a relationship, discharges aggression, makes charges of damage to the blamer, and at the same time covers over or gainsays the intense dependency, low self-regard and pervasive sense of shame that might be inferred from the literal content of the blamer's accusations. The act of blaming often contains direct reference to unfair exploitation of the blamer's vulnerabilities or defects; this is usually overshadowed, however, by storms of narcissistic rage, self-righteousness, and a sense of entitlement to justice. This exhilarated sense of self-righteousness and entitlement lasts only during the act of blaming and serves a defensive function in those in whom the residue of damage and humiliation due to desertion and deprivation by early caretakers are major issues.

Blaming transactions may be a vehicle for envy and often exert a self-fulfilling force on the blamed:

Example 7. Mrs. D (from the previous example), whose father and first husband were drinkers, savagely blamed her husband for his drinking even during the long periods of time when he was sober. It was often following blaming bouts that he would relapse into alcoholic binges. With the aid of conjoint and couples group therapy, Mrs. D was helped to appreciate that her anxieties were activated by issues other than her husband's drinking. She explored her past and how much her upbringing in a family similar to her current one had colored both her marriages. Her strong attachment to her mother and her fear of being like her mother, who both feared and attacked men, came to the fore so strongly in treatment that Mrs. D decided to visit her mother in a distant city to explore the "unfinished business" she had brought into her marriages. Her husband's drinking, job difficulties, and depression abated as a result of his own efforts in treatment and when the anxieties underlying her blaming behavior were acknowledged and brought into focus. The husband remained sober and employed after a lengthy follow-up period.

The blamer may experience blaming attacks as revolts against a long-standing attitude of subservience. Spouses who are the unprotesting recipients of blame are commonly clinically depressed. Women in such relationships are often, by their own admission, slovenly—poor housekeepers with almost no interest in sexual relationships. For the blamed, there is a loss of self-respect and resentment of the humiliation as well as the perpetration of the degraded status by inviting demeaning accusations.

Example 8.   Mrs. C (Examples 3, 4 and 5) consented infrequently to intercourse. She seemed even to invite verbal punishment from her husband. When her parents' marriage had dissolved, she went with her mother while her older sisters went with another relative. When her mother and sisters were reunited, she assuaged the wrath of her sisters by degrading submission by which she secured the relationship to them. She did so again in her marriage but at the cost of her self-respect. She seldom expressed her resentment as such, but her lack of interest in sex served to distance her husband, retaliate for his attacks, and invite more blame. Mr. C, for his part, felt deprived of sexual gratification, frustrated, and rejected.

Both parties in such relationships are intensely dependent and both have narcissistic preoccupations that make it impossible for them to feel that they have entered the marital relationship completely. For the one inflicting punishment, avoidance of humiliation is of paramount concern and can never be put to rest except during the act of blaming. For the one accepting (or inviting) the punishment, preservation of the relationship at the cost of self-respect has been a *modus operandi* for so long that a degrading form of relating is less anxiety provoking than is one offering mutual respect.

Example 9.   Mr. E was hospitalized several times for depression stemming, in part, from the consequences of his characterologic difficulties. His wife berated him for drinking even when, by her admission, he had been sober for many months. At length, his fury mounted and he did drink, losing his job and his self-respect and inviting more blame from his wife. The drinking served to justify his wife's blaming and to lower her anxiety about commitment to him and to the marriage. The cost, however, was his self-respect and chronic impotence. Job difficulties and serious depression resulted.

Collusiveness in such relationships takes place as follows: one spouse has a need to degrade by verbal bullying, and the other suffers these attacks in a fashion that locks the blamer into a relationship. Both are intensely dependent and need an exclusive relationship, no matter what the cost, and both have a terror of intimacy that the collusive giving and receiving of blame enables them to avoid. The spouse receiving the blame is often clinically depressed, frequently with attendant neurovegetative signs and, almost invariably, with loss of libido. There is rarely any gratification outside of the relationship; work and business relationships are described in a colorless, affectless way. If there are extramarital affairs, they are often revealed in ways that inflict more humiliation and punishment on the spouse. The inflictor of punishment is as incapable of autonomous gratification as is the receiver.

Calling blaming relationships sadomasochistic because of the repetitive and, in some ways, gratifying giving and receiving of punishment departs from the earliest understanding of sadism and masochism as organ pleasures of the neuromuscular apparatus. There is a certain amount of security, and even exhilaration, in the aggressive discharge that secures a relationship and avoids humiliation at the same time, but such exhilaration must not be confused with genital and sexual excitation. Furthermore, blame is of its very essence verbal, and although physical punishment may accompany blame, it is peripheral. The issues of reversing or receiving humiliation, protesting and simultaneously avoiding abandonment, and inflicting and receiving verbal punishment are paramount in the blaming relationship. As applied to blaming in the marital dyad, "sadomasochism" can only be used in a sense that is strictly adaptational, in which case, the term loses its usefulness as an explanatory concept.

Projective Identification

The term projective identification has several usages, each emphasizing different points. The term was introduced in 1946 by Melanie Klein to refer to the primitive defensive operation whereby, in fantasy, part of the self is split off and projected into another who is sadistically controlled and who carries that part. Melanie Klein intended this as a primitive variant of a phenomenon of vicariousness first observed in detail by Freud and discussed as "identification" (Breuer and Freud, 1893-1895; Freud, 1921). Knight (1940) was one of the earliest investigators to discuss the interplay of identification, projection, and introjection in primitive defensive operations, especially those that characterize the oral fixation in borderline states and alcoholics.

Projective identification finds its location in lower level defensive operations, particularly those reinforcing splitting (Kernberg, 1967, 1975; Malin and Grotstein, 1966).

For the present discussion, it is necessary to add to the strictly intrapsychic dimension of projective identification. The fantasy of splitting off part of oneself and projecting it into another is accomplished by invitation and provocation to collude, that is, for the other to act as though he or she actually carried that part. This point has been most often emphasized in the discussion of transference and countertransference phenomena with borderline patients (Klein, 1946; Bion, 1954, 1957, 1977; Frosch, 1970; Giovacchini, 1973; Kernberg, 1975; Ogden, 1979). The provocation to collude—verging on coercion to collude—then make projective identification much more complicated than an intrapsychic defense. The term, in its more sophisticated usage (Langs, 1976; Ogden, 1979) referring to a complex collusive defensive and gratifying interactional system, far supersedes the original intrapsychic usage and goes a great deal further in explaining the blaming situation.

But if blame is to be understood, more has to be added to explain projective identification as Melanie Klein described it. In the blaming couple and in the blaming collusive defense, which the term projective identification may describe in part, there is also a *disowning* both of the projected part and of the collusive process itself. Unless this is appreciated, neither projective identification as a mechanism, transpersonal or otherwise, nor the phenomenon of blaming, which may be seen as a specific type of projective identification, can be understood.

The concept of projective identification bridges the gap between the intrapsychic point of view and the systems point of view. The specifics of the vicariousness in the blaming system in the marital dyad is that it involves simultaneous expression and disowning of the same traits. It is not necessarily pathological to act in collusion with others so that they carry parts not compatible with one's identity. This happens regularly in close relationships and invariably in the family. The absence of the ability to live through people vicariously by identification is itself a sign of serious narcissistic pathology. In a family in particular, the traits of any of the members are available for all to identify with and to use—not only typical instrumental, integrative, expressive, and nurturing qualities in the parents, but childish and omnipotential ones in the children. What is of importance in relationships dominated by lower level defensive operations is exactly what is noteworthy in the blaming relationship. Not only the vicariously experienced parts but also the act of colluding is disowned. In less pathological close relationships, collusion may be inexplicit, but it is not disowned.

The charges in the blaming attack are almost all damage done to the blamer by variants of desertion, unreliability, abandonment, failure of the object to be competent—of letting the blamer down in one form or another. Close attention to the blamer's actual words will often reveal in a very obvious way allusions to damage, defect, or desertion. To the extent to which these are traits of the blamer carried by the blamed, one may say that projective identification in the Kleinian sense is operative. But the strict usage of projective identification fails to consider the sense of damage, narcissistic injury, and shame conveyed in the accusation and the use of the object to restore the sense of self by regulating emotional distance.

Another aspect of projective identification, that most emphasized by the object relations school (Fairbairn, 1952; Dicks, 1963, 1967), focuses on the role of projective identification in collusive relationships that allow each spouse to repeat (in modified form) traumatic relationships from childhood. Disowned "parts," as well as the failure to meet needs in general, are seen as attributes of the person being blamed. A two-fold identification takes place—the disowned and projected needs are identified with the blamed person; and the blamer may also identify with an internal representation of someone seen in the past as critical (A. Freud, 1936; Fairbairn, 1952). The assumption here is that early and basically unsatisfying and traumatogenic object relationships have been dealt with intrapsychically in a way that involves the internalizing and identifying acceptable parts of oneself with an object, a critical one, and externalizing unacceptable parts of oneself onto another, who, however stimulating, is ultimately disappointing. This "identification with the aggressor" may involve both projection and a primitive variant of projective identification. Exhilaration and a feeling of self-righteousness result from the identification with a critical, rejecting, bad internal object whose loss is feared. The damaging behavior is experienced as coming entirely from the other. The contribution of the object relations theorists to the concept of projective identification is a theory of preoccupation with past traumata and their residual developmental consequences, which are replayed in the process of projective identification.

Example 10.   Mr. C (Examples 3, 4, 5, 8) was born in wartime Europe to a mother who resented having a child, and especially resented having a boy. He was told that his father had died in combat before his birth. He was passed from his mother to aunts and a grandmother, all of whom showed open resentment at having to care for him. He was frequently dressed in girls' clothes. In his marriage, his rage at his dependency on women was understandable in the light of these early humiliations at the hands of female caretakers.

Mrs. C was the youngest of three daughters born to an alcoholic couple. When her parents' marriage collapsed, she went with her mother, much to the resentment of her two older sisters, who went with the father. When her mother deteriorated further, Mrs. C went to live with her father and sisters and adapted to the resentful sisters' hatred of her by enduring and even inviting bullying from them. Her behavior in her own marriage was the same. She felt most needed and most secure when allowing another person to use her as an object of rage. The price of such security was a chronic depression.

Conflicts in blaming relationships involving projective identification do not reach resolution. The blaming situation is a venue for constant replays of internalized past traumata that interfere with the integration of the self and with which there is constant preoccupation. The repetition should not be thought of as an unmodified repeating of something that actually happened; perception of frustrating relationships is modified internally by the vicissitudes of the individual's aggression and reprojected in altered form. Projections may be available for some alteration before being reintrojected (Klein, 1946). Likewise, perpetuation of the repeated relationship requires the collusion, coerced or willing, of the acceptor of the disowned traits. Such collusion may entail doing something active to confirm the blamer's expectations or being provoked to do something that may be so interpreted, such as responding angrily or leaving the field physically or emotionally.

Example 11.   Mr. F, a man in his 50s, had a history of overstimulation and abandonment by his mother. His father died when he was four. Thereafter, he slept in his mother's bed until she suddenly remarried three years later and placed him in an orphanage. In later life, he went from job to job, usually quitting and leaving town after he impregnated his latest girl friend. He subsequently married one of the women and continued to berate her verbally with threats of abandonment. His wife had been left by her own mother to her grandmother's care, taken back by the mother, and left with her grandmother again several years later after sexual advances were made by her stepfather. In the relationship and subsequent marriage both "replayed," in modified form, preoccupations with overstimulation and abandonment.

What is pathological about projective identification is reinforcement of lack of integration in the personality, the disowning, and the high cost of the pathological relationship system. In less pathological relationship systems, the projection of traits incompatible with one's identity into another who carries them is a use of vicariousness as a liberating and gratifying experience conducive to freedom and growth. In regressive, collusive relationships there is only a collusive permission to replay psychic trauma and to vent narcissistic rage over the residual defects to the exclusion of everything else. This replay of predominantly traumatic object relationships involving splitting may represent not only a set of expectations and anxieties concerning conflicted dependency and modification of dependent relationships by the workings of internal aggression, but also attempts establish omnipotent control. What was internalized was a notion of a desperately needed bond with the other that is traumatic, intensely dependent and, above all, precarious. Vulnerable to constant withdrawal and abandonment by the other, the relationship is replayed as a verbal reversal of humiliating helplessness that seems a masterful act of self-righteousness. Presumably, what was experienced by the blamer in a passive, powerless, victimized role is replayed with reversal of affect in the verbal role of blamer. Mastery, self-righteousness, and omnipotent control, so prominent a part of the blaming transaction, are quite the opposite of the presumed original feelings of helplessness and shame. In that sense, the defensive function of projective identification is partly successful in overcoming powerlessness, helplessness, and humiliation by reworking the original situation experienced in the act of blame. The sense of entitlement (Murray, 1964) indicates collusive permission to discharge verbally the aggression resulting from such situations and awareness of their antecedent developmental deficits.

Lifelong fears of loss of relationship, loss of fantasied omnipotence, being let down, and being shamefully fragmented and helpless are still in evidence in the background of the blaming scenario, but in the forefront are well-ordered verbal attacks, with the self-assuredness and exhilaration of the accusatory state. The mastery and self-righteousness, as well as the omnipotence, are to be had only in the act of blaming when the dyad is held in place, and so the blamer, to restore the sense of cohesion and well-being, must repeat the blaming transaction whenever his or her personality cohesion is threatened. Without recourse to blaming, the old infantile anxieties and the sense of defectiveness and shame reappear, especially when the collusive other embarks on some independent activity. Collusion (as the fantasy complementary to omnipotent control) is the hallmark of relationships characterized by projective identification. This collusion is, of course, evident in the blaming couple. One can understand the tenacity of these relationships only in terms of underlying collusiveness.

THE SYMPTOM

This brief consideration of the concepts under which blaming phenomena are subsumed has, it is hoped, furthered an appreciation of some of the infantile roots and forms of defensive operations often seen in blaming relationships without minimizing of the phenomenology of the blaming situation.

Blaming is aggressive. The accuser attacks as he or she blames. Gratification and restoration of a sense of self as well as dissipation of a state of shame accompanies the expression of anger at being deserted, at being let down, not being able to be dependent on the blamed. That is to say, the source of the blamer's sense of shame, the inflictor of the narcissistic wound that precipitated a fragmentation experience, has been attacked. In the attack the blamer may attribute his or her disowned traits to the blamed other. thus, the self is exculpated and the other person is held responsible for one's diminished sense of self and damaged well-being. Blaming allows verbal expression of anxieties about humiliations and disappointments that stem from frustrations in early caretaking and resonate with incompletely dealt-with anxieties about those earlier relationships, central and tenuous ones, that are repeated in the relationships with the blamed other.

I am not presuming that the repetition is the same as the original experience. Indeed, the difference is usually manifest in the increased sense of mastery and, certainly, in the reversal of affect and sense of entitlement that accompanies the verbal facility, sense of self-righteousness, and the omnipotent expectations of responsibility and care from the other. The blamer may, and usually does, feel competent and relieved, even exhilarated during the act of blaming. Sexual excitement may occur, but the act of blaming usually precludes rather than promotes sexual satisfaction; sexual sadism and masochism, even if they do occur, are not of central importance. The feeling of mastery and exhilaration is present only when blaming occurs. It is the sense of self in relation to an accountable other that is of primary importance. Blaming as a symptom works, so to speak, only when it is going on; and, while it is going on, there is an altered state of consciousness—unselfconscious, cohesive, relatively shame-free self in relation to another presumed to be both capable and accountable. When blaming is going on, a relationship is asserted that turns the tables, so to speak, on internal objects that are the residue of traumata in early life that have left the patient fragile, afraid of both intimacy and abandonment, and filled with shame.

Intimacy is avoided. Yet there is also in the act of blaming a collusion in the relationship with the one who accepts the blaming behavior (whether or not the assignment of culpability in the blamer's accusations is accepted), who accepts the dependency of the blamer on the blamed, who grants the blamer a certain entitlement to specialness in the relationship for holding the blamed person accountable. The entitlement is always to be heard beneath the rage and the show of apparent confidence and mastery that the verbal behavior presumes. This verbal ego strength and heightened sense of self serves to gainsay the weakness, helplessness, and sense of defectiveness and shame that the dependency on the blamed presupposes. This dependency is usually considerably less evident than the verbal dexterity and masterful attack, although it is certainly beneath the surface. The examination of a verbal transcript of a blaming transaction will show this dependency quite obviously (see, e.g., Examples 3 and 4). Blame restores self-esteem, particularly when weakness, dependency and helplessness have been chronically humiliating issues in the past and have been faced in the presence of precarious object relationships reprojected in the present onto the blamed.

Blaming has complex effects on the relationship of the blamer and the blamed. The blaming couple or family must be seen as a system of complementary and interlocking pathologies in persons whose behaviors perpetuate, maintain, and protect the system. The system is organized around expression and containment of vulnerability to disorganization, overwhelming shame, primitive rage, and fear both of abandonment and closeness while at the same time keeping the persons in the system from being flooded with the awareness of the inadequacy protested in the manifest blaming transaction itself. The parties keep at some distance by inflicting punishment and disappointment on each other, but at the same time there is presupposed and preserved an intensely dependent dyadic relationship that confers on both a special, all-encompassing, omnipotent status within the relationship.

By distancing the blamer from the blamed, the blaming transaction removes each party from consciously experiencing real obligations to the other, from real commitment to the relationship, from the terror of exposure that intimacy involves, from the risks and uncertainties that commitment entails. Indeed, both spouses may be securely locked into such a relationship for decades, yet maintain a conscious experience of themselves as on the verge of separation, on the verge of divorce, or as emotionally already out of the relationship. The state of mind achieved by blaming not only reestablishes a firm bond with the other but paradoxically preserves omnipotent possibilities for both in fantasy, usually *conscious* fantasy. Both can presume that they are actually outside of the relationship, and this distance frees both from emotional involvement with each other. At the same time, the blamer demands accountability from the other. The feeling of entitlement is the basis for a reproach that the imperfections of the other have caused damage and shame. The imperfections of the world and the complaints of the blamer against the world are embodied in arguments with the blamed. The blamed thus stands for the whole of the reality, which the blamer hates.

As noted, the voiced entitlement presumes a collusion; and the collusion is in keeping with the specialness, exclusiveness, and omnipotence of the relationship. Voiced angrily, the sense of entitlement is free from the self-consciousness and shame over neediness and defectiveness that might undermine it. Blame is likely to appear at times when one party in a relationship is seeking autonomous gratification; blaming serves to reestablish the dyadic equilibrium and to lock the other back into the relationship when he or she threatens to go his or her own way. The autonomy of the other may trigger a flood of anxiety about the blamer's fragility, weakness, and inability to manage in the world. Such anxiety may be warded off by a reestablishment of the blaming situation whereby the anxiety and narcissistic rage are experienced as coming entirely from the shortcomings of the other. The focus shifts from weakness, helplessness, and shame in the self to power and malevolence in the other. At such times as the blaming defense can be foregone, shame and anxiety of this type can be overwhelming.

During the act of blaming, the blamer does not experience blame as damaging and generally does not consciously experienced guilt toward the blamed. Blaming may, in fact, defend against the type of involvement with the blamed person that would give rise to feelings of guilt attendant on harming another person whose independent existence is truly valued.

Example 12.   Mrs. G, a woman in her early 50s, appeared for conjoint sessions with her husband, who was hospitalized for psychotic depression and a serious suicide attempt. She berated him for irresponsibility, minimized his incapacity, and demanded that he return to work in their small business. He attempted to do so, became overwhelmed, and was rehospitalized. He requested vocational training, agreeing with a recommendation that he get a less pressured, salaried job. After hospitalization, Mrs. G made the same demands, and he was again depressed. His wife could see only the gains from illness, which, though they were indeed present, were not the central reason for his incapacity.

The blamed person often does not feel damaged, hurt, or guilty. This apparent oblivion to the attack is indicative of the underlying collusion. The blamed person's sense of self is often buttressed by the blamer's attributions of power and malevolence. Blaming transactions differ markedly from those in which the other is overtly shamed. The blamed person, however, may harbor anger about whatever is healthy in the relationship that is sacrificed to maintain the blame system—especially social, sexual, or recreational parts of the couple's lives that become impoverished. This feeling—that if it weren't for the blamer, the blamed person could have a happier, more enjoyable life—serves to protect both partners from acknowledging overwhelming inadequacies in relation to social, sexual, recreational, or vocational endeavors.

If the blamed partner does not blame in return and receives no acknowledgment as an independent person, the blamed person may suffer a clinical depression. Conversely, depression may be seen in this situation as resulting from the lack of sufficient entitlement to blame persons who are representatives of dehumanizing bonds with internal objects. The blaming transaction engineers and covers over a regression from a mature empathic type of relationship, not only of spouses to each other but of the blamed person's relation to internal objects that have truly damaged him or her.

The blamer in a blaming relationship avoids risks, empathy, mutuality, guilt, estimating his or her own force in the world, coping with exploitation, enjoying sexuality, cooperating, and a host of other ways of viewing the other person as complete and independent and acknowledging relationships outside of the regressive dyad. This avoidance is evident in the negative symptomatology of the blaming couple. Their conflict covers up and holds in place what may be called an almost schizoid dyad, often one without any meaningful connections to the outside world, a unit of two, stable despite the appearance of perpetual instability. Their quarreling is a schizoid withdrawal mechanism to shield them from the rest of the world and from the constant threat of exposure as defective, unimportant, and inadequate.

Chaotic blaming relationships may be stabilized by a third party. This can happen in a number of ways. For instance, the object of blame may be a child on whom both of the spouses focus. Unfortunately, as Odier (1956) has noticed, this predisposes the child to acquire the same inadequacies and, in many instances, the same sort of marriage and the same subsequent fate as both parents.

The conflict put forward in the manifest content of the statements in the dissociated blaming state posits a regression from mature multiparty relationships inside the dyad and out. It preserves a fixation at a preoedipal and essentially omnipotent level of entitled specialness, dyadic collusion, and somewhat magically object-related specialness whereby all the world's imperfections are attributed to the shortcomings of the blamed. In the blamer there is a feeling of being damaged and cheated that is objectified in the outbursts and, with permission expressed tacitly, in the relation to the blamed. The ambivalence toward the blamed is manifest in a magical expectation that relief from all frustration should come from this person and that, at the same time, this person should have no autonomous life of his or her own. Any attempt by one party in the relationship to go his or her own way is usually followed by some incident that reestablishes a blaming situation and reunites the dyad.

RESTITUTION

Conflict in the blaming situation essentially holds the spouses' fixation to dyads in place. It allows the couple to avoid intimacy, involvement and risk, and at the same time serves to replay anxieties about object loss and loss of their fantasied special entitlement.

The fixation in the blaming relationship is usually shared by both partners. Bowen (1966) has noted that married couples are frequently at surprisingly similar levels of differentiation of self, despite any outward appearances, even where one of the spouses appears quite functional and the other grossly dysfunctional. At a deep level there is usually a similar psychological structure in spouses in any enduring marriage. Both tend to come from the same kinds of families, and the marriages of both sets of parents tend to be quite similar to the marriage that the spouses have entered. Their marriage, in turn, usually produces offspring predisposed to similar marriages. When the offspring of such marriages select each other for marriage, the situation, which Odier (1956) has called "the neurosis of abandonment"—perhaps a better term than any in current usage—becomes self-perpetuating.

Such people may attract each other by early recognition that both have similar anxieties and needs for optimal distance from intimates. This complementarity, of course, is usually experienced as a great comfort with each other. What is experienced initially as comfort, however may be later perceived as inadequacies disowned and blamed on the other for precisely the same reasons that the initial attraction took place. The initial comfort and the subsequent blaming both take cognizance of the same inadequacies. At a deep level of relating, an attempt is made to establish a dyadic relationship with one who objectifies all the shortcomings of an imperfect world that the blamer cannot tolerate.

Such marriages do break up, but not nearly as often as one would expect in view of the enduring pathology, obvious disagreement, and discomfort. The spouses' unhappiness with each other is offset by more basic underlying issues that hold the marriage together. When these marriages do break up, one may see the effects of destabilization in many forms: self-harming, addictive or other impulsive behaviors, or transient psychotic episodes that result from disorganization previously modified by the act of blaming. Alternatively, couples who lose the safety of a blaming relationship may endure a colorless life characterized by pervasive emptiness.

Example 13. In the course of treatment, Mrs. C's depression began to lift and, in the process, her inviting punishment (see Examples 3, 4, 5, 8, 10) diminished. Her husband's depression transiently lightened; but as her improvement continued, he got drunk and was imprisoned after being caught in an attempted burglary. His lengthy prison sentence interrupted the threat of his wife's improving in treatment.

Example 14.   Mr. F (see Example 11) replaced a long series of relationships in which he impregnated and deserted his lovers with a marriage in which he constantly berated his wife for shortcomings and threatened to leave her. In the course of concurrent individual and conjoint therapy, she made a significant move out of the victim role. This progress undercut his compulsively repeated attempt to deal with the trauma of overstimulation and abandonment by blaming. He became seriously depressed and was hospitalized.

The inability to maintain a sense of entitlement in the relationship with another person, who will then serve as a collusive object of blame, may lead to a chronic loss of personality cohesion and feelings of futility and emptiness, destructive juggernaut attempts at suicide, or successful suicides. That this potential chaos is prevented, the cost notwithstanding, by the blaming relationship places blaming among the restitutional phenomena—the way back to objects—most prominently seen as flagrant symptoms in neurotic and psychotic states. Such restitutional symptoms include the secondary symptoms of psychosis, such as delusions and hallucinations, and the neurotic compromise formations, phobias, obsessions, and conversion reactions. Although it may be said that any symptom can be understood as a restitution, the blaming relationship is a striking example of dyadic buffering of extreme propensities toward personality disorganization. Such a dyad is a transpersonal compromise formation that serves as a restitution and has both expressive and defensive properties. At such times when preverbal experiences have rendered the vulnerabilities, deficits, and shame from past traumata so prominent that there is always preoccupation with them, the blaming relationship serves as a blending of the angry, possessive preoedipal bond with the marital relationship. Within the dyadic situation of a marriage, there is an attempt to have a mature sexual relationship while at the same time avoiding the complex and uncertain possibilities posed by larger relationship systems that require greater ego strength and personality cohesion on which self-esteem depends. The dyad is maintained by reestablishing in fantasy a reversal of the experienced early trauma: the secure dyad that can involve only one other person to the exclusion of everything else and on whom all the shortcomings of a less than ideal world are blamed.

No account of blaming can really be complete without proper emphasis on the importance of restitution. Although the term restitution is usually applied to psychotic mechanisms, it may apply to other symptomatology as well. In the blamer, the presupposed sense of entitlement to blame is the beginning of restitution. It is an old therapeutic saw that one must get depressive patients angry and that anger must be mobilized in treatment.

This is an incomplete way of formulating what is an initial step in the understanding of many types of clinical depression. The patient with clinical depression does not have the feeling of entitlement sufficient for him to become part of a blaming dyad with major figures in his or her life or with the therapist. Depressives, while they are depressed, do not blame; and while they are actually involved in the act of blaming they are usually not depressed. Depression may, in the sense pointed out by this reciprocal relationship with expressed anger, be seen in the inability to blame. Delusional depressives, in my experience, never blame, and those more seriously depressed persons, delusional or not, that are psychotically depressed, do not do so either. It is almost as though their verbalizable idea of the world does not include the possibility of entitlement to blame. Schizophrenics, who may at times have labile accusatory outbursts (Lansky, 1977b), never have a feeling of entitlement sufficient for them to use blame as a steady modus operandi. Schizophrenic outbursts are either labile projective states or delusional attempts at restitution that do not involve a true sense of entitlement or a way back to specific objects.

From this point of view, the entitlement and collusiveness found in the act of blaming serves a binding function in the relation with the other. However turbulent that relationship may be, it presents a much more optimistic therapeutic situation than that found in psychotic states, where attempts at restitution do not establish a feeling of entitlement in a close relationship.

In relation to restitution, one can best understand the blaming dyad as a true compromise formation. Blaming occurs in a dissociated state in which the bond to the other has been disrupted. Blame, in fact, should be considered a signal that disruption has occurred and that repair is being attempted. The manifest content of the blamer's accusation usually refers to damage to the sense of self or capacity to bond resulting from the blamed person's actions that have disrupted the bond with the blamer (Example 3). The collusive blaming transaction enables the blamer to repair this fragmented, dissociated state and to reconnect—however unpleasantly—with the blamed other (Example 4). The blaming transaction, its manifest turbulence notwithstanding, purports to restore a bond that has been disrupted.

Such a view of the function of blaming as restitutive of a bond that has been damaged points to the fact that the other for the blamer is not only the felt cause of breakdown and dissociation, but also the all-important other through whom the blamer reintegrates as a self. Failure to understand this process of disorganization and repair—both occurring in relationship to the other—is failure to understand the level of personality organization of the blamer and *for what the blamer needs an object.*

One might say that this use of the object to maintain cohesion is an instance of what Kohut (1971, 1977) called selfobject functioning. Such a view, though correct, is incomplete unless it is realized that the blamed other, usually with a similar level of pathology, also requires selfobject functioning from the blamer and receives it in the act of blaming. The stable instability of the blaming relationship can be appreciated only if it is understood that both the blamer and the blamed restore their sense of self through the reestablishment of narcissistic equilibrium accomplished in the blaming transaction.

This view of the blaming transaction as following a disruption in a dyadic bond and attempting to restore that bond locates the blaming transaction as a regulatory mechanism that helps to modulate both fragmentation and shame in the marital dyad. Shame, which comes from the sense of defectiveness, fragility, emptiness, and loss of control, is compounded by the blamer's propensity to disorganize when the needed other is not at optimal emotional distance. Unacknowledged shame that turns to narcissistic rage is a loss of control that amplifies the shame even further (Lewis, 1971; Scheff, 1987). The blaming transaction, by voicing the damage to the self and by claiming a sense of entitlement—of accountability from the other—restores some measure of cohesiveness to the blamer who is struggling to repair the disorganization that has followed disruption of the bond.

BLAMING IN THE THERAPEUTIC SITUATION

The treatment of the blaming couple is a matter for separate study, one that ought not to presuppose that dyadic therapy is the necessary treatment, a possible form of treatment, or even the first step in treatment for people in such relationships. Nonetheless, consideration of the complexities of disruption and restitution in the blaming couple allows a perspicacious view of blaming in the therapeutic situation. It is important to see blame for what it is within the dyad to appreciate its conflict-mastering, cohesion-producing, and restitutive features and to place in this perspective its constrictive and destructive aspects.

Quite different problems in therapeutic understanding occur if the patient openly blames than if it is only implicit. If blame is explicit, a situation may occur that is quite typical of the blaming couple. Say the patient berates the therapist for disappointments and perpetually threatens to leave. If the therapist can recognize the collusive bond in the blaming situation and not be put off by the unpleasantness of what seems like perpetual berating and threats of leaving, a successful therapeutic bonding may progress even in the presence of surface chaos.

Example 15. A 23-year-old woman entered treatment for suicidal tendencies and depression. Treatment began and continued with the patient berating the therapist and threatening to stop. This behavior continued unabated several times weekly for several years. Quite by chance in a social encounter, the therapist learned that the patient's recent marriage had dramatically improved, as had her school, current career, and interpersonal relationships. The blaming and threatening to terminate within the (quite strikingly successful) therapy continued until the therapy ended.

Blaming may be implicit for a variety of reasons. The patient may be too self-conscious to blame in a professional relationship, or there may have been no indication from the therapist that blaming would be tolerated. Implicit blame may be seen in various ways: the blaming of others, self-reproaches, certain forms of silence felt to be reproachful, a sharp attacking tone in the voice when talking about misfortunes as though they were the therapist's fault; and many others. In such cases, the therapist is well advised to see the indirectness of the reproach as an opportunity to indicate to the patient (interpretively) that he or she can tolerate blame that is expressed indirectly.

Example 16. A woman in treatment complained about an auto accident that she had had on the way to the therapist's office. A sharp, sarcastic tone to her voice betrayed a veiled reproach for the failure of the relationship to really protect her. Interpretation to that effect was met with vigorous denial. Her associations, however, went to her shame about her demands on intimates as a result of which she had sought protection from inappropriate people or avoided involvements altogether, because at some level she sensed that her demands would be too great.

Example 17. A young woman, quite delinquent in payment of the therapist's fee, returned from vacation silent, depressed, and saying that she couldn't engage in activities or relationships as she had hoped she might. After many months of such blaming in the transference, the therapist noted that she reproached him as she had reproached her parents for not equipping her to cope with the world and that the reproach showed up (in both relationships) as a spiteful neglect of her financial responsibilities. This interpretation resulted in more explicit reproaches, more exploration, and the beginnings of replacement of her depressive, spiteful, and reproachful preoccupation by explicit acknowledgment of her own shortcomings. The therapist's tolerance of and explication of the regressive blaming dyad enabled the patient to gain a truly usable perspective on the high cost of her establishing such regressive dyadic relationships in other situations.

Understanding blaming as an interactional symptom highlights certain features of the therapist's part in the relationship. A feature common to virtually every type of therapy is the location of responsibility in the patient for what he or she does, feels, and thinks. In those predisposed to being part of blaming dyads, this therapeutic effort at responsibility assignment is usually received by a humiliation-prone conscience that experiences failure to meet standards or responsibilities as mortifying and humiliating blame and rids itself of that responsibility by low-level defensive operations (see Example 2). Accordingly, there is the risk that any location of responsibility in the patient for what happens to him or her—however tactfully and mildly presented—may be experienced as intolerable blame and humiliation.

In other cases, unwitting or unconscious transference-countertransference collusion may be in evidence. Emotional withholding by the therapist that goes beyond the need for maintain the therapeutic stance may represent an unconscious infliction of punishment or provocation to blame in the therapeutic dyad. Alternatively, the therapist may be provoked to blame the patient for something the patient actually does, such as violating the boundaries of the therapy, acting out, or in situations in which the patient reacts to tension or inattentiveness from the therapist.

Example 18. A young man with severe characterological difficulties, embroiled in a three-party blame system with his parents, regularly missed sessions with his hospital therapist, a psychiatric resident. He would frequently catch the resident between meetings with ward staff or in tense moments on the ward and make annoying requests to leave, to get extra sessions, or to have vague somatic complaints investigated. The resident's mounting fury was shared by the staff. At the suggestion of a supervisor, the resident brought up not only the provocation but the timing of the provocative behavior with the patient. Interpretation of the resident therapist's response led to the conclusion that similar provocations had drawn the angry attention of his (mutually blaming) parents onto himself and so dealt with both his fear that the parents' marriage would break up or that he would be totally excluded by the parents' attention to each other if it did not.

Blame by the therapist may be the result of his or her past experiences brought into the therapy and only minimally due to the particulars of the situation. This is countertransference proper. Excessive emotional withholding is a case in point, as are interpretations that are actually excuses for blaming the patient.

It is crucial that the therapist appreciate the restitutive qualities of blaming lest the process of the patient's establishing and maintaining the blaming dyad be seen only as an obstacle to treatment. Blaming is an indication that a disruption has occurred in the therapeutic bond. If the therapist is not put off balance by the neediness, demandingness, and aggressiveness of the blamer, he or she has an opportunity to study and to enlist the patient's curiosity about the nature of the disruption, the latent meaning of the patient's relationship with the therapist, and the process of repair to the disrupted bond that is embodied in the act of blaming. Blaming is a way of restoring a precariously held relationship despite the blamer's dissociative propensities, shame over the vulnerability to dissociation, feelings of dubious self-worth, and pervasive sense of being defective and poorly prepared for adult responsibilities. Such restitution is likely to fail if the patient has too much shame and self-consciousness either because of the professional nature of the relationship or because the therapist has indicated inability to tolerate the stormy symbiosis that the patient requires. Such intolerance may be a manifestation of the therapist's deep anxieties about the intensity of the hostile fusion, and his or her insistence on a less uncomfortable emotional distance may be rationalized by reference to principles of good techniques or by blaming the patient for being untreatable.

To follow the restitutive path inherent in the act of blaming, the therapist must indicate at some level that he or she can tolerate the patient's blaming. If this is done at the level of unconscious collusion, there is the risk that unresolved feelings of omnipotence on the therapist's part may collude with complementary unconscious expectations on the patient's part; and there may be a counterproductive collusion in assuming that the therapist is entirely responsible for the patient's well-being. A collusion of this type invites disorganizing regressions on the part of the patient to sustain such a dyad and hinders the therapist in helping the patient work through the anxieties that fuel the blaming dynamic.

More optimally, this necessary form of restitution—of which blaming is often the significant first step—is regarded receptively by interpretation that indicates, by implication at least, that the therapist is aware of and can tolerate blame, whether explicit or inexplicit. By accepting the symbiotic restitutive aspects of blame without colluding in the regressive and restrictive aspects, the therapist maximizes the opportunity to secure the protective features of the dyad and to work toward resolution of deep anxieties—especially shame-producing ones concerning neediness, abandonment, and incapacity for psychic survival that appear in the manifest blaming transaction and hitherto have formed an insurmountable preoccupation.

5

Preoccupation as a Mode of Pathologic Distance Regulation

NARCISSISTIC VULNERABILITY AND THE FAMILY

I have described defensive operations in narcissistically vulnerable families with chaotic symptomatology at the forefront of the clinical picture. This symptomatology includes chronic conflict or blame; impulsive action such as overdosing, slashing, or binge drinking; and overt shaming, often accompanied by violence. These chaotic, even explosive activities often keep from view other parts of the clinical picture that bind intimates together. Such symptoms are the components of a complex pattern of pathologic distance regulation, involving the rigid control of emotional distance from intimates so that they do not get too close or too far away. Control over distance protects against the personality disorganization to which such persons are vulnerable. Disorganization and the attendant reliance on others that results from it provokes intense shame.

Avoidance of personality disorganization and shame are the central defensive concerns of narcissistically vulnerable persons. They are ashamed of the exposure of their real, not fantasied, personality difficulties and of the interpersonal maneuvers that they use to control them. Defensive operations aimed at avoiding shame differ from those aimed against guilt for fantasied transgressions. For persons or collusive systems organized around avoiding shame, any form of being seen—including being

An earlier version of this chapter was the recipient of the Jacques Brien Award of the Los Angeles Psychoanalytic Society in 1982. It is dedicated to the memory of Jack S. Abrams, M.D.

communicated with and being understood—presents real, not imagined, risks and not welcome opportunities, as they do with persons whose dynamics center primarily on inhibition and guilt.

In this chapter, I describe a defensive pattern that is usually better hidden from view than are the manifestations of chronic conflict or chaotic symptoms. This subtle defensive style, which I have called pathologic preoccupation, is often used to hide ongoing emotional absence rationalized as duty that promises to result in great prestige or power for the family. I further delineate a specific type of pathological preoccupation that is an adaptation, within a context of intimate relationships, to a chronic sense of inadequacy. Schizoid and restitutive propensities are combined in a typical defensive constellation that wards off the awareness of narcissistic vulnerability. Other allegiances, usually projects of great importance to the family, are evoked to justify a self-absorbed modus vivendi that keeps intimates at such a distance that personality disorganization and shame do not occur. The use of preoccupation as a defensive mode does not preclude the use of other defensive modes in the same family system. Often in a single family, one may see impulsive action in one person inviting blame for another while a third preoccupied person remains in the field in (what seems to be) a detached way. Pathologic preoccupation may, superficially, appear indistinguishable from nonpathological conflicts that result from divided loyalties.

The preoccupation, or emotional absence, of one who is physically present has several theoretical implications: absence is a defense against the threat of too much closeness. It may also be a manifestation of the withdrawal typical in a low-grade depressive disorder. The preoccupied person has become so identified with his or her obligations or occupations as to be unable to put them aside. Pathologic preoccupation is experienced by intimates as remoteness, rejection, or outright narcissistic wounding and may precipitate other and more obvious pathology in them. Finally, preoccupation is traumatogenic; that is, exposure to a chronically preoccupied parent early in life may constitute a chronic emotional trauma with serious residua.

Preoccupied persons present many more difficulties for treatment than their high social and vocational functioning might lead one to believe. Often they are treated with psychoanalysis, family therapy, and even pharmacotherapy, without altering their tendency toward preoccupation. With such difficulties and potential treatment failures in mind, my approach here includes observations and clinical data drawn from both individuals and families. The observations of the family process and the transpersonal defenses within it are telling in ways that a purely individual perspective and treatment situation are not.

PREOCCUPATION: THE TRANSPERSONAL DEFENSE

Preoccupation is a central and, to some degree, universal phenomenon of human relatedness. The word *preoccupation* ordinarily refers to the inability to stop a previous mental activity; it is "a holding on to" the mental "occupation" of the immediate past. This is the way that it is seen in relationships between people. In the relationship of an individual to a system of intimates, preoccupation is seen in a second form, as a moving away of manifest thoughts from the immediate interpersonal situation *to* something else. When thoughts move away from an immediate relationship, the inattention may be (plausibly or not) rationalized as worry about (holding onto) some previous activity of overriding importance.

In family relationships, preoccupation may be obvious, or it may pass unnoticed because it is rationalized as serving a useful purpose for the group of intimates who might otherwise expect the preoccupied person to be emotionally engaged. The breadwinner, the caretaker, or the talented offspring may be preoccupied in ways seemingly crucial to the family's support, sense of hope, and collective self-esteem.

But for the pathologically preoccupied individual, attention to an activity valued by the family veils an essential inability to remain attentive and is a schizoid detachment from emotional interchange, which is a style that is not in the person's control yet poses great difficulties in close relationships. In the family system, the activity to which the preoccupied person is devoted may help ward off each family member's awareness of the person's narcissistic vulnerability and enduring sense of shame.

These defensive operations, however successful they may be at regulating narcissistic equilibrium, are costly. The toll of emotional absence is high for a marriage, for the children, and for anyone in the family with a visible sign of narcissistic vulnerability, as I point out in the clinical material that follows. In families organized around a pathologically preoccupied member, the treating clinician often discovers inattention verging on traumatic neglect in those relationships that initially may seem close, caring, and even "clinging."

Preoccupation is one of a variety of both personal, or intrapsychic, and transpersonal processes of defense. Because my emphasis in this discussion is on the transpersonal defenses and the resistances to treatment that result, my clinical data are only secondarily concerned with the internal conflicts against which the defense is aimed. To deal systematically with any defensive process, one must recognize, first, that a defense is taking place; one must note how it operates before trying to ascertain against what it is that the defensive activity is aimed. Passing unnoticed, pathological preoccupation can present immense obstacles to treatment. And, indeed, this self-absorbed relational pattern is often hard to discern because the cooperation of more than one person in its maintenance usually conceals its defensive nature. It is important to describe in detail the manifest style of this defense, for it has a good deal of prognostic significance for both individual and family treatment.

THE FAMILY SETTING

The study of whole families reveals the transpersonal defensive operations that, as resistances, usually find their way into the individual treatment situation. In fact, such defenses may not be recognized or may be only partially understood in individual psychotherapy or analysis.

Marriages dominated by pathologic preoccupation often consist of couples who appear close, caring, responsible, and committed to their obligations. This dutifulness, however, can be used to justify and conceal an emotional absence in intimate situations. In younger couples with young children, a normal degree of preoccupation is derived from split loyalties—the provider's concern for career, its demands, strategies, and obligations and the caretaker's concern with the children, with resuming a career, and with his or her relationship with the family of origin. In more immature and vulnerable couples, such divisions of loyalty may coincide with pathological ambivalence about the relationship or a fear of loss of self. Preoccupation of this kind screens and subserves emotional disengagement. It is a schizoid mechanism, in essence, in which split loyalties are superimposed on underlying splits in the ego. "Second" loyalties protect the preoccupied person against domination by or immersion in the immediate familial process and the fear of being used up by excessive demands. The preoccupied state serves as a stimulus barrier in the face of fears of loss of cohesion or personal integrity. The manifest content of the preoccupation—with a job, children, or other relationships that enhance the meaning of the self or with some special aspiration—supplies information about the narcissistic significance of the preoccupation, the threat to self, or the part of self felt to be lacking.

If all members of the family system feel the emotional absence is justified, that collusion will protect the preoccupied person's vulnerable sense of self against the threat of experiencing fragmentation, perhaps to the point of intense paranoid anxiety occasioned by intimacy and a debilitating rupture when separation is threatened. People in such relationships are, at a conscious level, worried about their obligations, not about intimacy in the family. This symptomatic externalization, or exteriorization, of the source of anxiety is the primary gain of the preoccupation. Secondarily, the preoccupied person has a rationale for perpetuating disengagement from or domination of the family process. The preoccupation constitutes, in effect, a transitional space that allows a greater freedom to act and feel, a space that does not encroach upon self-boundaries.

In contrast to marriages characterized by blaming, impulsive action, psychosis, or intractable depression, those under the sway of pathologic preoccupation are often highly functional in social and vocational spheres. Nonetheless, despite the seeming assets of such couples, cases in treatment may prove unusually refractory to change, even when the couple or family remains in treatment.

COLLUSION: CLINICAL MATERIAL

A preoccupied person's refractoriness to change is usually buttressed by collusion of the spouse. Later, children become entangled in the emotionally barren family system, which has become dysfunctional as a consequence of the chronic emotional absence of one parent and the collusive, enabling activities of the other parent. Both spouses in each of the marriages to be described readily admitted that preoccupation was a prominent feature of their relationship.

Cooperation and Vicarious Participation

Often one finds in marriages that endure that the spouse does not seem to object to the almost constant self-absorption of the preoccupied person. He or she may accept the lack of attention if the divided loyalty has a high instrumental or narcissistic value for the family. In clinical practice, this situation is typical in the families of professionals, students, and performers. The colluding spouse usually reveals complementary pathology: he or she aspires to the narcissistic enrichment or increased self-esteem gained from the spouse's preoccupation, yet feels deprived by other shortcomings in the relationship.

Example 1. A 56-year-old academic physician with diverse career ambitions took on added university burdens without pause. He rose to high rank while retaining his clinical, research, teaching, and administrative duties from the previous rank. These activities were supported uncomplainingly by his wife, who derived her sense of worth by supporting his professional activities far beyond what would seem necessary. She made elaborate preparations for relatively informal meetings, placed no limits on his professional pursuits, refused to have help in the home, and overidealized the caretaking roles of both her husband and herself.

The wife's idealization of the caretaking of both herself and her husband encouraged his almost constant preoccupation yet pushed both of them to the brink of emotional collapse. The father's familial responsibilities were limited to providing an income. He had no obligations at home and seldom

left his study except for meals. The wife served as a go-between with all of
the children and maintained a stereotyped and idealized view of herself as
a wife.

This woman had a distant father who had died when she was young and
a mother who was extremely critical of her. Revering doctors and the
helping role in general, she had adopted nursing as a career. The strain of
her constant activities betrayed itself in her evident depression, as she
found herself yelling at the children, overinvolving herself with her daughters, and succumbing to alcohol abuse. Treatment was sought when one of
the children rebelled and disturbed the family homeostasis.

Provocation or Invitation

The spouse who is not preoccupied may be lost in somatic symptoms or
blaming or complaining behavior in a way that obscures the defensive
operations of the preoccupied spouse and may actually encourage more
preoccupation.

Example 2. Mrs. B, a 36-year-old woman entered treatment wanting
help with her marriage. She was married to an accountant some years her
senior. This man was reclusive, parsimonious, fastidious, and critical of
any lack of orderliness in her activities. The couple had few friends. Her
husband had little to do with the children. Although highly educated, the
patient herself was employed as a waitress, a job far beneath the level of
her training and qualifications. The patient's mother sympathized with her
by agreeing that men were self-centered and inconsiderate but nonetheless encouraged her daughter to serve her husband unswervingly and
never to question the fact that she had to prepare every meal and select
every article of clothing he wore.

Mrs. B's father was an alcoholic who had caused the family much
embarrassment. She expressed her resentment in the marriage by over-
spending and writing checks on insufficient funds. More generally, she
attacked her husband's need for order in ways that also discredited her and
encouraged more and more emotional distancing. Her husband further
justified his need for order as being necessary to compensate for her
evident irresponsibility. The emotional equilibrium between the two was
maintained by countless transactions in which she appeared disorganized
and needy and he withdrew and criticized her.

Displacement and Scapegoating

Often a pathologically preoccupied parent is the hidden catalyst in clinical
situations characterized by blaming or impulsive action. It is common, for

example, for this kind of pathology to be found in the fathers of acting-out adolescents.

Example 3. A 16-year-old girl entered psychotherapy after reporting general distress and suicidal ideation directed toward her parents. The parents were themselves troubled that she was doing poorly in school and was sexually active, making unwise choices of boyfriends.

Miss C was the youngest of five children, the only one currently at home. Her father, a prosperous physician, retired to his study every night to do "his books" and seldom spoke to her or to her mother. In general, the family mystified the advantages of wealth and prestige.

The patient's mother was embittered and critical of the daughter but never inveighed against her husband. She indulged in tirades against Miss C for her sexual activities or her talking on the phone. Gradually, it became evident that the mother sank into depressions that were relieved only by these acts of blaming, which occurred when Miss C brought home unacceptable boys or talked on the phone for provocatively long periods of time. The mother's neediness and inability to differentiate herself from the identity she borrowed from her husband's professional activity now became the focus in the daughter's treatment sessions. When at last Miss C decided to go away to college, her sense of well-being increased considerably.

THE INDIVIDUAL AND THE FAMILY OF ORIGIN

The Therapeutic Dyad

A patient may be the kind of person who takes obligations all too seriously and sees himself as "compulsive," "insecure," or a "workaholic." He may have a low-key depression. The analyst may explain the preoccupation as a manifestation of compulsivity (with its attendant dynamics), as a tendency toward depression, as anxiety, or as insecurity. But the analyst's failure to understand the transpersonal defensive operations in preoccupied persons may also result in a failure to appreciate their richness, collusive use in the family, or significance in the transference.

Explanations of transference displacements ignore the kind of schizoid distancing from the interpersonal process that one finds in preoccupied persons. Drifting of attention during sessions, along with some connectedness to the process, may not be appreciated as a characteristic of narcissistically vulnerable persons, one that is accentuated in any sort of intimate relationship. Preoccupied persons disengage from immediate involvement and become absorbed with something else in ways that amount to a tacit commentary on the process, either on its worth or on the relationship itself. The clinician risks misconstruing a complex situation (all too simply) as the patient's defense against acknowledging attachment to the analyst.

Analysis and intensive psychotherapy are, in fact, not conducive to recognizing pathological preoccupations. In such treatment situations, we deliberately set the stage so that the patient is present with the analyst and yet at the same time is not required to be emotionally engaged, or perhaps even visually in contact, with the analyst. Self-absorption is system syntonic in the analytic situation. The analyst attends totally to the patient; the patient, in contrast, is instructed to heed only his or her free associations, distractions—in fact, his or her preoccupations. A circumstance is created that has the same defensive advantages as does preoccupation in the family. In any other setting, such self-absorption would assume obviously pathological proportions. But it is masked in the therapeutic situation because that is what the analyst asks the patient to do. Hardly frustrated by the dyadic therapeutic situation, preoccupation may never come into focus as an analytic issue. Patients who have had lengthy and supposedly successful analyses terminated by mutual agreement with their analysts may go at a later date elsewhere for marital therapy and be found to use pathological preoccupation as a major defensive style in their marriages.

Resistance

One of the main reasons for drawing attention to resistance in a therapy of any modality is that pathologically preoccupied persons have such a fear of intimate engagement, exposure, and closeness that they are particularly apt to discontinue treatment.

Example 4.   Fearing that he would ruin his fourth marriage, a 36-year-old physician sought therapy. Unlike his three other short-lived marriages, this relationship was based on love and mutual respect. Previously he had entered relationships as a self-appointed helper to depressed and alcoholic women. In contrast, his current wife was competent and caring. After a year of marriage, she wanted to get pregnant.

The patient was constantly on the go, with his expanding practice and a role in the development of a large organization with innovative programs. He was on call at several hospitals. His overwhelming schedule kept his wife off balance, relegating her to a subordinate role.

The patient's recollections of previous marriages and other involvements with women revealed a consistent theme of distancing women and keeping them off balance. He was struck with the persistence of these themes and began to wonder why he repeatedly suffered the same struggles. Yet his curiosity about these issues seemed to be short lived or at least intermittent. He spent a great deal of time in the sessions talking about his accomplishments, his importance in the hospital, and his ever-increasing recognition by newspapers and professional organizations. An air of defiance permeated the patient's discourse. Aggressive, he was also hungry for approval and talked like a man starved for recognition. As the sessions continued, the patient allowed himself some acknowledgment of his desperate needs for accolades, success, and power and, with this recognition, became more and more inquisitive about his early life.

Dr. D was the eldest of three brothers in a family that he saw as dominated by his mother. She demanded that his father and his brothers take care of her and pamper her. Dr. D had been an openly rebellious and oppositional child but secured his position in the family by means of his academic prowess. When his parents quarreled, he would hear his mother scream out, threatening to withhold sex unless his father sided with her against their son, the patient. His father gave in to what the patient saw as humiliating subjugation by his mother, a state of affairs that continued until his father's death.

The patient began to sense that his frenetic overachieving bespoke his deep anxieties regarding his helplessness and fear of surrendering to women. These anxieties became increasingly apparent in the transference, in his terror of yielding to me. For a short period, his marital tensions lessened. But his defenses reasserted themselves, and resistance overtook the treatment. After a few months of therapy, more and more sessions were canceled by his secretary, who said that Dr. D was out of town, tied up by an emergency, or working up an unexpected admission to the hospital. Despite repeated interpretation and invitations to explore his anxieties regarding closeness in the treatment situation, Dr. D continued to find reasons to avoid the sessions and finally broke off the treatment.

The collusive behavior of a spouse who acts to provoke or fix emotional distancing may produce similar resistances. Let me return to Example 2:

Mrs. B began analysis. Although she continued to complain about her husband, she showed a warmth in the sessions that seemed to belie any ambivalence toward me; the analytic relationship appeared not to have any negative valence. The analysis broke off, however, when her financial disorganization culminated in an impulsive investment loss that prevented her financially from continuing the analysis and even from paying the current bill. Her husband's and her own self-fulfilling and protective prophecies had been fulfilled and perpetuated.

FAMILY OF ORIGIN: SHAME AND THE STRUGGLE AGAINST IDENTIFICATION

It is a strikingly common clinical finding that in the preoccupied person's family of origin, the parent of the same sex was seen as contemptible, shameful, or helpless in the context of the parental marriage. When questioned, the preoccupied person openly rejects a comparison with this parent. There is seldom an outward similarity between the parent as described and his or her offspring regarding achievement. Yet the patient manifests an unconscious, but pronounced struggle against identification (Greenson, 1954) with that parent.

Example 5. In conjoint therapy, a 29-year-old schoolteacher complained about her husband, a 30-year-old attorney who had recently left his law firm for a partnership in another firm that he had been working toward over the past two years. He ignored his wife except insofar as she was useful for developing contacts and entertaining them. He was distant, preoccupied, brooding, depressed, and tired—in other words, preoccupied—when he was with her alone, with the children, or with her family, with whom she remained close. Mr. E looked down on his wife's friends and would associate only with "contacts," professional people who could advance his business or prove to be referral sources for his law practice.

Mrs. E's husband talked with great difficulty and embarrassment about the family in which he grew up. His mother had been a controlling, self-centered person who despised his father, a successful contractor who nonetheless had lacked the professional standing and cultural refinement that Mr. E's mother felt was her due. Her open contempt for her husband was in sharp contrast with her idealization of her son and especially of his professional attainments, which were considerable. The father protested only feebly at this view of himself and participated with pride in the family project of advancing the son's career.

As the treatment progressed, Mrs. E began to dislodge the burden inherent in defining herself merely as her husband's helpmate (and appendage) and to begin doing things with her own friends. She began increasingly to assert her independence and insisted that Mr. E take his turn watching the children while she went out. In turn, he became anxious and gave her some brochures for a business venture, asking that at least she distribute some of these to her friends during the evening.

On one occasion, Mr. E spoke of his virtually nonexistent relationship with his own father. Mr. E. recalled being drawn to the father of one of his friends, a warm man who spent evenings and weekends involved in sports and hobbies with his own children and their friends. Mr. E cried openly now. The comparison of the two fathers caused him intense shame and pain without any relief. Despite intense efforts to become involved with his own son, Mr. E confessed that he found it very difficult to be the type of father he felt he should be. Instead of participating in sports or play, he took his son on business errands on the weekends. He phoned after the session to say that he would not return for further treatment.

Example 6. A couple sought conjoint therapy after the death of their adolescent daughter in a daredevil car accident. The initial phase of their treatment pertained to their reaction to the death, which in all likelihood had been a suicide. It gradually became apparent that the deceased child had been an emissary to both spouses in an unhappy marriage and that she had felt considerable responsibility for their difficulties. The wife complained to such a degree that her husband was alienated by her coldness and excruciating attention to detail. He was a lawyer and spent most of his spare time with his investments and with male friends, to the exclusion of his wife.

Mr. F had been reared by an elderly aunt who took care of him while both his parents worked long hours at a small business that, they said, required their every waking hour. This aunt had constricted his activities, preached utopian socialist politics, and deluged him with invectives against his father, who, she said, abused his mother and drank. Her attacks on his father increased after his mother's death when the patient was eight. Afterwards, he lived with the aunt and had very little to do with his father.

As their treatment progressed, Mr. and Mrs. F decided to see separate therapists, with only occasional conjoint sessions. In Mr. F's therapy, his need to distance his wife was clarified both in the light of the genetic issues in his upbringing and, more immediately, as a response to his wife's cold, distancing behavior. Interpretive work, linking his anxieties regarding his wife to his unconscious fear of his aunt and further noting his identification with his devalued father, crystalized his horror of being impinged upon and overwhelmed by vengeful contemptuous women. His maneuvers to keep his wife unbalanced and at bay, as well as the inadvertent choice of a mate with whom he could replay the childhood scenario, appeared increasingly intelligible.

A family session was held when the F's eldest son was in town for a short visit. He described Mr. F similarly to the way Mr. F had depicted his own father, as ineffective, devious, abusive, and absent as a source of structure and support.

Mr. F returned to his own therapy horrified, shamed, and depressed at the comparison. Aware that there was considerable evidence to support it, he was also furious at the son's preemptive, competitive, and demanding attitude toward him. Scrutiny of this view of his son led him to see that he himself had had competitive and hostile feelings toward his own father, brought on by his aunt's assaults and unmodified because of his father's remoteness. The result was a damaged and devalued paternal introject against which he had struggled but with which he had identified in assuming his own parental role in the family.

Mr. F was able to use the therapy sessions to reveal to me and himself just how he had undercut his children's independence, keeping them dependent on their parents and immersed in their parents' marital battles. In the midst of realizing that he and his wife had encouraged incapacitating irresponsibility in a second son, he began consciously to entertain the possibility that the deceased daughter had been driven to suicide by his absence and entanglement in the marital conflict. He continued in therapy long enough to arrive at a consistent set of expectations of the irresponsible son and left therapy when that son left home.

The pathologically preoccupied person's inner struggle against a past identification derives from representations of the family of origin in which the same-sex parent was seen as an object of contempt or shame. It is important to underscore this struggle against such an identification, because in a highly responsible and accomplished person manifesting pathological preoccupation, it may be far from clear how powerfully active is the unconscious struggle not to become such a shameful person in one's own marriage. And this is so despite the apparent absurdity of comparing the preoccupied person with his or her parent. This unremitting internal battle and the pervasive sense of imminent shame that accompanies it makes closeness, communication, and being understood both in the family and the therapy threats rather than opportunities for satisfaction. When the therapist seems to get too close and the intimacy of the process intensifies, the fear of exposure produces disruptive treatment resistance. Such resistance is usually rationalized as a preoccupation, that is, a divided loyalty interfering with the treatment sessions.

BINDING AND UNBINDING: VULNERABILITY AND PROGNOSTIC CONSIDERATIONS

The function of the preoccupied person's transpersonal defensive operations, the cost of the processes of defense, and the state of the ego being defended can be put in perspective by locating preoccupation among other types of collusive activities in families.

The phenomenology of the collusive relationship—the details of the patterns of manifest defensive maneuvers evident in both the patient's activities and the responses of intimates—in families is useful for the assessment of the degree of personal and familial narcissistic vulnerability. Defensive operations attempt to adjust emotional states that arise simultaneously from the threats of merger or exposure and of separation. Whether these defenses are binding or unbinding, that is, whether they hold relationships together or push them apart, and whether the binding is labile or relatively stable have a great deal to do with the amount of external tumult in the patient's life and, therefore, with the overall cost of defense. Such externals, of course, also affect the internal equilibrium of the narcissistically vulnerable person. The ego's anticipation of the extent of its resources that are bound up in distance regulation is related to its availability for relatively conflict-free areas that have not been plunged into the chaos of disruptive distance regulation. The ego must adapt to the consequences of its own distance-regulating propensities, that is, the cost of warding off closeness (the risk of merger or exposure) or of too much separation (the risk of abandonment and lack of cohesion). So the structure of typical distance-regulating defensive operations in the family situation tells us something about the internal situation, especially about the cost to enduring subliminatory channels necessitated by maintaining intimate relationships at a safe distance. The phenomenology of transpersonal defense, then, gives us some insight into the structure and cohesion of the personality. Interpersonal responses to narcissistic wounding (somewhat reified for purposes of exposition) follow a continuum from weaker to stronger ego: disengagement, blame or impulsive action, preoccupation, and integration.

Disengagement

Some types of pathological distance regulation fail to bind relationships together. Persons whose support systems often have eroded use defensive operations that repel rather than bind and do not offer reciprocally protective collusive opportunities to their circle of intimates. Demandingness, devaluation, and manipulativeness (Bursten, 1972) are among the transactional styles that put excessive claims on others in an attempt to restore distance and regulate self-regard. Sooner or later, families and therapists alike are likely to become exhausted and leave the emotional field. These are cases in which restitution fails (Lansky et al., 1983). Such persons may, in the short run, control by intimidation or guilt induction, which for a time may bind relationships together. But such binding is usually precarious: intimates often become resentful, exhausted, or reactive to the emotional bombardment and, sooner or later, leave the scene. When this happens, the sense of one's destructiveness to relationships is confirmed. Such failures of (external) restitution may confirm a state of internal despair and shame that presages completed suicide or repeated fantasied attempts to take in lost internal objects by means of continuous rather than episodic substance abuse.

Blame or Impulsive Action

In defensive operations characterized by blaming attacks, overtly chaotic relationships containing uproar and conflict, although they may seem to be falling apart, are actually bound together by the blaming transaction. Such blaming episodes frequently follow behavior by the blamed person that invites blame. The volatile transaction binds the blamer to the blamed in ways that exclude others from the labile dyad, at least during the blaming transaction (mother and daughter in Example 3). There is, then, a constricted and labile restitution that comes at a high cost to all activities and relationships outside the dyad. Such blaming transactions may be parts of family systems that also include impulsive action such as slashing, overdosing, binge drinking, or impulsive sexual activity. Whether or not they coexist, blame or impulsive action that is overtly disruptive behavior is almost always found to follow a change in optimal distance among intimates in an attempt to restore distance.

Blaming attacks or impulsive actions may be characteristic responses to narcissistic injury in persons with extremely liability to personality disorganization but who can nevertheless become party to these chaotic patterns of collusive activity in relationships of surprising durability. In such relationships, narcissistic injury may be followed by impulsive sexuality, binge eating, binge drinking, or suicidal bouts. These events invite blame by another and thus have an organizing and mood-regulating effect among intimates, albeit a disowned one that produces in the impulsive actor a lowering of self-regard, an inner sense of incohesiveness, and a lack of integration. The cost of such distance regulation is extremely high. For the blamer or impulsive actor, cycles of personality disorganization (and attendant shame) followed by attack or impulsive action (and attendant guilt) may erode any enduring subliminatory channels, and so the ego's sense of its own integrity is not buttressed by stable and relatively conflict-free spheres of accomplishment, either in work or in close relationships.

Preoccupation

In preoccupied persons, overt, excessive closeness among actual persons is adjusted by covert emotional absence during physical presence. Collusive relationships are usually enduring. Binding or restitutive propensities are immense, and wide subliminatory channels are kept open. If the preoccupation, for example, the work of a "workaholic" justifies his inability to relate in close relationships, then the situation is of the type currently under discussion. Work accomplishments are often overvalued or mystified, for example, in the specialness conferred by the preoccupation on those in the family. The preoccupied person responds to chronic narcissistic vulnerability by being present as an absence. There is narcissistic value in the specialness, but this type of relatedness can be quite toxic to people in the immediate emotional environment and is often found in the parents of patients with severe narcissistic character pathology.

The preoccupied person's ego is capable of meeting responsibilities to intimates and to vocational and community involvements and so promotes a view of the self as basically loving and responsible, rather than—as is the case with blamers and impulsive actors—destructive and hateful. Although these ego strengths may provide much in the way of subliminatory channels and maintenance of self-regard, one also finds more rigidity and less access to modification in these patients than their stability and attainments might suggest at first.

Integration

If a high degree of structuralization is present, but in a fully restitutive way, and is accompanied by emotional presence, one may say that the impingement imposed by divided loyalty has been integrated. Instead of resulting in a pathologic preoccupation, it has been sublimated and is no longer pathological.

Transactions that fall short of being integrated give the vulnerable person control over distance from the prevailing process. Such pathologic distance regulation, often utilizing a collusively validated preoccupation, substitutes and compensates for a lack of normal feeling of worth and cohesion in intimate relationships. It justifies an emotional withdrawal for the purpose of completing the self, a self buttressed by the importance of the second loyalty. Both the distance-regulating power and the narcissistic value of the second loyalty defend against a sense of shame and avoid the awareness of narcissistic vulnerability. The shame arises in part from the vulnerability, the lack of cohesiveness itself, and the unconscious identifications against which the preoccupied person struggles.

CONCLUSIONS

The kind of pathologic preoccupation discussed here overlies a set of collusive defensive maneuvers that rationalizes and compensates for a split in the ego with schizoid propensities and a fear of being exposed as defective. The result of rationalizing such a split by means of the claims of divided loyalties is a mystified absence while present.

Pathologic distance regulation must be understood through the manifest defensive operation of narcissistically vulnerable persons, that is, by the nature of binding and unbinding that occurs among real people, not just in fantasy. The understanding of unconscious fantasies of splitting and object control—projective identification—complement but do not replace observations of defensive maneuvers that constitute pathologic distance regulation. Though unconscious fantasy plays a role in distance regulation, details of such regulatory activities in actual relationships are a separate source of data and cannot be gleaned from associative material only. In view of these complexities, it is premature to adopt definitive treatment strategies and even goals for treatment. Nonetheless, a perspicacious view of the phenomenology of pathological preoccupation is of importance to any focus of therapeutic attention.

6

The Explanation of
Impulsive Action

PRECONCEPTIONS

The presence of impulsive action is an ominous prognostic sign in what might otherwise appear to be an optimistic clinical picture. Impulsive actions include binge drinking, compulsive overeating, compulsive heterosexual or homosexual activity, wrist slashing, overdosing, suicidal crises, or bouts of blaming in conflict-ridden marriages—instances of seemingly isolated bits of chaos in an otherwise understandable and workable picture. Impulsive action, however, is an indication not only of clinical complexity but also of the possibility that treatment will fail. It demands the fullest understanding, even in cases that appear to be quite simple.

The reasons behind unacceptable or uncontrollable action should be explored in the therapeutic setting. Those reasons may be conscious or unconscious and explanations for them accurately but incompletely reflected in the clinical situation may incline analysts to make intuitive or theoretical constructions about what has transpired. Such constructions may eventually hold us captive, for they find selective confirmation and often dovetail with explanations consciously or unconsciously given by others, especially the patient. This tendency toward premature acceptance of explanations obscures our understanding of what I believe to be a complex process of disorganization and restitution in which impulsive

An earlier version of this chapter was the recipient of the Edward Hoedemaker Memorial Prize of the Psychoanalytic Association of Seattle in 1983.

action is the striking surface feature. Our need to explain often keeps us from appreciating the full complexity of impulsive acts.

On the level of common intuition, an obvious explanation may be, for example, that people who eat excessively do so because they are hungry or because they lack sufficient will power to control their eating. This kind of explanation conveys a more or less common sense notion of force—of "impulse" and something opposing it. Theoretical notions of wish, drive, or frustration tolerance posit a similar picture and appear to explain impulsive activity: one can understand a desire, the wish to consummate it, the temptation not to, and the effort required to resist it. So it appears plausible that people eat because they are hungry, have intercourse because they are sexually aroused, or quarrel with a spouse or slash themselves because of the vicissitudes of aggressive drives. However, these explanations, based on intuitive notions of force—drive, wish, low frustration tolerance, and insufficient will power—do not really explain impulsive action. Compulsive eaters seldom feel hunger, binge drinkers are usually not addicted to alcohol, compulsively promiscuous women often feel no desire and do not reach orgasm during compulsive sexual episodes. Very often patients will say as much, but therapists may discredit their statements as evasive or defensive attempts to disown both unacceptable activities and the parts of themselves that engage in such activities.

Impulsive action is really not understandable as an excess of drive or desire or a lack of will power or ego strength. A somewhat more sophisticated view is that consequences of such acts are intentional; that is to say, they are adaptive or outright manipulative attempts to control intimate persons in the patient's life (or the analyst in the transference). Accordingly, overeating may be viewed in terms not only of hunger but also of the wish to be fed or to retreat from an overwhelming situation. A wide variety of impulsive acts, including wrist slashing, suicide attempts, and overdoses, do have the effect of regulating distance in close relationships. This effect can be presumed, in many cases, to be the intent of such actions, which may indeed control those who are concerned about the impulsive actor, who gains special caretaking or exemption from responsibility. Attention to control of people close to the patient illuminates the distance-regulating effect of impulsive action, but not the disorganization in response to which control of distance is felt to be necessary.

Explanations may go beyond the language of force and of adaptation to include that of meaning. Impulsive action can be understood as a dramatization of life themes that are "acted out" instead of remembered and that pose resistance to the process of treatment. This definition extends the original usage of the term "acting out" that Freud (1905b) posited in the discussion of the Dora case and in his papers on technique (Freud, 1914;

see also Breuer and Freud, 1893-95; Ekstein, 1965; A. Freud, 1968; Sandler, Dare, and Holder, 1973). "Acting out" originally referred to a dramatization of some conflictual situation rather than its recollection in analysis. The term has another connotation within the family context if a patient has become a delegate, so to speak, who enacts the repressed wishes of close, usually parental, figures (Johnson and Szurek, 1952; Vogel and Bell, 1967). The vulnerability of the patient's unconscious to respond to that of the analyst has also been pointed out (Searles, 1965). But the patient's enacting of disowned or repressed wishes of those close to him is a matter quite separate from the specific dramatization that replaces recollection in the analysis of neurotics. "Acting out" carries with it so many misleading assumptions that it must be considered an overused term (Greenacre, 1963). In the sense of action replacing recollection in the analysis of neurotics (Freud, 1905b, 1914), the term acting out is of limited usefulness for our understanding of impulsive action.

Impulsive action is often a part of a larger picture that can be understood as an attempt to recreate and master situations that were traumatic in the past. The problem of repetition, whether or not one uses the term compulsion to repeat (Freud, 1920; Loewald, 1971), is a difficult one for psychoanalytic theory. Repetition of major life themes cannot be ignored in the explanation of human action. Repetition aims, however unsuccessfully, to solve something troubling the patient. Although impulsive action may be a part of activities that constitute acting out or the compulsion to repeat, those terms do not explain impulsive action itself. The confusion of impulsive action with thematic repetition often mistakenly implies that an understanding of the *meaning* of impulsive action will result in control of it.

There is a risk, then, of accepting explanations that are not based on a grasp of the whole structure of the process of impulsive action. Interpretive efforts based on such explanations address only a part of the picture. These interpretations may be correct but may nonetheless miss more covert aspects of the process being interpreted. Following Glover (1931), 1 would call such interpretations inexact.

The patient too gives explanations for his actions. He may offer them consciously in his rationalization of the act, or they may be inferred from his associations concerning the activity. These associations constitute, at some level, the *patient's* explanation of impulsive activity. Exploration and interpretation of the patient's immediate associations to an impulsive act give much more limited access to the actual process of which impulsive action is a part than is commonly acknowledged. The associative method points us to the patient's fantasies about the act, fantasies that are themselves the results of defensive activity that give the patient a feeling of control over the process; at the same time they also disguise the process of disorganization. Thus they are compromise formations and, like dreams and screen memories, must be considered material for continued analysis rather than the actual bedrock of analytic work.

The patient's conscious or unconscious explanations of impulsive action may dovetail with the analyst's explanations in ways that seal the process off from therapeutic scrutiny and eventual modification. The possibility of such dovetailing should alert us to a serious type of stalemate resulting from such transference-countertransference collusions.

I shall attempt to delineate a structure common to a great many psychopathologic phenomena and not limited to those treatable by psychoanalysis or psychoanalytic psychotherapy alone. Impulsive action includes a range of experiences felt by both patient and analyst to be impulsive intermezzos split off from the mainstream of the patient's continuous experience of self. The exact boundaries of the concept cannot be firmly drawn at the outset of this discussion. Impulsive action may be part of a clinical picture too peppered with chaotic activity to admit of analytic scrutiny. Many addictions and perverse activities are varieties of impulsive action. At the other extreme are those instances of impulsive action often unappreciated in unmodified psychoanalysis in which processes of disorganization and restitution are subtle enough to defy detection in the analytic situation. Such activities include marital quarrels, spending sprees, criticism of children, problems regulating food and intoxicant intake, and rage attacks that are obliquely reported as hostility to the analyst. These phenomena may be incompletely analyzable unless they are recognized as subtle variants of impulsive action.

My clinical material is intended to illustrate the structure of impulsive action. The pathology described is by and large more severe than is usually found in patients for whom unmodified psychoanalysis is the treatment of choice. (Only Example 6 was in unmodified psychoanalysis.)

A NATURAL HISTORY

I contend that there is a natural history to the kind of vulnerable ego that expresses itself in impulsive action. That natural history is indicative of the structure of the disruptive ego in which it eventuates. The sequence of events may be so woven into character style and characteristic relationships with intimate persons that the patient, the analyst, and intimates in the patient's life all fail to recognize them. A process involving disorganization and restitution with the same essential features is common to many impulsive actions. It is common to have specific impulsive behavior crystalize and repeat itself: eaters eat, drinkers drink, blamers blame, slashers slash. Although a person may show more than one type of impulsive activity, a clinical picture often reveals a predominant kind of recurrent impulsive activity.

I describe in this chapter a five-stage sequence of disorganization and restitution that is split off from the ordinary continuity of thought and action. These phenomena are extremely widespread and are likely to be seen under circumstances in which only part of their structure is apparent. For these reasons, I am presenting the stages of unfolding impulsive action in an unequivocal, even reified way: (1) a precipitating experience, an outer event often having the meaning to the patient of a narcissistic exposure or wound (this is commonly a loss, a separation from an intimate or one in the transference but may also be, for example, a job loss or a health problem, an increase in intimacy, or a withdrawal of attention); (2) an inner reaction to this precipitating experience that is hard to define and is often discussed in analytic literature under the terms fragmentation anxiety (Kohut, 1971), separation anxiety, paranoid anxiety (Rosenfeld, 1964), dissociation, and elsewhere as the experience of absence or aloneness (Erickson, 1970). (These experiences are difficult to characterize because an adequate shared language for discussing such absences is extremely sophisticated and cannot be presumed to be present); (3) the impulsive activity itself, which can be described behaviorally (I am limiting the scope of discussion to isolated, discrete impulsive acts); (4) manifestations of shame or guilt in response to an awareness of the act of defenses against such awareness, which are often woven into the character structure or manifested by a splitting-off of consciousness (binge drinking is a notable example); (5) a distance-regulating effect on intimate persons, often but not always serving to restore an optimal distance disturbed by the precipitating experience.

After discussing these elements, I touch on the implications of such a view of impulsive action as a manifestation of a vulnerable or split ego for interpretation in the analytic situation.

My purpose is to draw attention to a pervasive sequence of disorganization and restitution that is endopsychically perceived and evokes so much superego anxiety—especially shame—that the entire sequence becomes split off from the continuous stream of consciousness of self. I have used several different frames of reference and have drawn heavily on extra-associative data from the present and recent past. The breadth of my topic is such that truly convincing clinical material would be unwieldy. Accordingly, I employ case vignettes to clarify and illustrate the points being made, not to preclude other possible formulations.

THE PRECIPITANT

Impulsive behavior often occurs after a change in a relationship with a significant person, both as a reaction to the narcissistic injury resulting from the change and as an attempt to control it. Such a precipitating event may be an actual separation, temporary or permanent: a vacation of an analyst or other important person, the breakup of a relationship by death or divorce, or even the dissolution of a relationship because of maturation. In patients with extreme narcissistic vulnerability, the precipitant may be an event as subtle as neglect, transitory inattention, a short absence, exclusion from a conversation, or the depression or withdrawal of the emotional availability (Mahler, 1971) of a significant person.

Binge Drinking

Example 1. Treatment of a father and son both hospitalized on the same psychiatric ward showed that the son's impulsivity waxed and waned with the vicissitudes of his father's depression. Cycles of impulsivity and industriousness on the part of the son were correlated with shifts in his father's moods, and a convincing interrelationship could be posited. The father had been admitted for alcoholism, depression and job losses. When the son returned from off-ward passes intoxicated and remiss on his job, father felt self-righteous, masterly, and in control of himself. When his son, heeding his father's apparent wishes, controlled himself, started working, and began to be independent and sober, his father sank into a presumably mysterious depression. Alcohol binges and job irresponsibility on the son's part soon followed. His father's depression rapidly lifted and was replaced by feelings of self-righteousness and mastery as he blamed his son for impulsive drinking. The son's impulsive alcoholism could be seen as a response to his father's deep depression. The father's mood lifted rapidly and dramatically when he could experience drunkenness and irresponsibility as belonging exclusively to his son. The younger man's alcohol binges served to restore his connectedness with his emotionally depleted father by reestablishing a relationship in which his father could feel self-righteous.

Relationships that become too close may precipitate an impulsive action that restores a more comfortable distance.

Suicidal Crisis

Example 2. A couple appeared for therapy because of the husband's premature ejaculation. The wife, in her early 30s, had never had orgasm during intercourse. The husband, in his mid-50s, was previously divorced and had a caring relationship with his younger wife but was troubled because he did not satisfy her sexually. As conjoint therapy progressed through caressing exercises to genital contact and intercourse with the wife on top, he achieved more and more ejaculatory control. As she came closer and closer to climax, however, she also became suicidal. Eventually, she made an impulsive suicide attempt and was hospitalized. Her suicide attempt and hospitalization gathered others around her but also put off the entire project of sex therapy and the intimacy it required. The disorganizing effects of intimacy and of impending sexual satisfaction became the subject of her subsequent psychotherapy.

Often the precipitant for an impulsive act can be understood only by an appreciation of a changing emotional climate in a constellation of relationships among persons on whom the patient is dependent. This change may occur where there is a split in the pattern of the relationship. For instance, one party (or parties) may become increasingly protective of the patient in a way that provokes another party (or parties) to become angry at the protective situation and to see it as manipulative. The precipitating situation frequently has obvious similarities to the emotional climate in the family of origin that the patient felt the need to control.

Impulsive Drug Use

Example 3.   Mr. C, a 49-year-old man, was hospitalized repeatedly for "depression," which he attributed to his circumstances. On one admission, his trainee therapist, a protective woman, was slow to see the interpersonal manifestations of his character pathology, much to the dismay of an experienced ward staff. The latter viewed him as an irresponsible substance abuser who was very much responsible for his difficulties with his ex-wife, job, parents, and a recent girlfriend. The trainee and the permanent staff became polarized. As intrastaff tensions mounted, Mr. C's agitation grew uncontrollable. He ingested PCP, telling his therapist that it relaxed him. Her acceptance of this explanation increased the conflict between her and ward staff, and meetings addressing staff tensions focused on this issue. The patient's response to the therapist's inquiries about the drug use was that he was deteriorating—losing form, getting hopelessly lost. He said he couldn't control himself. He couldn't be responsible, nor could he even think. Divisions existed between those staff members who felt the patient's distress and those who saw the control and manipulation of the therapist.

The family history revealed a strikingly similar constellation of intimates. Mr. C's father considered him (youngest of four) the only loser in a successful family. His mother, however, considered him her favorite and proclaimed that he was her reason for living, excusing all his irresponsibility. His mother's attitude granted him special status but also intensified his father's resentment of him and widened an already serious marital rift. His panic attacks and failures served to exploit the marital tensions and also to control the marriage by shifting his parents' attention from their problems to his. The patient's adult years had been characterized by a series of involvements with overprotective women whom he drew into relationships that infuriated those from whom these women protected him. Eventually the women themselves gave up on him. As his therapist became more protective of him. Mr. C disorganized and his condition deteriorated. Her protection intensified the dislike of him by others on the ward staff, thus repeating the same kind of split that had characterized the parental marriage. The therapist's exclusive attention to his anguish and her neglect of his irresponsible behavior amplified his regression and stimulated more drug ingestion. Mr. C's escalating frequency of impulsive drug use secured him in a dependent relationship with the therapist and also discharged his rageful feelings of powerlessness and envy at the therapist's impingement.

Other patterns in early relationships may predispose certain people to disorganization when similar situations occur in later life (Lansky, 1980). These include parental conflict not initially involving the patient but for which the patient feels responsibility and that he therefore attempts to control; and increasing emotional absence in a parental marriage characterized by one preoccupied parent and one who is depressed (Bosormenyi-Nagy and Spark, 1973). One person's withdrawal of emotional responsiveness precipitates impulsive activity in a second person, which justifies self-righteous attack (blame) by the first, in a way that restores emotional equilibrium to the blamer. (See Example 1.)

A wide variety of circumstances can pose the threat of narcissistic injury and thereby precipitate impulsive action. Since there is a narcissistic element in every unconscious conflict, the surfacing of any unconscious conflict has an element of narcissistic injury (Wurmser, 1984, personal communication) and can, in principle, precipitate impulsive action.

THE PRODROME

In the prodrome, or endopsychic perception of personality disorganization, an experience of disorganization, of dissociation, of emptiness, or of disintegration is often felt as the presence of persecution. The emptiness involves a fantasy of a void that is somehow *fillable* by a consummatory "impulsive" act together with a specific craving to complete it. That act becomes the consummation in action of a preoccupation and, in some sense, discharges it.

The prodrome includes the registration of the precipitating event, but is most difficult to identify from the patient's account of what transpired. Since the experience is entirely subjective, it is impossible to know about except from the patient's report. In the patient's recollections of his conscious experience, it is often unlocatable, indescribable, obscured so much by what precedes and what follows, and so foreign to the usual capacities of language, that all or part of it may not be conceptualized or even registered in conscious experience.

A person in a prodromal state usually fails to realize what goes on during or preceding such a state, especially if he is held captive by an explanatory notion of his own about the act or is flooded by shame or guilt. He may have a conscious recollection of a furtive, frightened state or about the craving at the very end of the prodrome, which culminates in a consummatory impulsive act (as I illustrate later). Usually, however, there is very little conscious registration of the reaction to the precipitating event or of the sense of absence, nor awareness of the craving to complete the act. Reflecting on the events surrounding an episode of impulsive action, the patient may recollect anger in reaction to the precipitating event, attempts to restore control over that situation, a kind of craving for the consummatory act, a struggle against it, or shame or guilt about his lack of control. Sometimes states of fragmentation (Kohut, 1971) and paranoid anxieties (Klein, 1946; Rosenfeld, 1964) may reach consciousness, but the sense of a lack or of an emptiness (Erickson, 1970) felt in fantasy to be fillable or dischargeable by a specific consummatory action may not be felt as such and, in any event, it is something our language in inadequate to communicate dealing as it does more easily with presences or behaviors than it does with absences. Our conscious awareness and recollections of a sense of absence are very much colored by our language or lack of it. Accordingly, such a sense of absence is most likely to be unavailable to the recollection of the patient and the scrutiny of the analyst. The patient will best remember the act itself and occasionally will be aware of the disorganization, furtiveness, or craving. Associations or conscious rationalizations usually concern the act itself and minimize the subjective experiences that immediately preceded the impulse to complete the act.

On occasion, patients will recall an actual persecutory feeling preceding the consummatory act. This feeling of persecution indicates an interpretation in fantasy (explanation to oneself) of a sense of fragmentation following an absence so that it is experienced (by the defensive workings of unconscious fantasy) as a presence. The lack of something is felt to be evidence of persecution by someone.

There may be the added dimension of interpretation in fantasy of an absence or disorganization as an emptiness of or lack of something accompanied by a fantasy of restitution—that the lack may be restored by a consummatory act. Often, but not always, the act involves stimulation of a mucosal area and the filling of a cavity—lips, palate, anus, or vagina. This zonal libidinal investment makes the restitution of the lost internal object. (See Examples 5 and 6.)

Appreciation of the subjective and fantasied states between the precipitant and the impulsive act is crucial to our understanding of what has transpired. Those states reach the impulsive actor's awareness only with difficulty and usually incompletely. The states are often covered over by the flamboyant aspects of impulsive action and are usually glossed over by some explanatory simplification. The prodromal phase is the bridge between the fragmented response to the precipitant and the restitution accomplished by the impulsive act itself. The restitutive process begins with the workings of fantasy in which an absence is felt to be persecution by or lack *of*. The disorganization is thus transformed in fantasy into a problem capable of solution. The isolated, helpless, fragmented state is interpreted in fantasy as a state that can be ameliorated by changing a relationship to an object. The disrupted state is transformed by the defensive activity of fantasy into something that is resolvable by activities that control distance by the patient's taking something in (introjection) or putting something out (projection). This working of unconscious defense transforms an experience of inner dissolution into one of fantasied transgression and control (I took in, I put out). Such defensive reworking restores the experience into the ego's fantasied omnipotent control.

Wrist Slashing

Example 4. Mrs. D, a 31-year-old divorced woman, was transferred from a locked hospital ward to an open one in which intensive impatient psychotherapy could be attempted. She was noted to be repeatedly suicidal. "Suicidal" had several meanings: she "felt" suicidal and communicated this to caretakers, who became duly alarmed because of several kinds of impulsive action, especially overdosing and wrist slashing. These actions, although of low lethality, took place in an affective and communicative climate that aroused alarm that Mrs. D would commit suicide and resulted in ward restriction and a general pattern of overregulation that only made matters worse.

In a hospitalization of nearly a year's duration, Mrs. D was treated with intensive psychotherapy and weekly family therapy. She began to be more in touch with feelings of terror and anger without disorganizing and slashing impulsively. Many months of therapy transpired without an impulsive act. Since difficulty separating from the hospital was anticipated, a date was set several months in advance for her discharge from the hospital. As the date approached she became more and more agitated.

About a month before discharge, during a visit from her mother (with whom she intended to live after discharge) she had an explosive episode during which she slashed her wrists superficially. Questioned about this, she said that she had awakened—some 10 hours prior to the visit—confused, perplexed, agitated, and in need of an outlet. She identified this state as one that always preceded an impulsive action, usually a wrist slashing. She would feel the need to slash, finding immediate relief if she did so—less if she merely overdosed or broke furniture. In retrospect, she was not only ashamed of the activity but horrified and depressed that she had become unable to hold together a job, a marriage, or even an existence outside of the hospital. Some months before, she had reached the stage where she could recognize her perplexity and put herself under some sort of staff observation until the confusional state had passed.

With the pressure of approaching discharge, these disorganized prodromal periods were more lengthy and severe. The impulsive act was seen by some of the ward staff solely as an attempt to forestall discharge and thereby to bind the relationship with the hospital. This attempt at control was indeed present but could be usefully approached only in the context of disorganization and restitution that was heightened in the phase of separation from the hospital.

THE ACT

The impulsive act is usually accompanied by a discharge in tension and a sense of relief. Something must be said about discharge because it is far from clear how impulsive acts are consummatory, how they release tension or relieve anxiety. On close examination, it is usually evident that compulsive eaters do not feel hunger at all, that habitually promiscuous women often do not experience orgasm or even sexual arousal when they have intercourse (Example 6), that wrist slashers are quite frequently not suicidal at the time they slash (Example 4, see also Rosenthal et al., 1972), that marital clashing does not arise because each spouse expects that the other will change (Example 3), and that episodic binge drinkers are not driven by the tension of physiological withdrawal when they drink (Example 1). What seem to be explanations of episodic impulsive activities are in fact often misleading and illusory. Freud's (1900) earliest (and ongoing) preoccupation with the explanation of human action by reference to a decrease of accumulated tension in the central nervous system—expression as discharge on the model of the orgasm—has not proved to be a sufficient explanatory model either for human action or for the theory of expression of emotions. The relief caused by performing an impulsive act has an enigmatic, fetish-like component (Sperling, 1974). There are specific conditions for discharge that must be understood. In general, a disproportionate amount of attention to impulsive activity in the context of psychoanalysis and dynamic psychotherapy has been aimed at *explaining* impulsive action, that is, at ascertaining its meaning as verified by the patient's associations. This explanatory task often substitutes for a comprehensive appreciation of its *structure*—the sequence of disintegration and restitution of which impulsive action is one phase.

The specific crystalization of a consummatory act somehow relieves a kind of tension, fills a felt emptiness, restores a sense of self or a relation to a lost object. Explanations solely in terms of force, adaptation (i.e., manipulation), or meaning may keep us from appreciating that in complex ways, involving both internal fantasy and control of external objects, such acts attempt to restore an optimal distance to objects. Impulsive action, then, is an attempt at restitution of optimal distance that compensates for a vulnerability to personality disorganization.

Impulsive Homosexuality

Example 5.   Patient E, a man in his 40s with a history of dozens of jobs as a waiter, had a typical cycle of impulsivity. He felt drawn to the headwaiter; he would then become demanding and quarrelsome with him, provoking him to anger. He then would grow agitated and disorganized. He would phone his wife, say he had to work late, and go to "the baths" desperately seeking anal penetration. He wound up furious and disappointed when, as usual, somebody sucked his penis and brought him to climax, because what he craved was not that discharge but, quite the contrary, to have the lack (felt in his anal mucosa) filled up with an erect penis. This craving followed panic when he got close to a male superior. His persecutory feelings found expression in his provoking the headwaiter and thereby creating circumstances where he felt attacked. This persecutory experience immediately preceded the conscious craving for anal penetration.

After his father died when Mr. E was three, his mother called him the man of the house and had him sleep in her bed. When he was seven, she remarried, and he was placed in an orphanage. He had several kinds of romantic lives apart from his homosexual sprees: one was to impregnate women and then leave town; another was a very romantic relationship with a woman he later married; and yet another was a degrading relationship with a woman whom he treated contemptuously and needed to abuse.

Mr. E's impulsive homosexuality was always precipitated by closeness to the headwaiter. It proved unreliable as a method of distance regulation with the boss and failed to preserve the relationship. As a result he regularly lost jobs. These cycles of impulsive action did, however, protect his marriage as an enduring, albeit unhappy, relationship. A similar stability was found in the therapy, where he again used impulsive activity to keep from getting too close to the therapist and safeguard against the relationship's falling apart.

What happened repeatedly on the job was avoided in the marriage and the therapy. Mr. E showed a particularly strong preoccupation with castration, which became apparent as therapy progressed. These dynamics became evident from his need constantly to impregnate women, his search for anal penetration as reassurance that he possessed an erect penis, his persistently inviting attacks from male superiors, and in his associations, which revealed that he viewed waiting on tables as an essentially feminine, castrated role. Interpretations of the impulsive act in terms of the castration complex provided only part of the picture. Interpretative work that clarified and dealt with his disorganization and his paranoid anxieties in situations involving closeness and loss—within the transference and in the marriage—stopped the pattern of impulsive activity completely.

REACTION TO THE ACT

Awareness of one's responsibility for habitual impulsive activity carries with it such shame or guilt that strong character defenses develop to ward off these feelings. With the recent attention to narcissistic phenomena in the last two decades, psychoanalytic thinking has been moving toward the appreciation of primitive shame and humiliation (Kohut, 1971; Lansky, 1981a; Wurmser, 1981), which is often a more fundamental defensive concern than is guilt.[1]

The reasons for the comparative neglect of shame are complex. Perhaps it is because shame cannot be conceptualized in the same mechanistic way that guilt has been—as the internalization of expected punishment—that shame dynamics have been so neglected. Shame results from being exposed as lacking or defective, unworthy, or unlovable before the gaze of another. Shame is public and is grounded on actual interaction, whereas guilt is private and is rooted in fantasy. Shame is an ultimate and irreducibly human phenomenon that cannot have a mechanistic model. Indeed, Nietzsche defined man as "the animal with the red cheeks."

One's shame at being found to be out of control, defective, weak, or impulsive is often more powerful than one's guilt at having transgressed or spoiled or injured loved ones. Hence awareness of one's personality disorganization is likely to be more disturbing than awareness of the consequences of an act. It is a common psychoanalytic error to incline one's explanations toward the more easily conceptualized notion of guilt

---

[1] I am using "guilt" in this context to refer to consciously felt remorse. Unconscious guilt, with its powerful effects on the individual's intimate relationships, is a topic beyond the scope of this chapter.

than toward the more immediate sense of shame before the gaze of the analyst, just as *actions* come more easily to attention than *absences*, guilt dynamics (involving actions that transgress or injure) are often first to hold us captive rather than shame dynamics (which involve exposure as lacking, out of control, or defective). The two may occur in combination, and either may be the motive for intense defensive operations that range from the penitent, reparative, obsequious or abstemious lifestyle of the habitual drinker when not drunk, or a degraded view of some promiscuous women as sexually "easy" and therefore bad, to a set of object choices that includes fellow binge eaters, fellow drinkers, sexual partners suitable only for promiscuous relationships. Any tendency to overemphasize *behavior* rather than paranoid fears, fragmented states, and experiences of emptiness or absence may incline both patient and analyst toward explanations involving transgression (guilt dynamics), rather than narcissistic mortification and dependency on selfobjects (shame dynamics). In some patients prone to humiliation, guilt conflicts may defend against shameful awarenesses that are even more mortifying (see Example 6).

The sense of mortification on realizing the consequences of one's impulsive action (guilt) and the shame suffered as a result of awareness of absence and fragmentation give rise to character defenses aimed at protecting such mortifying awareness from occurring. The defenses against shame and guilt may exclude or include integration of the impulsive action. If they include it, a whole character style—for example, as violence prone, street addict, prostitute, or chronic hospital patient or criminal—can arise. If character defenses exclude the impulsive act, a splitting off of ego states occurs so that the activity is experienced in a disowned way. The following clinical examples of promiscuity, impulsive homosexuality, blaming, and alcohol binges illustrate impulsive activity split off from otherwise more integrated character structure. The more tightly the impulsive activity is integrated with the rest of the character structure, the poorer the prognosis. Patients who are chronically manipulative (Bursten, 1972) or grossly obese or who gravitate to circles where they are expected to drink constantly are less amenable to change than are patients for whom impulsive activity is an unintegrated split-off part of the personality.

Shame and humiliation at the awareness of self as fragmenting are usually more mortifying than guilt, the experience of oneself as transgressing. Accordingly, the patient's focus on the consequences of his action is often found to have the defensive function of deemphasizing the shame-producing prodrome (or the relation of the prodrome to the precipitant) in favor of the guilt-producing act or attack on objects. Recollection of a transgression, in effect, serves as a screen memory, defending against the awareness of fragmentation experiences. As a result, the patient is defensively oriented to represent himself in a guilty rather than a shameful light.

Most important, this defense may dovetail with the analyst's preference for a focus on the more intelligible guilt (based on behaviors) rather than shame (being seen to depend on the other to avoid disintegrating). If this occurs, a process of partial or inexact interpretation may take a path of apparent verification when, in fact, it has served to seal a major defensive maneuver from analytic scrutiny.

The defensive functions of unconscious fantasy show the same movement. At first, the patient sees himself as alone with feelings of fragmentation, incompleteness, and isolation. Then he suffers premonitions of persecution or of consummatory acts that define him in terms of a relationship and transform the difficulty into something that needs to be done, that is, the act itself, which takes something in or puts it out. This defensive movement in fantasy proceeds from an apperception of a defective or fragmented state (about which the patient is ashamed) to something that the patient psychically takes in (introjects), expels (projects), or controls (about which he feels guilt).

Promiscuity

Example 6.   Miss F was a young woman with a long series of unhappy relationships with very self-centered men. She described pacing back and forth in front of the building in which her analyst's office was located. She felt confused and terror stricken, fell, got up, and ran. The persecutory malaise evolved into an urge to go to a nearby pickup bar and find a man. A predictably brief sexual encounter followed. She felt neither arousal nor genital excitement—only intense dread and a need, one which for years had been incomprehensible to her, for her vagina to be filled. She had had dozens of such encounters, preceded by such prodromal states, without arousal or orgasm. She was orgasmic only by masturbation, using a vibrator.

Her immediate associations were to a situation some years before in which she feared that her mother, a cardiac patient, would die if she knew that Miss F was pregnant. Both oedipal competitive and preoedipal envious aspects of her fantasied attack on her mother were found to contribute to Miss F's pervasive sense of guilt. At another, more fundamental level, however, was her even stronger sense of shame that she could not control herself and would be found to be worthless in the sight of everyone. Details of this primitive shame were hard for her to put into words and had to await a lessening of her sense of guilt when her transgression against her loved one was understood. Neither the shame nor the guilt could be analyzed separately. Analytic uncovering of competition and of envious attack promoted an integration that decreased her guilt to the extent that shame at her inability to regulate herself could come into focus.

This young lady avoided seriously intentioned men in favor of self-centered ones, in part, to keep from awareness her lack of control that she felt to be so shameful. She adopted a lifestyle of habitual promiscuity consisting of brief encounters with men who had not reached her level of professional or educational accomplishment. She came to have a view of herself as "easy" and degraded and worthless—so much so that she removed herself from her home town because of her reputation. She became sexually eager only in situations that were conducive to sustaining this degraded view of herself. She bristled with excitement, but not sexual arousal, over what invariably turned out to be brief trysts with self-centered men. She became bored with or uninterested in any seemingly worthwhile suitors who showed serious interest in her.

During her analysis, Miss F's sexual involvements served to distance her from the analyst emotionally when she felt needy and depressed and to talk about other relationships that were thrilling, however short lived and damaging they might be. Subsequent associative material revealed a similar engineering of short encounters at times of tension in the relationship with her mother. Brief sexual episodes thus served to offset the dangers of fusion with her mother and loss of her. Once in the analysis, when her anger at the analyst reached such an intensity that she threatened to stop, she "wound up in bed" with a close friend's husband and reaffirmed her need for analysis to understand her compulsion to do so. The impulsive promiscuity disappeared completely after several years of analysis, when a full picture of her pattern of impulsive action and its relation to the transference had been understood and interpreted.

Distance Regulation

Finally, there is a homeostatic mechanism that attempts to restore the equilibrium that was disrupted by the precipitating factor. The impulsive action and characterological response to it may regulate distance between persons who are getting either too close or too far away, moving too independently, or felt to be exerting too much pressure for recognition. It is this distance-regulating aspect that is often visible in the transference and can be understood in terms of the patient's past history in intimate relationships and the patient's subsequent need to control his or her intimates. Analytic scrutiny of the psychic disorganization and loss of control often demonstrates that they result from the same disruption of relationships that the impulsivity is designed to restore. For example, constant parental quarreling that made the patient feel he must hold the parental marriage together may be a symbolic factor in the origin of his vulnerability to disorganization. At a later time, the same type of quarreling may precipitate the impulsive act, which exploits and tries to control it.

The distance-regulating function may be evident in the countertransference, that is, the enormous pull on the analyst or therapist by the process of impulsive action to become oversolicitous, regulate the patient, or withdraw emotionally. Any departure by the analyst from a position of empathic neutrality risks the reestablishment of the sort of unstable relationship characteristic of such patients—one that is rejecting because it is too removed or one that is intensive and thus risks envious regression in the patient or exhaustion and rejection by the analyst.

Example 7. (A Blaming Situation): Mrs. G was 10 minutes late for a conjoint therapy session and Mr. G verbally exploded, hurling vile epithets at her for her immaturity and unreliability. Reflecting after the outburst, the couple agreed that such blaming was typical of a marriage of several decades' duration. The therapists attempted in vain to find a recent source for such anger that might have been displaced on to the issue of lateness. However, repeated blaming episodes showed convincingly that a few minutes' tardiness or a brief lapse in Mrs. G's attention or emotional absences were sufficient to precipitate her husband's violent blaming attacks. These restored the wife's attention, although at a high cost to the marriage. Lapses varied from short delays, conversations with others that excluded Mr. G, or even his feeling excluded when the bathroom door was closed. Mr. G's persecutory feelings found expression in the act of blame itself, in verbal attacks on Mrs. G for letting him down and causing him frightful anguish.

Mrs. G was the youngest of three daughters of an alcoholic mother and a violent father. The parental marriage broke up with the father taking the two elder daughters while Mrs. G remained with the mother. Her mother's capacities deteriorated, and Mrs. G was sent back to her father. Her adaptation to the older sisters' resentment was to indulge herself in whining submissiveness, which invited physical abuse and served to placate and gratify those on whom she was dependent. Her inviting and tolerating abuse in the marriage served both to hold the marriage together and to ward off closeness.

Mr. G was born in wartime Europe. In combat at his birth, his father was killed in battle. Thereafter his mother made no secret of finding him a burden and finally left him with her mother and sisters, none of whom wanted to raise him either. His vulnerability to desertion by women and his rage at them were both expressed in the blaming transaction with his wife.

Despite their manifest vicious bullying and contemptuous features, these attacks restored a situation in which the couple became intently locked in, their relatedness excluding the children and later the therapist, when their anxieties were high. Despite the surface unpleasantness of the marital quarrels and the fact that they took place many times daily for several decades, the couple had never talked of divorce and did not complain about the marriage. Indeed, these harsh exchanges were noted only incidentally in a setting where family involvement was part of the workup of every patient.

Distance regulation is not just maneuvering by the patient to preserve his cohesiveness by keeping intimates from getting too close or too far away. Impulsive action may embody the patient's hopeful claim to a relationship in which he can truly regress, be sick, and even be destructive (Winnicott, 1956, 1963). Manifest disruptiveness and anxiety make the hopefulness difficult to see. Nonetheless, such regressive action is the patient's attempt to get from intimates enough of what he needs in the hope of getting beyond the effects of the early deprivation that has left such costly limitations on his later life.

THE PSYCHOANALYTIC FOCUS

My illustrative material contains data that go beyond the associative methods and frames of reference that are clearly outside the psychotherapeutic dyad. My purpose is to illuminate a structure common to many kinds of impulsive action, not to put forward a treatment approach or a rationale for the selection of treatment strategies.

Some types of impulsive action can be dealt with entirely by psychoanalysis or psychoanalytic psychotherapy. In such cases, the analyst attempts to get an analytic focus on the premonition or experience of ego disorganization that serves as a nidus of an explanatory fantasy that evokes zonal fullness or emptiness as a restitutive pathway toward the optimal distancing of objects. In other cases, both chaotic symptomatology and the need to contain it may necessitate either modifications from an interpretive approach or other types of treatment altogether. Some patients with a great propensity for ego disruption are not treatable by interpretive means, but this realization should not blind us to the need for a psychoanalytically illumined focus on any sort of impulsive action, no matter what treatment approaches are taken.

There are many countertransference obstacles to such a focus: from chaotic and anxiety-producing symptoms; from simplified views resulting from splitting off of the impulsive activity from the mainstream of conscious experience; and from the analyst's discomfort with the patient's intense superego anxieties, especially shame. Such countertransference difficulties often become embedded in and rationalized by the analyst's preconceptions—"explanations" of impulsive action that draw from accurate, but incomplete, views of the clinical picture.

The whole process I have described should be included in the analyst's view of what has transpired when he communicates to the patient. Over-emphasis on the external events—the precipitant, the impulsive act itself, and the control of significant objects—at the expense of understanding the subjective phenomenology may make the patient react to interpretive work as blame and may inflict further narcissistic injury, which perpetu-ates the disorder and complicates it. Too much focus on the transference, however accurately portrayed, if it is not tactful and empathic, may be justified by conceptualizations that overemphasize external events: the "compulsion to repeat," envious attack on the analyst, self-sabotaging maneuvers that hold dependent relationships together, control of signifi-cant objects including the analyst, justifying secondary gains, and others.

Overemphasis on the feelings that accompany the prodrome or the reaction to the act, to the exclusion of the rest of the process, results in an approach to the patient's material that is closer to sympathy than to empathy and fosters splitting. By such a stance, the analyst may collude with the patient in ignoring the consequences of his actions. By equating the analyst's with the patient's point of view and fostering idealization, a sympathetic response from the analyst undermines a focus on the negative transference and any possibility of working it through.

These overemphases reflect and perpetuate either true countertrans-ference difficulties or ones that emanate from an incomplete or faulty understanding of the clinical picture. The structure of impulsive action must be grasped at some level if one is to do competent clinical work, especially if stubborn treatment situations or seeming treatment failures are to be examined.

The vulnerabilities to personality disorganization that underlie cycles of impulsive action often result from defects in empathic nurturance early in childhood: from parental absences or changes in nurturance resulting from character pathology in parents; from parental inattentiveness be-cause of depression or preoccupation or schizoid tendencies rationalized as withdrawal justified by divided loyalty to family or business. Frequently the patient is found to have been the object of parentifying, scapegoating, or blaming maneuvers of parents, or of actual physical or sexual abuse that went on with the knowledge of the parents or even involved them (Lansky, 1980, 1981a).

Analytic interventions should be aimed at conveying the analyst's awareness of the ego's struggles with these vulnerabilities. Reconstruc-tions are important only insofar as they outline the ego as preoccupied with certain defensive tasks and trace throughout time the actual structure of the ego's activities that deal with these preoccupations. Identifying and dating traumata in the clinical setting are not in themselves curative, fully explanatory, or conclusively verifiable. The actual symbolic significance of the impulsive act or its derivation from an infantile experience or from the relationship to the analyst likewise illuminates the experience of an ego that is preoccupied with the threat of disorganization, that undergoes an experience felt to be a lack, that interprets this as an emptiness, that crystalizes the emptiness into a consummatory act, and that acts in a mysteriously restitutive way generating shame and perplexity and necessitating considerable character armoring and sometimes changing an entire life style.

Basically, interpretive efforts involve the analyst's understanding of the ego as preoccupied and communicating this understanding to the patient in an accepting way. Such an insight is usable if it acknowledges that the patient's ego is vulnerable to disorganization and that it arranges interpersonal situations to compensate for this vulnerability by regulating distance to intimate persons to avoid disorganization. Seen in this light, any contrast of interpretation with empathy posits a false antithesis. If interpretation puts emphasis on the act itself, the precipitant, or the controlling of objects, it is likely to be experienced as blaming and unempathic. It is not that interpretation per se is not empathic, but only that overemphasis on these aspects tends to be perceived as blaming and, for that reason, unempathic. If interpretation is skewed toward the subjective side, that is, toward the experience of emptiness and fragmentation, of anxiety and shame and guilt, without attention to what has actually transpired (or its adaptive significance), then the analyst errs on the side of sympathy, and he may produce an equally destructive countertransference dilemma.

Neither blaming nor sympathy really constitutes empathic interpretation, interpretation that *starts* from the patient's experience but remains aware of the effects of what the patient does in the transference and how he affects others. It is only by reference to the self preoccupied with defects as it acts in attempts to restore defects to its integrity that interpretation and reconstruction can be accomplished. These are not antithetical to empathic contact with the patient; they include it.

Blaming and sympathy are two prominent types of countertransference polarities based on explanatory pictures that may hold the analyst captive to a limited view of the process. *Explanation*—covert or overt—is an activity based on preconception. It is not to be confused with the type of understanding that follows interpretive illumination of what process the patient is struggling with. In the case of impulsive action, if we cannot transcend explanation, we cannot explore the limits of what can be accomplished by interpretation.

7

The Borderline Father
Reconstructions of Young Adulthood

In this chapter I hope to shed light on the impact of borderline psychopathology on the transition in young adulthood from the developmental tasks of adolescence, to the tasks, fatherhood in particular, of adulthood proper. The tasks of adolescence include separation from family of origin, consolidation of sexual identity, and the beginnings of the abilities to work and love in adult life (Blos, 1974). By the end of young adulthood, say at the age of 25 or 26, a healthy or even neurotic person should have some ability to work and form a satisfying, generative love relationship. Interference with these normal developmental tasks by borderline pathology affects intimate relationships, the capacity to work, the capacity for a stable marital relationship, and an expanded capacity for involvement in relationships that are not tied to immediate defensive needs. These developmental attainments are sharply, and sometimes decisively, tested in the young adult man by his emergence into fatherhood. In the paternal role, the young adult must be able to provide emotional and material support for mother and child and to tolerate the loss of the exclusiveness of the dyadic relationship in the marriage.

The effects of borderline pathology on young adults are less easily assessed than might at first blush be imagined. The true extent of the patient's psychopathology is difficult to glean from the treatment situation whether psychoanalysis, psychoanalytic psychotherapy, hospital treatment, or family therapy, whereas in the intensive treatment of adolescents, a clear view of psychopathology is more easily obtained. The young adult facing crises of commitment to vocation, spouse, and parenting,

113

however, is seldom phase-appropriately dependent on others in the same way as is an adolescent. For that reason, such a patient is likely to become symptomatic in a way that masks those dependency needs and renders him less accessible to sustained treatment.

Although the basic psychopathology is substantially the same as it is in adolescence, role expectations in young adulthood are sufficiently different from those in adolescence to increase substantially the sense of shame over defects in self-regulation and other limitations that are posed by the disturbance. Shame and massive defensive operations aimed at minimizing shame may be a larger part of the clinical picture and prove to be greater obstacles to treatment than they are in adolescence. The marriages of borderline men often are dominated by impulse-ridden behavior. These symptomatic impulsive actions—suicidal bouts, broadcasted infidelities, intimidation or violence, and addictive self-soothing—have a distance-regulating or binding effect on relationships: they keep those relationships from getting too close or too far away and keep the symptomatic person from being flooded with shame. Analytic scrutiny of such patients invariably reveals the emptiness, depression, fragmentation proneness, excessive reliance on relationships to secure cohesion, and the shame they feel both over their propensity to disorganize and over the limitations such pathology places on their strength of will in job, marriage, and parenthood. A full view of the young adult borderline father's struggles, of the extent of his pathologic internalizations and structural defects, makes understandable the force with which these difficulties propel him into collusive symbiotic relationships, usually chaotic ones, that to some extent accommodate to and cover over the basic pathology (Lansky, 1981a). These collusive relationships are so costly in activity and resources that they preempt generative middle adult tasks. Furthermore, by sealing the couple together in a protective dyad, they also tend to interfere with any sort of treatment that might uncover the inner struggles of the spouses and further flood them with shame.

Some insight into this difficulty of access into the inner life of the young adult borderline father was gained from research on psychiatrically hospitalized fathers undertaken in a hospital setting. This chapter draws heavily from this psychoanalytically informed research and from intensive extra-associative clinical data: the admitting circumstances, ward behavior, the clinical course of the hospitalization, results of group psychotherapy for fathers, and supervision (by the author) of individual and family therapy. Especially illuminating were interviews with each father admitted to the ward for a one-year period. These interviews took place shortly after admission and were recorded and transcribed. The research interview covered the hospitalized father's relationships from an intergenerational perspective: how he viewed his relationship with his own father; whether he saw his mother as helping or hindering that relationship; his view of his relationship with his wife and whether she helped or hindered his relationship with his children; and, finally, his view of his relationship with his own children, and his view of his own strengths and shortcomings as a father.

Research endeavors within the context of sustained clinical treatment provided the unique perspective of reconstructions of early adulthood made by borderline fathers in mid-life, say 30s through 50s. Often this perspective seemed more complete than one gleaned from young adult borderline patients treated during adult life or from relatives of such patients. This observation merits commentary.

Direct clinical contact with young adult borderline fathers, either in treatment themselves or related to patients (e.g., husbands or fathers of abused wives or children) is often obviated by symptomatic impulsive actions. Such symptomatic acts cover over conflicts surrounding shame and its exposure. The midadult borderline fathers, by their own admission, were not very accessible to either treatment or self-scrutiny as young adults, and indeed reports by these young adult borderline fathers were uncommon in our clinical setting. When such young fathers did present as patients, it was often for symptomatic impulsive action. Such impulsive action, as I have already discussed in this volume and elsewhere (Lansky et al., 1983), has a distance-regulating function. It serves, by intimidation and other means, to hold relationships together, to keep other people from getting too close or too far away. Many young adult borderlines are either not in close relationships at all or are in ones that are so characterized by emotional turbulence and guilt over the patient's impulsiveness that they make scrutiny and psychotherapy—both of which risk exposure and further shame—almost impossible.

It is perhaps for these reasons that data gleaned later from midadult borderline fathers show a more balanced picture. The fathers from whom we learned the most had all gone through relationships in which they married and entered tumultuous collusive relationships organized around hiding massive inadequacy. Splitting and trading of dissociations (Wynne, 1961) were ubiquitous in the men's relationships with wives, all of whom had endured strikingly similar trauma from their families of origin. In the paternal role, these men were much more overwhelmed, fragmented, shaken, chronically preoccupied, and unable to relate than their clinical picture suggested at the time. They reacted to their deficits by escalating cycles of impulsive symptomatology—by violence, drinking, suicide attempts. They tended to select women with very similar backgrounds, who subsequently paired off with the children in ways that excluded the fathers. These fathers responded to feeling excluded from the mother-child dyad by impulse-ridden symptomatology.

These symptom patterns escalated to abusiveness and irresponsibility to the point where the father finally felt himself thoroughly rejected. He became more symptomatic and was often ashamed to return to the family fold. The men who told us the most had gone through a period of sustained depression and helplessness at the time they stopped symptomatic acting out and reentered relationships with their offspring, who were by then adolescents or adults. The case material from which these conclusions were drawn is voluminous. From that material, I have drawn two clinical sketches illustrative of the fathers who were able to tolerate treatment to the extent of reconstructing views of their young adult years. In what follows, I summarize some pertinent features in the developmental struggles of the young adult borderline father that shed light on the difficulties in the transition from adolescence to the more generative tasks of middle adult life.

Both the clinical sketches and the material from the research interviews include reconstructions of young adult life. Neither is a reconstruction in the strictly psychoanalytic sense (Freud, 1937). In the clinical sketches, the reconstructions are made by the men themselves about their young adult lives at times in their middle adult years when they faced particular crises with their children within the context of a supportive treatment setting that allowed them to face these crises without disorganizing.

The reconstructions in the research interviews are based on my own synthesis of data compiled from these interviews and amplified by clinical data on the same patients. The illustrations are illumined by a psychoanalytic understanding of borderline pathology and particularly from insights gained from object relations theory (Dicks, 1967) and from the intergenerational study of the family (Bowen, 1966).

CLINICAL ILLUSTRATIONS

Example 1. A 35-year-old father of two young children was admitted to a locked ward after cutting his wrists. This slashing had followed an attack on his wife, who had flaunted an affair in front of the patient and his children. She had defiantly and publicly taken a lover to register her refusal to continue to endure the patient's indignities and abuses. The patient had been hospitalized several times previously after suicide attempts. He had had longstanding difficulties with job failures and substance abuse. He had been a serious drug user since adolescence.

He was one of three children, a disappointment to both parents, but especially to his father. He complained bitterly about his father's total inability to understand him and his total lack of involvement with him. Asked what he thought might have been different if he had had a different kind of fathering, he replied, "It's hard to say, because I never really had anything. I would like to think that there would have been things different. Maybe I wouldn't have been so involved in drugs. I think there's a connection there . . . . I missed not having a father that really cared about me. The stuff that I really enjoyed he didn't enjoy, so he went his way and I went my way. I didn't enjoy school. He wanted all of us to go to school. So I got pressure there. I enjoyed athletics—he didn't. So there was nothing for us to get together and talk about. I was more in my mom's mold, so my relationship with him was really distant. It got to the point where we wouldn't even talk. That went on for years, and I would always go to my Mom if I ever needed anything or any advice . . . my mother, and not my father."

His standing in his marriage for a time felt like a reversal of the humiliation he had felt in his educationally oriented family. There he had felt himself regarded as the outcast, the defective, and the one in disgrace. He had married a prostitute whom he had met in another country. He insulted her, ignored her, and scorned her as beneath him in status and poorly educated. He had thus passed on the devaluation and abusiveness that he had gotten from his family of origin to his wife, who for years endured these indignities. He had kept her at a distance with his drug usage and preoccupation with drugs and drug problems. He was aloof and outright hostile to her. When she protested strongly enough, he became suicidal and was admitted to the hospital.

At the beginning of his treatment, he presented himself as utterly without ambivalence in the paternal role, saying, "I just turned all my love and everything toward my two kids. It was scary, because if something happened to them, I don't know how I would react. I love my kids; they're precious to me. I love being a father." Only later could he admit difficulties in the role: "There's so much anxiety to parts of it, you know—sometimes after working on all the frustrations with [my] wife and everything, I'd catch myself taking it out on the kids, but I'd try and stop that." He at first idealized himself in the paternal role. This was the only relationship in which he had ever felt worthwhile: "I'd play with them, I'd dance with them, I'd do all sorts of stuff. I'd act like a kid with them, and that really would upset my wife, but my kids would love it. They just love me. My girl wants to live with me. When I see my two kids, my anxiety level goes down. I really feel relaxed with them, because I know that they like their father. I see so much of myself in my daughter, and I think she's real precious to me, real special."

This patient engaged actively in treatment and began to acknowledge the extent of his difficulties. He participated in psychotherapy and was able to profit from a group for hospitalized fathers that was part of the ward program. A crisis in treatment came when his wife announced that she did not want care of the children but intended to leave them in his custody and to live with her lover.

Having actual caretaking responsibilities thrust upon him precipitated a phase of reconstruction. He became horrified and overwhelmed, recalling that while he was on drugs and living with his wife and children, he had never acknowledged the extent to which he became terrified and disorganized. He now feared falling apart, having rage attacks, and being utterly unable to function when the children needed him. He was terrified at the prospect of having to be the stable person in their lives. This was the first time he had squarely acknowledged the anxiety and shame he felt at his fragility and the first time he talked about his difficulties in a way that showed him as a vulnerable person who had brought about most of his difficulties. The prospect of turning for help either to his parents or to his wife because he could not manage his children alone was humiliating. These inadequacies and his shame when they were exposed proved to be a major focus of subsequent therapeutic work. He was able to recall experiences of disorganization that he had covered over with use of drugs, with violent outbursts, and with suicidal episodes.

Example 2. A 47-year-old divorced father of four sons who was treated for a number of years as an inpatient and an outpatient was interviewed during a brief hospitalization some years after treatment efforts had begun. He had first come to the ward suicidal and had had a lengthy stay there, he had unusual difficulty facing a discharge without an upsurge of suicidal feeling. He had aroused both sympathy, because of his deep pain after his family's rejection, and alarm that he might attempt suicide. His eliciting both sympathy and fear that he would kill himself intensified a split among ward staff, with his therapist and several staff members overwhelmed by how seriously damaged he was and others on the staff feeling that he had maintained his hospital stay an unreasonably long time by deliberately contrived declarations of suicidality. At this time in his treatment he characterized himself as a man alone in the world. Closer examination revealed that he had been in contact with his ex-wife, with his sons, and with his grandchild and that his mother lived in the area.

The patient's early life history was replete with overwhelming trauma, abandonment, and abuse. He was the fifth of six children born to immature and constantly quarreling, physically abusive parents. His mother deserted when the patient was five. His father and paternal grandparents tried to keep the family together but soon gave up and placed him in an orphanage. There he was exposed to both physical and sexual abuse. He was moved from foster home to foster home. His vulnerability to personality disorganization, his spite and envy, and his coexistent need for and hatred of caretakers clearly stemmed from this chaotic upbringing. His difficulties leaving the hospital and his discharge were further complicated by his developing diabetes mellitus, which he deliberately exacerbated by dietary excesses, giving staff further fears that he would not comply with treatment and would commit suicide by neglecting his treatment regimen.

The ward staff had to deal with immense countertransference difficulties in response to his deliberately placing his life in danger. This man was finally offered a treatment package that involved hospitalization for brief crisis periods only along with continued outpatient therapy with management of medication. Management of his spiteful, regressive acting out was successful enough that the patient calmed down and began to become reinvolved with his father until the father's death, with his mother, to some extent with his ex-wife, and more particularly with his children and grandchild. Focus on the patient's very early family relationships and the futility and emptiness he had felt as the legacy of his early upbringing resulted in a lessening of his reluctance to become involved with his family. The futility and spite abated somewhat, and he was able to garner some supportive contact from these family members. A major therapeutic breakthrough enabling him to do so followed the ward staff's bringing into focus and dealing with his hostile dependency and his indirect hints of intent to suicide. These regressions had begun to exhaust supportive relationships on the ward and were emblematic of his spiteful, hostile-dependent relationship with caring people in his life. With his hostile dependency brought into focus and worked through even minimally, he was able to increase contact with his family members. He often sank into depression but did so increasingly without indirect threats of suicide.

His lengthy involvement with the hospital staff resulted in enough working through of his tendencies toward control of relationships by suicide threats. Hand in hand with his relinquishment of his self-defeating control maneuvers was an ability to reflect both on his own vulnerabilities and on his father's. This reconstruction came some months after one of his sons had gone through a suicidal crisis. The patient was able to reflect on his father: "My Dad—I didn't know him until I was six or seven. My parents split and they put me in a state home, and then I didn't see him until I was 14. I kind of felt that if he wanted to see me he'd come and see me. That made for bad feeling between us, so when I got of age, I just didn't bother going around him too much. It was my wife who insisted that I see him . . . during the last part of his years. . . . I was there for a while, we went on vacation together, our family and my Dad, and my brothers. I got pretty close to my father there at the end, before he died. A lot of things, a lot of feelings changed. I kind of understand some of the things he went through because I went through them myself, so I didn't feel so angry. I think I still have a lot of anger, but it's tempered *right now* . . . understanding what happened to him, what he went through, especially when I started having trouble with my own wife. I could understand why he tried to stay away from his kids. I had to make an effort to go see my kids when I was separated from my wife, too."

He talked with sadness about his poor relationships with his own children. "I felt like a father ought to be there when you need him, and be able to talk to him, and get answers from him. I felt that way when they asked me, but I kept them at a distance, I think, because of my father. And I was doing all the right things, but I didn't let my feelings get involved. Then I started having troubles with their Mom. All these feelings came out, and I didn't know what to do with them. . . . I had guilt about not being able to feel love or to feel satisfaction, or anything."

He praised his wife's support of him until the marriage broke up, but then, "she was kind of hurtful. She seemed to think I should be doing a lot more than I was doing at the time. I can understand my wife. I can understand what my dad went through. When we split up, I'd go see my kids. I'd get hysterical. I'd just go down the road, laughing and crying at the same time, because of all the feelings that came up. I had to leave them. I couldn't stay with them. All these things were going through your head, and you just get really depressed, or angry, really angry, but I still have to deal with it, and I have a hard time with it. It's very difficult. "

One of the most painful things for this man was to carry with him simultaneously feelings of his failure with his own children and the feelings of bitterness he had toward his own father. To his horror, he had turned out the same way: "That seems to be a big part, to me, of what I can't handle— the fact that I turned out like my father. My kids went through the same things I did. Because all the time I was growing up, I was so angry that I swore that none of my kids would ever be like that. . . . I think I felt a lot like my dad. I just wanted to stay away completely from them, because there were too many feelings involved, but then I remembered what I went through as a kid, so I go see them even if it really bothered me. I go see them, and I think I feel a little good about that. That I do that. I still have a lot of guilt doing it, but I do feel that I did try to do something that my Dad didn't do. I tried to be able to handle something that he couldn't have. . . ."

These were new gains for this deeply disturbed man. He recalled that in the early years of marriage things had been tempestuous and wild and impulsive: "I still have difficulty . . . some of the things I know now don't seem to make them any better. That's the thing that's making it difficult this time. All this time, since 1968 when it all happened. I think a lot of it's pure being confused and mixed up. I don't like the feelings at all, and I'd like to see them change. Before I didn't really care." His capacity to withstand disorganization and to bear feelings of depression and helplessness had enabled him to reenter a relationship with his children. This reentry, in turn, had given rise to the flood of shameful, embittered, and painful memories that became a reconstruction of his early years as a parent.

These reconstructions of young adult life came many months after the research interview. Such reconstructions have similarities to and also significant differences from reconstructions that are confined to the analytic situation. This man's reconstructions of young adulthood came about in the context of psychoanalytically illumined general psychiatric care in hospital and after hospitalization—not in psychoanalysis or in lengthy psychoanalytic psychotherapy.

Like specifically psychoanalytic reconstructions, they took place in an atmosphere conducive to both support and self-scrutiny. Some sense of safety had to be felt in three sectors for the men to endure the pain and shame of acknowledging their vulnerabilities and deficits: their early upbringing had to be recalled and the overwhelming affect surrounding such recall tolerated; the current familial reality had to involve facing a rapprochement with children; and the relationship of the borderline patients with the hospital staff (often a provocative and turbulent one) had to have been sufficiently addressed so that the disruption, splitting, and provocation that occurred on the ward emerged, was dealt with, and subsided. These three sectors are homologous to the alignment of genetic uncovering, acknowledgment of current reality, and working through of transference resistance that must occur in the strictly psychoanalytic situation to pave the way for psychoanalytic reconstructions.

RESEARCH INTERVIEWS IN A CLINICAL CONTEXT

The following generalizations highlight prominent issues in the lives of the borderline fathers in our study. The issues raised illuminate the predicament of these men as young adults. The reconstructions arose from psychoanalytically informed intergenerational histories and extrapolations from what many of the men recollected at varying phases of their treatment.

The most significant clinical breakthroughs occurred for these fathers in later adult life when they faced rapprochement with adult or adolescent children after years of absence from their families. Reparative fantasies at this time were common: fathers volunteered to work in child abuse centers; they imagined that they would be much better in the role of grandfather than they had as fathers. They began to have different recollections of both parents and especially recollected their fathers as much more fragile and inadequate the more they could acknowledge these feelings in themselves.

Developmental History

Intergenerational interviews with hospitalized borderline fathers gave a consistent picture of the internalizations that propelled these patients into their young adult relationships, especially marriage. Generally, in the hospitalized borderline patient's discussions of the members of his family of origin before he was 10, his memories showed consistent representations of a father who was a failure both at work and in the family. On recollection, the patient's attention tended first to go to his father's bluster, cruelty, intimidation, criticism, and outright debunking of all the children in the family, usually the patient in particular. Commonly, the future borderline patient became involved in a marital dispute between his parents with the conscious thought that his involvement protected his mother; only later did he realize that his activities had provoked his father to anger. Further reflection by the men who were able to become curious usually focused on the intense inadequacy and poor sense of self that their fathers had handled by employing violent, intimidating means to gain some sense of control and of respect within the family. These borderline patients lamented the fact that their fathers had had no involvement with them in homework, socializing, or such masculine endeavors as fishing or team sports. There was no warmth, no guidance, no structure, no involvement at all. All the hospitalized borderline fathers voiced intense bitterness about this lack and carried with them conscious resentment that they had not been prepared for adult life, that they had been cheated, that they themselves had evolved as defective, and that this defectiveness showed up directly in their own ability to be a father. Their discourse was peppered with self-pity, blaming, a sense of damage, rage, and a sense of entitlement—all typical features of narcissistic injury in patients with borderline organization. What often unfolded in these patients' treatment, if they were able to become reflective was a horrifying feeling of identification with father, a premonition that they were doomed to be like him, and a struggle, albeit a hopeless one, against that identification (see Example 2).

The borderline patient's parents' marriage was usually portrayed as an armed camp with open resentment between the parents. Father was seen as violent, inadequate, often drunken, and almost always contemptible. Mother was typically viewed in a confusing, unintegrated way. She was first described as a victim, a well-meaning, nurturant, protective woman brutalized by the patient's father. If the patient was able to engage in psychotherapy, this view invariably deepened. Memories of mother changed from a portrayal of a loving, victimized, caretaking person to a depiction of one who was also devious, failed to integrate the family, formed coalitions (often very seductive ones and very often involving the patient) that humiliated, rejected and provoked the patient's father to anger. In the midst of her husband's anger, the patient's mother did nothing to help the relationship between the patient and his father. The patient attributed this divisiveness and troublemaking—a lack of the integrative capacity that Atkins (1984) has called transitive vitalization—not only to mother, but also (and in a strikingly similar way) to his wife. This split maternal imago left the patient alternating between rage, when he considered mother's (or wife's) divisiveness, and depression and guilt, when he considered mother as protective, devoted, and victimized.

Each patient, without exception, reported striking defects in nurturance before the age of 10 due specifically to character pathology in one (or usually both) parents; some involvement on the part of the patient in the parents' highly pathological, tension-ridden marriage. The patient often was parentified (that is, made to feel responsible for meeting the parents' emotional needs) scapegoated, or blamed; and he often sustained physical or sexual abuse which went on with knowledge of one or both parents (Lansky 1980).

Psychopathology

Derived from this typical constellation in family of origin was the borderline patient's struggle against malignant aspects of his identification with his father (Greenson, 1954). This identification included the adoption of father's abusive repertoire of behaviors, usually ineffective ones, for assuring his place in the family: intimidation, violence, drunkenness, and debunking. The patient also identified, on a deeper level, with the father's inner sense of inadequacy, weakness, and worthlessness. Further complicating these identifications was the patient's (conscious) awareness that he wished his father dead. Such death wishes should not be confused with their less toxic variants inherent in the oedipal rivalry found in neurotics and normals. These wishes reflected a view of the patient's father as so contemptible, hateful, attacking, and basically worthless that his significance had to be denied entirely. The entire positive valence of the paternal representation (Loewald, 1951) was missing. What seemed to be so devastating for these patients' sense of self is that they internalized these damaged models and, in later life, felt themselves to be equally worthless and not entitled to respect or authority from their own children (see Example 2).

The confused views of mother reflected a widely split maternal imago, both components of which had devastating effects on the patient's self-regard. From the aspect of his mother that he protected and saw as caring and victimized, the patient derived a sense of himself in his family of origin as preemptive, out of place, in some strange way too close, and, fundamentally, more of a fake than a real protector. The aspect of mother that proved divisive, undermining, contemptuous of her husband and resentful of a strong male affected the patient's view of himself as a husband. Wives were seen as undercutting, divisive, and tending to form hostile coalitions rather than to integrate within the family. The split in the marriage of the borderline father's family of origin was mirrored in a subsequent split in the patient's ego, a split that powerfully affected mate selection. In a seemingly uncanny way, these men selected for wives the same kind of women that had mothered them.

The result of these deficiencies in the patient's nurturance, then, was not only an extreme narcissistic vulnerability but compensatory mechanisms to deal with the vulnerability that reinforced splitting and compounded the original difficulties with a pervasive sense of shame, worthlessness, despair, and dirtiness.

Defensive operations aimed at minimizing personality disorganization and controlling shame had a constricting effect on the men's potential to make their marriages successful. They had an intense fixation to dyads and an intolerance of any attachments their wives made that might threaten the exclusivity of the marital dyad. Their vulnerability created a need for a collusive, two-person protective relationship that would keep the patients and their spouses from disorganizing and being flooded with a sense of inadequacy. Often the borderline fathers tried to control these difficult marital relationships with some kind of intimidating impulsive action, such as suicide attempts, intimidation or violence, or drinking binges.

Mate Selection

This type of borderline pathology propels the patient to rely on transpersonal defensive operations; that is to say, on a collusive marital dyad where the couple is bound firmly, if symptomatically, together, but one in which intimacy is warded off (Lansky, 1981a). The superego pathology—that is, the struggle against identification with father and the denial of the need for father—together with the unintegrated maternal introject, is replayed in the marriages of such patients. Their defensive needs for cohesion-producing, collusive relationships that compensate for and fend off feelings of inadequacy supersede needs based on generativity or desire. Mate selection is narrowed to potential spouses with similar developmental histories and defensive preoccupations.

The prevalence of similar personality organization in borderline patient and spouse is striking (Bowen, 1966). When asked about their earliest recollections of courtship, the patients studied often recalled relief and comfort with the future spouse. Later they felt anger, disappointment, and contempt, for reasons strikingly similar to the reasons that they felt comfort. The marriages of these young-adult borderline fathers were similar in essential features both to the parental marriages of the patients and their spouses. Some of these patients came from less impulse-ridden families characterized by high-achieving, generative parents who lacked a capacity for intimate relations and showed up as chronically preoccupied or depressed parents.

THE NATURE OF COLLUSION

These patients described their wives as close, often clinging; emotional; and demanding. Frequently there was a trading of dissociations (Wynne, 1961). The patients were often unable to experience their own feelings in close relationships and selected women who had intense, often uncontrollable feelings, which their husbands could comprehend and to which they could react. When children arrived, the fathers often projected "weak" and "bad" onto the children, or onto the wife to sustain a view of themselves as powerful. This projection was often buttressed by intimidation or violence, which evoked feelings of weakness and fear in spouse and children. This splitting came at an enormous cost to the family equilibrium. The wife often intensified a tendency to project the good onto the child and the bad onto the husband. Her splitting reflected her own split maternal imago, (no matter what the sex of the child who was the recipient of that split representation). Themes from both families of origin are replayed. The young-adult borderline father thus became, both in reality and in his own fantasy, a horrifying copy of his own father, and his wife, the very worst likeness of his own mother.

THE DISTURBANCE POSED BY FATHERHOOD

The developmental difficulties that were bound at first in the marital dyad underwent a severe upheaval with the arrival of children. Father felt deprived of the exclusive marital dyad; mother's need for closeness was met by the baby. The result was an unmanageable amount of jealousy and envy, which disequilibrated the borderline father's defenses and often resulted in the personality disorganization, shame, and subsequent symptomatic action that the marital dyad had hitherto controlled. Such tendencies to disorganize might have been minimized by a mother capable of integrating husband's and children's emotional needs, but these fathers almost invariably had married women who, because of their own propensities to splitting and fixation to dyadic relationships, either could not or would not provide such emotional support. There was, then, a significant disruption and disorganization following the birth of the baby. This disorganization generated an enormous amount of shame. What often appeared clinically at the time was a picture dominated by violent, intimidating, and impulsive activity on the young father's part that covered over the shame, or by drinking, which enacts and expresses hostility, the need for control, and the need for self-soothing. Given that the same conflicts surface to some extent in any marriage when children arrive, the pathology of both parents amplify the predicament for the borderline father.

MASKING

There is a need to mystify and cover up these struggles because acknowledgment of them generates overwhelming shame. Shame, unlike guilt, becomes more painful when it is exposed, and as a result such patients will often engage in desperate maneuvers to avoid being exposed as out of control, inadequate, or dependent on others for personal cohesion. For the borderline father, such maneuvers are felt to be confirmation that he is the same as his own contemptible father. The masking of these difficulties is so pervasive an activity, and exposure such a threat, that they can be acknowledged only in later adult life.

The reconstructions of these fathers shed light on the relation of the manifest symptomatology evident in young-adult life to the more fundamental disturbance of cohesion from which these difficulties emanated. These borderline men were so constituted as a result of their developmental difficulties that their vulnerability to personality disorganization was high. Fragmentation experiences occurred after narcissistic wounding that came from deliberate shaming by an intimate or when intimates became either too close or too far away. Viewed in this light, both symptoms could be viewed as efforts to control close relationships so that people would be neither too close nor too far away.

ESCALATION OF PATHOLOGY

Dovetailing pathology between husband and wife made narcissistic wounding a constant threat after children were born. The wives' splitting mechanisms usually resulted in role assignments that made the child the good object representation and the borderline father the bad. These role assignments added further rejection to the father's burden and stimulated more symptomatic impulsive action to restore his sense of self and a feeling of power in the family. Those very compensatory mechanisms confirmed the role assignment and further reinforced the wife's splitting. The wife became more firmly bonded to child or children in ways that further excluded the borderline father.

The same kind of vulnerability and impulsivity usually resulted in work failures, and these men often went from job to job. They had less status, less confidence, and less pride in their vocational accomplishments as time went on, until finally they became devoid of any source of self-respect in this area. There was an escalating erosion of generativity and a loss of sources of the positive self-regard that comes from the sense that one has provided well for those one loves. The borderline fathers' sense of deserving authority and status decreased, and their shame increased. There was more depression and more substance abuse. In that way, the borderline disorder fed on itself. Not uncommonly father was entirely cast out of the family (Lansky et al., 1983). Some of the fathers had these escalating cycles through several marriages, with the same results.

These fathers had no sense of the value that came from an imminent sense of worth and generativity in the paternal or spousal role. To meet their own internal defensive needs they often had to negate the importance of their own fathers. They struggled with an identification with a man held in contempt by his own wife, a man who used violent, intimidating means to hold on to any semblance of respect from his family. At a deep level these men saw themselves faced with divisive and basically contemptuous women who could only relate in dyads and who maintained themselves by hostilely excluding others. Their familial situation was compounded by their (accurate) sense of themselves as having caused trouble, become rageful, not provided their children with what they needed, and, in fact, giving to them the same deficient parenting that they had received from their own fathers and damaging their children in the very same ways that had so damaged them. The impetus these men got from internalizations of their families of origin was insufficient to allow them to enter into the sustained generative relationships in work and love that are the foundations for what is commonly called self-esteem. The cycle of worthlessness, disorganization when excluded from the dyad, attempts at intimidating control, shame, and guilt escalated to the point of total failure of intimacy and total rifts in the family, with mother and children banding together to provoke and exclude father.

Many of the men we studied made serious suicide attempts, and most of them exiled themselves from the family after their attempts at intimidating control failed. All the fathers in our sample had a very harsh view of themselves as fathers. Ultimately, they were as critical of themselves as they were of their own fathers.

The failures of adult generativity, of course, resulted in depression, increased impulsive symptomatology, and self-soothing through substance abuse. The men carried with them an inner sense of themselves as damaged, cheated, entitled to justice, and truly defective, but, at the same time, as intrusive, demanding, destructive, and controlling. In short, they were utterly confused about what they were entitled to and felt incapable of meeting their responsibilities.

CONCLUSIONS

The view of young adulthood revealed within the clinical setting or in the research interviews was not fleeting or peripheral in the lives of these patients. These were not ephemeral recollections, but genuinely expanded views of reality that linked hitherto mysterious calamities that "happened" to the patients to what they actually did. These insights paved the way for an increased tolerance for superego pressures—shame, guilt, and anxiety—and a heightened ability for these men to see the realities of their intimate relationships as clearly resonating with their own psychic realities. Their views of reality were quite painful but, like any psychoanalytic insight, gave these patients more opportunity to comprehend their difficulties and work toward overcoming them.

The two sets of reconstructions give similar pictures both of the core disturbance as it presented in young adulthood and of why the disturbance was so difficult to acknowledge and, hence, to lessen. These reconstructions are striking enough in their essential features and consistent enough in the sample studied that they can usefully be compared with pictures of the world of the young-adult borderline father that do not derive from reconstructions. We may learn more about those views of the world from the treatment of young-adult men faced with the predicament of entry into fatherhood or from the prospective study of at-risk adolescents or recently married young adults.

—— IV ——

Shame and Symptom Formation

. . . Later, I think you'll learn
That now as before you have done yourself no good
By gratifying your temper against your friends.
Anger has always been your greatest sin!
                                        Sophocles
                                        Oedipus at Colonus (852-855)

8

The Psychiatrically
Hospitalized Father

THE PROBLEM

Within the past decade and a half there has been increased interest in the
study of the father, both in the context of child development and in the life
cycle of the father himself (Cath, Gurwitt, and Ross, 1982). Interest in and
knowledge about fathers has, however, lagged behind interest in the
individual child, the mother-child unit, or the mother alone (Howells,
1970). The reasons for this neglect are complex but in some part involve
the difficulties in understanding the role of father and the sorts of activities
that constitute fathering. These conceptual difficulties are greater with
activities that constitute fathering than with activities that constitute mothering. Mothering is usually thought of as involving the experience-close
caretaking, that is, feeding, cleaning, physical soothing, of the mother-
child dyad. It is clear for purposes of observation and study what at least
some of the activities are that constitute mothering and how they may be
observed.

For fathering, though, there is seldom this sort of clarity. Fathering may
involve parenting that is experience-close, but by and large the activities
that fathers themselves consider to be appropriate fathering are experience-
distant, and difficult to capture convincingly in observable terms: provi-
sion of support, protection, discipline, a sense of justice, and a sense of
leadership. Few of those activities can be reduced to observable behaviors
between father and child that are suitable for study. The problem of
studying fathers, then, is inseparably linked to the problems of studying

131

whole, or even extended, families. The data are complexly interactional, difficult to define with certainty, and contained in units of observation that may be both large and fluctuant.

How a father is evaluated by himself and by others—what kind of job he does, and in what kind of esteem he is held—is often as much of a measure of the marriage (i.e., of support or sabotage from mother) as it is of the father's activities considered alone. Volatile, strife-ridden marriages may be taken as evidence of a father's weakness, even if it is the mother who erodes the sense of stability with activities and commentaries that undercut the family's sense of stability. In a better-bonded marriage, mother may compensate for a weak or even remote father. Hence, fathering has to be studied in the full family context, whereas significant aspects of mothering do not. To these complexities must be added the ubiquitous fantasies about what is wanted from parents: "I want my mother" is usually a regressive wish appealing for caretaking and exemption from responsibility; "I want my father" usually reflects a wish to master the world, not to avoid it. Some of these conceptual difficulties explain why until recently there was a dearth of academic and clinical interest in fathers and, in particular, why there has been a paucity of information on the psychiatrically disabled father in the role of father. As a matter of fact, a literature search failed to turn up a single source on the hospitalized patient as father. This communication is an attempt to approach the topic.

Obviously, any major illness will have a substantial effect on the father's performance of his role, not only because of the consequent limitations on the father's actual functions, but also because of the strength and power that the father gives to the family in the fantasies of family members and of the father himself. Thus, in addition to impairing the instrumental contributions of the father, illness also inflicts narcissistic injury on the father and on the family as a whole.

A study of family systems usually shows that predicaments or crises that present as clinical disruptions follow a change in family equilibrium. Disruption follows the sudden upsurgence of previously disowned infantile elements in the family system. This may happen, for example, when the family homeostasis changes after the birth of a first child. The combination of added demands on father, a decrease in attention from and caretaking by the new mother, and competition with the new arrival may change a previously well-compensated family system to one that is dysfunctional. The same may happen if physical illness in an older father necessitates his wife's employment and occurs at a time when children are also becoming financially independent. The narcissistic issues often subsumed under the vague and overused term "self-esteem" are found to be intimately related to the parental role and are crushingly disturbed at such times of disequilibrium. Less well studied is the relation of psychiatric symptoms to the role of father. Such symptoms include psychotic episodes, suicidality, violence or intimidation, episodic substance abuse, and depression. I do not presume that difficulties with the role of father *cause* any of these symptoms, but only that the symptomatology itself is intimately bound up with the role of father in a way that is difficult to study yet is crucial to understand in any treatment strategy.

Because in the Family Treatment Program families are seen in every case and the index population is largely adult and male, the setting is optimal for observing the difficulties of the hospitalized father. Yet, for reasons not apparent on first glance, most fathers were loath to comment on their difficulties in functioning as fathers. Identifying their difficulties in other ways, they spoke of voices, drinking, violence, being suicidal, depression, anger at their wives, or anger at children. The staff on this program, highly sophisticated in the treatment of hospitalized patients and specialists in family psychiatry, also had difficulties focusing on the paternal role. Part of the staff's difficulty arose from clinical apprehension that the issues were too threatening to the patients and could be brought up only with the risk of mortifying the patients. Staff had countertransference difficulties—emotional difficulties with men who were felt to be broken or defective; and they had unusual difficulties maintaining focus on these men on the paternal role. There was, then, a diffuseness of focus on difficulties in the paternal role, not only on the part of fathers, but also in their families and in the people who treated them.

This generalized diffusion of awareness to difficulties in the paternal role could not be attributed to mere ignorance or lack of focus on the problems of hospitalized fathers. Rather, it seemed to be a defensive process of overwhelming magnitude, one that came into focus only gradually. I use the term "defensive process" without any presumption that the origin of the patients' basic difficulties was basically interpersonal or that the treatment was basically dynamic or interpretive. I am, rather, presuming that any approach or sensible treatment strategy must consider what sort of emotional struggles keep the areas of great difficulty so much in darkness that they cannot be examined, discussed straightforwardly, and diminished.

A view of the clinical picture is blurred by this diffusion of awareness. For that reason, it is important that we be mindful of the concrete particulars of the setting in which the issues faced by hospitalized fathers come into focus. Our treatment staff went through an unfolding awareness of the central role of shame and narcissistic mortification in these men and of the high cost of maneuvers to protect themselves from such mortification. These defensive maneuvers included the diffusion of awareness of difficulties in the paternal role. The more we understood these fathers' struggles, the more their struggles seemed always to include one between *concealing* to avoid being seen and seeing oneself as defective and the opposite effort (with which we wished to ally our efforts)—revealing and clarifying the issues so they could be faced. Our knowledge of the plight of the hospital-ized father grew with the deepening of our understanding of conflict and defense tied to shame.

As a general psychiatric inpatient unit with around-the-clock staffing, we at the Family Treatment Program were in a good position to observe the general disruptions that range from psychotic decompensation and its attendant symptoms to suicidal thoughts and actions, violence and intim-idation, and episodic and continual substance abuse. We have come to see many of these symptoms, however chaotic they might seem, as the patient's attempt to restore an optimal distance from supportive persons, both to keep them at a distance and to lock them into a relationship with the patient. We have a clear view of the impact of illness on the father's role.

The intake meeting is used for examination of the circumstances leading to hospitalization and a workup of the family from an intergene-rational perspective. Family sessions continue weekly and explore condi-tions under which the temporary containment by the hospital can be replaced by containment outside the hospital, by the patient himself, by the family, or by other support systems. These sessions may evolve into ongoing family psychotherapy sessions.

We have come to conceptualize the hospital as a temporary container for chaos when such containment cannot be provided by the patient's personality system or external support systems, including the family. We have also come to focus on the benefits and difficulties of the symbiotic relationship created by a few months in the hospital. The temporary containment and relief from responsibility are often offset by the enor-mous shame the patient feels when he sees himself as needing the hospital for well-being, by the resultant envy and hatred, and by the controlling maneuvers (such as binge drinking, suicidal gestures, or violence) that forestall discharge and preserve the relationship with the hospital. They also divert attention away from the hospital dependency that so upsets the patient. Often the patient's controlling maneuvers exhaust support sys-tems. Family may become depleted and exhausted and may give up on the patient. We have come to see the *absence of family* (Lansky et al., 1983) as a source of data with major diagnostic and prognostic significance, never as a variant of normal.

To focus further on the problems of hospitalized fathers, we began brief (30 minute) intergenerational interviews for all fathers admitted to the ward who consented to have them. These interviews were tape-recorded sessions with a three-generation perspective. Each patient was asked first about his father: what the relationship was like, what was good, where it fell short, how any shortcomings were felt to have affected the patient's subsequent life and his own ability to be a father. Next, they were asked about the women in their lives: wives, ex-wives, mothers of their children or step-children and whether they helped or hindered the paternal role. Lastly, they were asked about their own relationship with their children: good points, regrets, role of their illness, what they might need to help them.

A group was offered to hospitalized fathers. Patients had received the first offer of a group with much enthusiasm, but the group was very poorly attended. The few who came were very chronically ill men with years-long relationships to the hospital and damaged self-images. All were chronically suicidal. All were directly involved with their own children's care, usually with some help from an ex-wife. A second group was formed from men who had had the intergenerational interview (40 fathers were offered the group). About 12 participated, but most of them attended for only a short while and then dropped out, most saying explicitly that they could not handle the upset that the material stirred up. The majority were divorced. Most felt rage, helplessness, and depression at the small or absent role they played with their children. Many had been ordered by courts to stay away either because of attempts to intimidate the family or actual violent episodes, or because they could not provide the support for the family mandated by law. All felt helpless, humiliated, and untenured. There were varying degrees of acceptance of responsibility. One man complained bitterly and vociferously of his ostracism from the family, but neglected to mention that in a fit of rage, he had beaten his infant son to death. The group was designed to be exploratory and supportive rather than confrontive, but all the men found it painful, anxiety provoking, and humiliating to talk about their difficulties and lack of status in the family. Those who were not directly involved with their children dropped out; several asked for (and were given) sessions conjointly with children to help with the issues raised.

The intergenerational interview and the father groups gave us considerable insight into the diffusion of awareness around problems of fathering. These hospitalized fathers were so overwhelmed with shame—the pain of seeing themselves, and of being seen, as defective in the fathering role and deprived of status—that most could not bear to address their difficulties. Over 90% of the hospitalized fathers agreed to be interviewed, and most of them showed interest in the fathers' groups; however, less than one-third attended, and most of the fathers that did attend left, saying that the pain was too great and the hopes of improvement too dim to warrant further suffering.

CLINICAL ILLUSTRATIONS

Illness: Schizophrenia

Example 1. A 35-year-old Hispanic man had been transferred from another inpatient unit as an undesirable—a "manipulator," a chronic schizophrenic beset with murderous rage and suicidal thoughts. His course in the Family Treatment Program was unlike that in the previous unit, and he profited immensely from a several months' hospital stay. Despite the evidence of years of almost unremitting psychosis, and despite his describing his illness clearly, his family had refused to acknowledge that he was ill. His wife and adolescent son both treated him as contemptible and lazy and acted as though he could pull his life together simply by willpower and industry. His many suicide attempts could be seen both as precipitated by this lack of understanding and acceptance and as attempts to gain some control of his role in the family.

After he left the hospital, his suicidal ideation recurred intermittently, but he did not make further suicide attempts. He was readmitted, floridly psychotic, after a family quarrel in which his son had mocked perils he had undergone in military combat and his wife sided with the son. In the intergenerational interview, he expressed high regard for his father and some understanding of his wife's inability to accept the fact that he was ill. He presented a consistent picture of himself and his struggles in all treatment settings: in ward meetings, family sessions, and in the fathers' group. He had a persistently painful view of his broken, constantly fearful psychotic condition with very little surcease in awareness of the contempt in which he was held in his clinging, albeit hostile family. Conjoint family sessions were of great help in enabling his wife and son to comprehend the nature and extent of his illness and to respond more realistically to his limitations.

Illness: Alcoholism

Example 2. This 47-year-old man was admitted on a drinking binge after several months' sobriety in a rehabilitation residence for alcoholics. He had been alcoholic since his teens. As is typical of alcoholic fathers, he described his own father as an alcoholic man, violent when drunk and absent emotionally (and usually physically) when sober. He said with bitterness that a better father would have provided the substance to his personality that he knew he had never had. He had been separated from his mother at birth, and told, for reasons not clear to him at the time, that she had died. He first met her when he was in his 20s after he found out that she was still alive. She was a severe alcoholic and had removed herself from the family. Alcoholism had eroded both his vocational and his family functioning, and he had left the area where his wife and children lived some years previously.

In the intergenerational interview, he described a visit back. His drinking had gotten out of hand and he embarrassed himself while drunk and left, much as his mother had done when he was small, vowing never to return until his drinking was in control: "A lot of times, I thought of going back home and it'd be different, and, well, while I was thinkin' it, I'd be drinkin' at the same time. If I could ever get my drinking under control, I could have a decent job and go back and see them and maybe prove to them what I'm doin'. Maybe it could work then, but I couldn't go back, you know, with the drinking. It'd just be the same thing over and over. They'd say, 'Daddy hasn't changed a bit.' When I get sober, I get depressed and confused and worried and wonder if I can change this and that and then I take a drink and [cries]—It's depressing to think about all this."

In these two cases, vulnerabilities from illness, no matter what dynamic issues were in evidence, interfered so much with the father's instrumental and narcissistic equilibrium that treatment strategies had first and foremost to deal with control of the illness and acceptance of chronic illness within the family. These were defeated men who viewed themselves as too broken to function in the role of father. Such views were not so much depressive fantasies as realistic appraisals of the effect of illness on the men's functioning. The schizophrenics in our sample tended to rate their own fathers and wives as highly supportive and to see their own difficulties and their illnesses as standing in the way of good fathering. The alcoholics who drank continuously rather than episodically always reported poor relationships with their fathers: absence and brutality were ubiquitous. These fathers would try to hold onto their families by means of abusiveness and intimidation at first and later to be so ashamed of themselves that they stayed away from their families. They usually rated themselves as poor fathers and felt their (usually ex-) wives to be vengeful and angry.

System Disruption: Personality Disorder

Example 3. A 57-year-old man was admitted in a turbulent state after a vague communication of suicidality told to his first wife. That woman, who had divorced him some 20 years before, brought him to the hospital, where he was admitted in part for safekeeping but in the main for evaluation of difficulties with his second wife and stepson and of depression accompanied by mild neurovegetative signs. He described a very difficult childhood. He had never known his father and had been raised in orphanages. His first marriage had ended 20 years earlier. His explanation for that failure, like so much else in his discourse, was vague and evasive and failed to give a clear view of his role in the marital difficulties. He remarried soon after the divorce. He described himself as steadily employed and stable with his new wife and her son by a previous marriage. Two years prior to admission he had had spinal surgery, which incapacitated him. His wife had to work to support the family. His stepson, nearing maturity, failed (he said) to show him any respect and his wife sided with her son. He became sullen, angry, and began drinking heavily. He attempted to convince the wife to move out of the area and leave the stepson behind. He berated the stepson as lazy, parasitic, manipulative, and sneaky in getting undeserved caretaking and special status. He seemed to show no awareness of these claims as (projected) self-reproaches for his status with his wife and later with the hospital. His previous stable compensation had come undone when the combination of physical illness, loss of status as breadwinner, and competition with his stepson flooded him with the infantile neediness, shame, and depression that precipitated his hospitalization.

In this case, overt family disruption made it sensible to approach the problem first from the point of view of the family system. The patients with personality disorders and no more than episodic substance abuse all tended to complain of poor relationships with their own fathers, whom they described as often violent, drunk, and absent. A bitterness pervaded the interviews, and the fathers tended to link directly their own massive problems in fathering with the deficiencies in relationships with their fathers; wives were regarded as undermining and favoring the children over their husbands; there was a varying, but usually deficient, perspective on their own role in their difficulties.

Symptoms: Hallucinations

Example 4. A 36-year-old man was admitted for hearing "voices" (auditory hallucinations) accompanied by florid, front-rank signs of schizophrenia. He talked of the "voices" and "needing a job" as his major problems. Fuller workup showed that this man was desperately trying, in spite of a severe psychosis, to maintain a job while living in his parents' house. Asked about the "voices," he said, "They tell me to castrate myself." Asked further about this, he replied that he should be castrated for being unable to keep his ex-wife away from other men and unable to be an adequate father to his children. His ex-wife, his children, and his parents had taken his protestations about "needing a job" and only being impeded by "voices" quite literally and had failed to see obvious manifestations of gross psychotic illness. The wife had divorced him and remarried. She would not allow him to see the children unless he paid the child support ordered by the court. She refused to come to family sessions. His parents came to weekly conjoint sessions, and after acquiring some appreciation of the illness, became more supportive and less inclined to literalness when he talked of "voices" and "needing a job."

Symptoms: Suicidality and Episodic Substance Abuse

Example 5. A 38-year-old father of two young children was admitted to a locked unit for "suicidality" after cutting his wrists. The slashing had followed his throttling his wife. He had attacked his wife after accosting her in front of the children with her lover, whom she refused to leave. She had taken the lover in part as an act of defiance and despair. He had many times been hospitalized as "suicidal" after experiencing some failure or legal difficulty connected with substance abuse. The types of drugs he abused had varied through the years, but he had been a serious user since midteenage. She had remained loyal, to the point of taking meals to the hospital.

He had met his wife while in military service in another country. She had been a prostitute. He saw her as beneath him in status and poorly educated. His marriage for a time reversed the way he had felt in his educationally oriented family, in which he was felt to be the outcast, the defective, and the family disgrace. Both parents, but especially his father, disapproved of him. He passed on the abusiveness and devaluation he felt he had received from his father to his wife, who for years endured his indignities without protest. He kept his wife off balance by drug use and talk of drug problems. He was aloof and outright hostile to her, and became "suicidal" and hospitalized when she verged on rebellion.

He was admitted to the Family Treatment Program after being several days in a locked unit and feeling "depressed," that is, in a period of active upheaval. He spent enormous energy in psychotherapy sessions, family sessions, and the fathers' group. He began to focus on his difficulties in the paternal role. At first he claimed to be entirely devoted to his children and that his difficulties lay elsewhere—with symptoms, marriage, job. As he concentrated on maneuvers to extrude himself from the paternal role, he became "depressed" in a different way. Ward staff felt him to be "slower" and less turbulent. He had clear neurovegetative disturbances. Vigorous antidepressant treatment was pursued. He was helped more by monoamine oxidase inhibitors than by tricyclic antidepressants.

Meanwhile, his struggles in the fathers' group were with his involvement with children. These struggles came to a head when his wife announced that she did not want total care of the children and suggested that he take them. He was horrified and overwhelmed, saying that while he was on drugs and living with his family he had never realized the extent to which fear was part of his life. Now he feared falling apart, fragmenting, and having rage attacks when his children needed him. He was overwhelmed at having to be the stable one in their lives. This was the first time that he had come to grips with his anxiety and shame over his tendency to fragment and the first time he talked about his difficulties in a way that clearly showed him as the vulnerable person and the author of many of his own difficulties.

Symptoms: Violence and Intimidation

Example 6. A 42-year-old man came to the hospital and requested help for "homicidal impulses." Asked about recent circumstances that might have set him off, he said that his 18-year-old stepdaughter, after living with him and his wife for six years, had gone to live with her biologic father following an argument over the use of the car.

The patient was working toward a doctorate in education, a notable attainment for a man from a deprived background. He admitted that saving face and "looking good" were important to him and acknowledged rage, self-pity, and suspicion of others' motives were important parts of his makeup. He did not tell the staff that his wife, tired of years of his blustering and threatening, was about to leave the marriage, and probably the state.

We gained some appreciation of the anxiety he generated when he mentioned murderous impulses, while at the same time he was vague about the extent to which he had control over himself, and then blithely asked to go home on pass. An emergency staff meeting was held. The patient nonchalantly claimed that he only wished to go to the library to work on his thesis. When the staff's anxieties and his comparative indifference were pointed out to him, he became angry and said that he should not stay in treatment if we felt that he spread anxiety. The anxiety-provoking aspects of what he said were clear: first he would stir up anxieties about loss of control of his violent feelings and then would ask for a pass from the hospital in a dispassionate way that induced panic even in very experienced staff members. The staff responses compared their own to the patient's wife's feeling of terror over the years at similar episodes of intimidation. Her reluctance to stay in the marriage and her wish to leave the state seemed more understandable when his panic-inducing method of holding on to intimates was elucidated.

In Examples 4-6, the relationship of symptoms to the family systems perspective was met initially with the kind of diffusion of awareness of difficulties in the paternal role that has been discussed. The *symptom* proved to be the gateway into the difficult family situation to which it was related. Symptom and system required different treatments, but both had to be addressed. The key to integrative treatment proved to be the appreciation of shame in the patient's struggle and in the therapeutic process.

Particular note must be made of "depression" as a symptom understood apart from the patient's connection to close persons. In this sampling of very disturbed men, virtually every crisis and exacerbation was accompanied by some form of clinically significant depression. Such depression should always be taken seriously and treated with the best possible means as a symptom with its own set of treatment criteria. Nonetheless, the failure to integrate depression with the entire clinical picture, that is, letting it become a split-off entity treated as "endogenous" or entirely *sui generis*, can result in a disastrous failure to achieve an integrated view of the case. All the examples showed severe depression in one or another part of the clinical picture, but the depression could often be appreciated in relation to helplessness felt in the paternal role, especially when pathologic distance regulation (usually intimidation) and diffusion of awareness began to subside, that is, when the patient began to give up controlling and denying and started to face his problems squarely. All these patients had "endogenous" patterns of depression, with neurovegetative signs and some response to antidepressant medication. But, in each case, the depression also signified a loosening of omnipotent defenses and, after the depression cleared, a greater ability to face the problem and thus a greater chance to modify it. Depression, then, could be seen in a more integrated way as a phase through which these fathers passed—with pharmacologic help—on the way to acknowledging their difficulties rather than trying to cover them up in some impulse-ridden way.

EXPANDED VIEWS OF CONFLICT

The ambiguity and diffusion of focus on the paternal role came into sharper view when an appreciation was attained of the intense pain, shame, and narcissistic mortification these men felt on failing in the paternal role. Splitting-off of symptoms from the totality of the patient's world made it seem as though voices, suicidality," "violence," "drugs," or "drinking" were the problem; and not that the disturbances behind these symptoms fed into a virtual destruction of paternal identity by rendering these fathers incapable of providing their children with the mastery, structuring, discipline, and authority that they (often idealistically) attributed to the paternal role.

These deficits were often covered over by flamboyant and intimidating controlling maneuvers to retain some sort of power, control, and status in the family. The more broken, chronically disabled men adopted an identity as "ill" and, if they did not avoid their families altogether, attempted to win over their children by ingratiation, bribery, or guilt induction. These men often had a history of exerting control by some intimidating combination of impulsive symptoms: drinking, violence, suicide, threats, or drug use.

For the group of fathers currently employing these intimidating modes of distance regulation, one could feel the tremendous impact of, for example, drinking bouts or threats of violence, as they held the family under the father's control, as they covered over the intense shame and helplessness that the father felt on being unable to relate and unable to provide those things that he himself felt a good father should provide. All those fathers who used such intimidating impulsive action had had fathers whom they saw as strikingly like themselves. This method of object control by intimidating impulsive action carried with it a precariously untenured status, one of ruling by force, but only temporarily, until their dependent wives and children managed to escape. The wives of these men had usually colluded at first but ultimately became exhausted and frightened and usually opted out of the marriage. In these impulse-ridden men, overt clinical depression often presaged a willingness to face the reality of their deficits and bear the attendant shame.

Shame is central in these maneuvers. For the broken men who adopted a status as chronically ill without apparent protest, the defeated "patient" status was accompanied by almost daily suicidal feelings. For those fathers whose clinical pictures were less clear because of impulsive actions or other split-off symptoms, both the splitting and controlling served to protect them from being overwhelmed and totally mortified by shame over their deficits. These deficits were real, never imagined, tendencies toward fragmentation, inability to relate intimately, and massive ambivalence and hate in close situations. Often the shame surrounding these deficits was obscured by impulsive actions and subsequent guilt.

The struggles of these psychiatrically hospitalized fathers surround shame-producing deficits, which may have been obscured by guilt-producing actions, isolated symptoms, or disowned and resented symbiosis to the hospital. The struggles and conflicts surrounding shame must be considered in any treatment strategy, not just those that are basically dynamic or interpretive in nature. If they are ignored, treatment responses are likely to be heavily swayed by countertransference, for example, by the therapist's intolerance of powerful, upsetting affects, rather than being guided by a comprehensive appraisal of the patient's needs.

The therapist is at risk of becoming overwhelmed, lost in depression, helplessness, or futility and feeling that the situation is hopeless. Such a therapist may miss opportunities for simple interventions, such as educative approaches, symptom-oriented strategies, crisis intervention, or family sessions. At the opposite extreme of obliviousness to the massive defects in capacity, the mortifying narcissistic injury can result in oversimplified strategies that fail to help with the major struggles. Only a full view of the world of the psychiatrically hospitalized father, upsetting though this is likely to be, will enable the therapist to choose strategies that will be helpful with the central issues and at the same time minimize the overpowering and unremitting sense of shame that these men carry with them.

9

Violence, Shame, and the Family

Violence is commonly equated with the destructive actions that are done by the violent person. Given that one may provoke or pacify and so alter violent behavior in someone else, the problem is usually seen as coming from and belonging to the violent person. I contend that a more useful focus for the problem of violence is transactional, that the violent act is better understood as emanating from a system of intimate relationships and, specifically, that violent action often serves the purpose of controlling distance in the intimate relationships of persons who are so constituted that a change in optimal distance results in disorganization of the personality.

This transactional focus, useful though it be, is not easy to attain, partly because of the violent person's efforts to conceal both personality vulnerabilities and the need to control intimates so that he will not be flooded with shame. Another difficulty in the path of the therapist's gaining a transactional appreciation of the problem of violence is that significant persons in the social systems involved often remain out of view. In this chapter, I draw heavily on experience in a hospital setting with violent patients and their families. The systems view of violence gained from experience in that setting may be applied to other (usually outpatient) settings that provide a less complete picture of violence as a transactional mode of relating.

Faced with a potentially violent patient, the therapist may feel panic and a feeling of loss of control. A lack of alliance with the patient in controlling the violence may erode the therapist's poise in the role of

144

professional. If the therapist does not recognize that the feeling of helplessness and loss of integrity are provoked by a defensive process that the violent patient generates, that therapist may lose perspective and overlook an important fact: that the very same process, a process that includes both the patient and the therapist or institution, provides crucial information about how the violent patient handles chaos in interpersonal situations and about how the patient's defensive maneuvers may keep helping persons feeling off balance and ineffective and eventually cause them to respond by being overcontrolling or rejecting. If such information is overlooked, the therapist may have much difficulty finding an optimal approach to the patient. An integration of treatment that maximizes personal responsibility may be lost. The entire process may usually be better understood when compared with other supportive interpersonal situations, especially the patient's current family and the family in which the patient grew up.

The therapist may see dynamic understanding either as irrelevant or as an activity for calm reflection after an emergency situation has subsided. But the transactional dynamics of the emergency situation itself can be worked with only while they are operative. They involve intimate relationships that have changed from an optimally supportive distance. These dynamic factors are much more pertinent to the management of the potentially violent patient than are the dynamics of unconscious hostility, that is, the attempt to discover whom the patient might hate.

The transactional view recognizes an understanding of defects in self-regulation that flood the patient with shame. The focus on unconscious hostility involves aggressive transgressions, about which the patient feels guilty, at least in fantasy. An erroneous view of the significance of dynamic understanding—the view that ignores the transactional and loses perspective on the process that results from panic and feeling out of control—may cause the therapist or the institution to regard violence only as a disturbance in the patient. Rather, it is a *process* that demands understanding, for not only does the patient's violence affect supportive relationships but the supportive relationships also affect the patient's propensity to act violently. Interpersonal processes go a long way to amplify or diminish a tendency to be violent regardless of the nature of the underlying defect that causes that tendency. The therapist, in a state of panic evoked by the violent situation, may abandon efforts to understand the process in favor of an urgent attempt to control the situation by overemphasis on regulation, diagnosis, management, or some sort of restraint. Such diagnostic and therapeutic zeal is often far from benign. The patient may be flooded with the sense of shame that comes from feeling either overregulated or emotionally distanced when helping persons lose empathic contact with chaotic parts of the patient's personality.

The therapist may see violence as an eruption of something that must be held down by regulation of movement, by physical restraint, or by chemical restraint, usually with neuroleptic drugs. A model based on *holding down chaos* diverts attention away from the activation of interpersonal vulnerabilities of the patient that precedes a violent eruption. That vulnerability is often exposed when the patient feels ashamed about dependent relationships, especially where there is a change in optimal distance from intimate persons or when they get too invasive or too distanced emotionally or physically. The "holding-down" model often justifies a type of overregulation that humiliates the patient and complicates the return to self-regulation, say, after a brief hospitalization. While helping persons are overregulating the patient they cannot assess the degree of vulnerability or of internal control present, nor do they promote development in these crucial areas.

A violent situation often provokes the therapist to advise, exhort, confront, or threaten the violent patient, as though the patient were ignorant or had lacked willpower and the therapist could direct the patient to avoid these shortcomings. Advising, confronting, regulating, and threatening are neither harmless nor neutral to such patients, almost all of whom are exquisitely prone to humiliation. Patients tend to respond to such behavior either with a disowning sort of indifference to the whole situation that makes the therapist even more anxious or with a kind of shame at perceiving the therapists' condescension, shame that predisposes the patient to more violence. Instead of helping the patient control aggressivity, the therapist's behavior activates some of the very vulnerabilities that proceed to violent outburst and is much more likely to amplify the difficulty than to diminish it.

Another common response to a violent situation is to focus on diagnosis as though the discovery of an etiology—perhaps paroxysmal, perhaps neurologic, perhaps psychotic—would entirely explain the violent act. Even though episodic dyscontrol may be a manifestation of neurologic impairment in violence-prone persons, such patients are still vulnerable to interpersonal processes, especially those that shame them. Ictal phenomena themselves do not result in purposive acts of violence (Delgado-Escueta, 1981). Consideration of neurologic abnormality is a part of the workup of the violent patient, and specific medication is often part of the treatment. Overemphasis on diagnosis, however, may result in the therapist's overlooking aspects of the patient's supportive relationships that precipitate or calm violence. An understanding of those relationships is often crucial in the management of violent patients.

CLINICAL ILLUSTRATION

Example 1. A 38-year-old man with well-demonstrated grand mal seizures was referred for a workup of psychosis and for violent behavior attributed to his paroxysmal disorder. His seizure disorder was responsive to mysoline. He had had a rage attack and destroyed property in his home. He said he had stopped taking the mysoline because he did not know where to get more. He referred to taking his medication as "eating mice." This and other peculiar thought connections had prompted a psychiatric referral. Details of the "rage attack" were investigated: the patient's wife, an older woman who had been his caretaker for years, had become overburdened with his care after many years of exclusive dedication to him. She had left on vacation with a lady friend a day before the patient stopped his medication and had his "attack." The outburst consisted of his breaking one of each of her favorite set of dishes and stemware. He was readmitted summarily to the hospital. His wife was contacted and cut short her trip to return to him.

The wishful fantasy that one can control chaos by finding the diagnosis does not always bear fruit. Furthermore, the crucial therapeutic issue of who is responsible for the violence may become obscured if the therapist overemphasizes diagnosis and is not attentive to the fact that—even when there are etiologic factors present that have specific treatments—a responsibility-enhancing and empathic process is a major factor in diminishing violence. If the patient is ashamed of the vulnerabilities that precede violent outbursts, and if the therapist is uncomfortable dealing with these vulnerabilities or intimidated by the patient, they may both risk colluding and accepting an explanation that is put in terms of a neurologic disorder or a psychosis rather than responding to, say, temporary or permanent separations in dependent relationships. That neglect may escalate to disastrous proportions, especially around the time such a patient is separating from the hospital or other supportive environment.

In general, any movement away from emphasis on the process and toward overregulation or emotional distancing risks amplifying violence and allowing the patient's ego to remain weak because pathological defensive operations are not interpreted.

There is also the risk of mistaking intimidation for actual violent activity and thereby confusing manifestations of a specific underlying disorder, often treatable with medication, with defensive processes treatable largely by interpersonal means.

My emphasis on process does not imply that all, or even most, violence is entirely a result of malignant interpersonal processes, but rather that violence, whatever its origin, acts on such processes in ways that interfere with the supportive presence and emotional availability that calms violent tendencies. Violence attracts chaotic, rather than stabilizing, relationships and distracts attention from the very vulnerabilities that have to be addressed if the tendency toward violence is to be significantly mastered. I am advocating, therefore, an integrative approach, not one entirely based on process. The clearest pathway to such an approach is often the study of the family of the violent patient both as it is affected by violence and as it increases violent behavior by overt or subtle humiliation of the patient.

Our sample drawn from the Family Treatment Program was not a random one. All the violent patients in this study were men. Compared with other samples, the acts of completed violence tended to be relatively minor; most were threats, hittings, or aggressive activities that fell short of inflicting permanent damage on other people. The program has a surprising number of transfers from the general medical-surgical hospital of neurologic diagnostic enigmas that have violence as part of the clinical picture. Our diagnostic categories include psychoses, personality disorders, and disorders with demonstrable neurologic lesions. All the patients considered had a major psychiatric diagnosis, the pharmacologic treatment of which was a necessary element in the management of violence.

We have come, over the years, to develop a "container model" that is derived from our work with families (Bion, 1977; Lansky, 1981b). The hospital is viewed as a temporary container that sustains the patient when his personality system and the family system are unable to contain his chaos. The patient comes out of an inadequate container into the hospital containment system for a period of a few weeks to a few months and then goes to another situation, which, it is hoped, can contain his chaos: his own reconstituted personality system, the family system, or some other supportive or custodial system. We have learned to compare our containment function to that of the patient's family. This approach has led to an understanding of "violence" as a transactional process that may be generalized to many other clinical settings.

We find important clues to understanding the current process by comparing it with that in the patient's current family and his family of origin (Lansky, 1980). Our observations on family process include those on families that have deserted the patient. Abandonment by the family system, either by exhaustion, intimidation, or the family's unreliability, is crucial information. We have gained a good perspective on the effects of process on violence as well as violence on the process. Similar observations have been reported for suicidal patients and those with other impulsive activity in the clinical picture (Lansky, 1982a).

Our data do not permit conclusions either demographically or etiologically on violent patients in general. We do, however, see features of clinical processes typical enough to warrant attention to them as general. Violent acts are usually part of a complex interaction of circumstances and vulnerabilities that include the following.

(1) Violent patients have a vulnerability to personality disorganization. Such vulnerability is related to, but far more complex than, specific abnormalities of aggressivity or lack of control, such as the excessive rage

in brain damage, in characterologic disturbances, or psychotic propensities to violence. Violent patients have some combination of characterologic, psychotic, and neurologic difficulty that makes them not only volatile, but also more than usually dependent for their personal cohesion on supportive personal relationships. Without these, there may be disorganization that culminates in violent activity. Violence proneness has an final interpersonal pathway: vulnerability to change in interpersonal processes. We have found consistently that violence-prone patients on our service are extremely vulnerable to personality disorganization. This propensity is usually masked by the patient's presentation of himself as powerful and intimidating.

(2) Most violent acts have precipitants, usually alterations in optimal distance from persons who hold the patient together emotionally. A dependent relationship may be threatened when the person on whom the patient has been dependent leaves or becomes more independent. Likewise impingements from persons who provide support may be experienced as overregulatory and smothering if not outright disorganizing. The patient's awareness of being dependent on relationships that have gotten too close or too far away produces intense shame. So does the exposure of a need for dependent relationships. Overt shaming by those on whom the patient is dependent is a common precipitant of violent action. The nature of the relationship and optimal distance within it may be assessed by comparison of the family in which the patient grew up, his current family, and relationships with helping persons in the treatment situation. Optimal supportive distance with the vulnerable patient may be critical in diminishing a propensity toward violence. The effect of the process on violence is discussed later.

(3) The prodrome, or the dissociation or disorganization of the personality in response to the precipitant, is the least visible of the events here described. This type of disorganization and dependence on others for personal cohesion floods the patient with shame when the disorganization is seen. The prodrome culminates in the feeling of drivenness to complete a violent act. Patients' experiences of disorganization after a precipitating event may include fragmentation, paranoid ideation, or rage. In some cases, the patient may not have conscious awareness of any prodromal stage at all. *It is this experience of disorganization and helplessness at the hands of others that is often reversed (in fantasy and, later, in reality) by completing the violent act. The disorganization and helplessness are induced in others rather than experienced by the violent person himself.*

(4) The violent act covers over the process of disorganization. Many things can be denoted by the word "violence"—anything from uncontrolled striking out, to premeditated attack, to broadcasting of lability, threatening, intimidating behavior without attack and a host of others.

Grouping these together tends to confuse them and their various functions. *Violent acts should be distinguished from intimidating behavior.*

(5) Guilt about the act takes attention away from the disorganizing prodrome and places it on the consequences of rage or harm to others. It is often prematurely assumed that the patient is guilty about the act rather than shameful of his own disorganizing propensities (in the prodrome).

(6) Control of the interpersonal situation. The communication of a propensity for violence, especially if the communication is indirect, mobilizes people. Pathologic distance regulation—keeping intimates from getting too close or too far away—is often a major defensive operation of violence-prone patients. Such control of intimates may become a chronically intimidating lifestyle. Both for treatment considerations and for purposes of research, it is important that control of objects by intimidation not be confused with the violent act itself. The two are not the same.

EFFECTS OF VIOLENCE ON THE PROCESS: INTIMIDATION

The effect of violence on the process is often missed when the therapist gets swept up in panic, that is, overregulated and controlled by the patient, and responds by overregulating and controlling the patient. If the patient is subtly or indirectly threatening but does not acknowledge this, the therapist's panic escalates more than if the threat is direct and can be addressed. Very often patients create anxiety-laden, intimidating situations when a dependent relationship with family or hospital is threatened. The patient disorganizes, then communicates violence in a way that gathers people around him. Helpers placate the patient. The whole process takes attention away from the dependency of which the patient is ashamed. The controlling aspect of intimidating behavior is often called "manipulative," the implication being that the patient wishes only special status, caretaking, and evasion of responsibility. It would be more accurate to say that what is "manipulated" is the control over dependent relationships that keeps the violent patient from fragmenting and being flooded with shame. The patient may maintain control by repeated communications that arouse anxiety in others, and that are addressed in terms of "violence," but not in terms of the interpersonal process that goes on.

Example 2.   A 44-year-old Hispanic man came to the emergency room requesting help for his homicidal impulses. He said that his stepdaughter, 18, decided after a quarrel with him to return to live with her biologic father.

The patient, a Master's Degree candidate, had come from a deprived background and felt a good deal of rage which he related to his upbringing, his social position, and his race. He was admitted after a good deal of persuasion from the resident physician, who saw him in the emergency room. After his admission he talked about his intent to kill his wife, his stepdaughter, and perhaps her biological father because he had been humiliated by the stepdaughter's leaving.

The day after admission, he requested a pass to do research work at the university library and became incensed when the staff showed reluctance. He proclaimed that he had to do work on his thesis and that he would sign out if he were detained. His demanding a pass at the very time that he agreed to hospital admission kept the staff frenzied, off balance, and afraid of offending him to the point where he might leave. The staff discussed the matter, met with the patient and pointed out to him the manner in which he spread panic by broadcasting his dangerousness and then asking for a pass as though he were entirely intact. He became enraged on being told that he spread panic and accused the staff of manipulating him. When the details of his conduct and communication were pointed out, he mentioned, for the first time, that his wife had said the same thing when he brought guns home and threatened to use them, and that she had left the state after he threatened to kill the daughter.

This method of filling people with anxiety and controlling them with indirectly communicated intimidation enabled him to avoid feelings of being dominated, helplessness, and shame. When this was pointed out, he experienced his anxiety and fear of domination directly. The emergency situation calmed to the point where he experienced the treatment program as supportive enough for him to face his own limitations and vulnerabilities.

In a hospital, a patient in therapy may talk about things that have nothing to do with violence, intimidation, or with his attachment to the hospital itself. The patient may appear to be actively engaged in therapy. However, an emergency situation may follow, near the end of hospitalization. At this time (if they have not been addressed) issues of dependency, shame about it, use of intimidation as a means to control helpers and cover up vulnerability, and a tendency to disorganize will reemerge. At the end of the hospitalization, the patient is faced with the same vulnerabilities with which he started.

These situations may be immensely compounded and thoroughly mystified if there is a questionable neurologic disorder in the picture, for example, if the patient has unexplained neurologic symptoms or if a paroxysmal disorder is suspected in a clinical picture with loss of control.

Example 3. A 26-year-old man was evaluated for workup of an unexplained neuromuscular abnormality, a demonstrable weakness in his legs that defied neurologic explanation. A detailed workup, including electromyography and an amytal interview had failed to demonstrate the specific etiology for the symptomatology. The patient let it be known that he was an expert marksman and shooting instructor. He had taught the use of rifles, handguns, and hand-to-hand combat in the military service. His hospital room was filled with photographs of himself with his many guns and with books on guns and martial arts. He talked of his volatile Mediterranean background but refused to give any information about his family, past or current. He claimed to have almost killed a nursing assistant and another patient. These near killings consisted of menacing and posturing, not physical attack. The ambiguous lethality left the neurology service perplexed enough to seek psychiatric consultation and eventual transfer of the patient.

During his psychiatric evaluation, his supposed muscular weakness was found to be unaccompanied by changes in reflexes or muscle tone and to be present only when he was aware of being watched. The staff, taking up the question of why he had been allowed for some weeks to remain in a wheelchair, began addressing a host of indirect indications of his potential for violence—unverified stories of beatings, reminders of his skill in combat, allusions to his gun collection, veiled threats, and the like. As the intimidating quality of these communications was raised among the staff and with the patient, he became more and more depressed, gave up his physical symptoms entirely, and grew more and more rageful, especially at female staff members. He then appeared as a vulnerable man enraged about his own neediness, which made him too closely bound to female caretakers and to the hospital itself for discharge even to be considered. Specific attention to his depression, with a lengthy termination phase, made it possible for him to leave the hospital.

It is common for neurologic diagnoses, definite or possible, to be considered as a larger part of the clinical picture of violent patients than they should be. Even a questionable electroencephalogram may be presumed to explain violent acts that really would not be sufficiently explained as a clearcut seizure disorder. Ambiguity in the neurologic situation frequently shows up in consultations that conclude that no decisive diagnosis can be reached but nonetheless recommend treating the disorder with anticonvulsants. This lack of integration distracts attention from the problem of responsibility: what the patient is or is not responsible for. It also takes the focus off of the tendency to disorganize when intimate persons get too close or too far away.

Patients' communications that intimidate, indirectly, and control intimate people are extremely costly defensive operations. Relatives, loved ones, and helping people in or out of hospitals sooner or later become exhausted or tired of intimidation and, subtly or overtly, reject or desert the patient. The patient's awareness that he habitually intimidates intimates who finally leave increases his desperation and the risk of violence to self or others.

Intimidation is extremely difficult to manage. If helpers are not at the optimal distance, the situation becomes more volatile. If, for example, they confuse intimidation with violence and become oversolicitous or overregulatory, they promote excessive dependency, reinforce intimidating behavior, and generate both shame and envy. If, on the other hand, the distance is too far or if close persons are emotionally withdrawn or separations are at hand, the patient is exposed to the same disorganizing propensities that generated violence in the first place. Only if intimidation is addressed directly in the presence of an emotionally adequate distance that remains supportive can the defensiveness subside with minimal risk.

Accordingly, a major therapeutic goal is to determine what is the optimal supportive distance so that caretakers will not be exhausted and patients will not be flooded with vulnerabilities beyond their tolerance and react with impulsive violent action in order to regulate helpers to a more comfortable distance. This whole situation is much compounded, of course, when helping persons or family members have some emotional stake in participating in a relationship that involves violence. Violence proneness in the patient may justify overregulation, or self-righteousness on the part of family members, or they may have a need to exploit either the patient's aggressiveness or his disorganizing propensities for reasons of their own. Helpers or intimates can then experience the patient as out of control and themselves as caring, dutiful, and intact.

Example 4. A 32-year-old man and his 46-year-old wife were seen in emergency conjoint consultation after he struck her. Both spouses were horrified, and the husband agreed that hospitalization might be the best way to start the lengthy treatment that he wanted. As he attempted to explain his view of his difficult marriage, his wife disorganized him with repeated humiliating comments about his inability to hold a job. These comments came at a time when he was talking about matters other than the job. When he did talk about work, she interrupted, first to say how immature he was compared to her previous husbands, then how strong and manly he was. The combination of building up and undercutting his sense of manliness was brought into focus.

As the therapist commented on the process, the husband became more and more calm and talked more and more about his depression and about his relationship with his father, a military drill sergeant who had filled him with talks of heroic exploits and then mocked his every effort to impress, undercut his integrity, and debunked him publicly. The patient's volatility decreased, but his depression, neediness, and vulnerability increased. As his wife continued debunking him during sessions, he became more and more focused on her disorganizing transactions. He began to see these in the light of his struggles with his father and became less ashamed of himself but more depressed. After the fourth session, he left his marriage and the hospital for another state and phoned the therapist for an appropriate referral for individual therapy. On follow-up some months later, we learned he had followed through with treatment.

Collusion in relationships with helpers—family or professional—that require another person to be off balance or out of control are a constant risk with impulsively violent patients.

EFFECTS OF THE PROCESS ON VIOLENCE: FRAGMENTATION

The act of violence and the intimidating effect of violence on the process tend to cover up the effect of interpersonal processes on violence, in particular, the vulnerability of the patient to disorganize and then to respond violently—either when he experiences dependent relationships as shameful or when he becomes aware that he disorganizes when optimal distance from cohesion-producing persons is not being maintained.

Usually, violent patients show both an excessive need for supportive relationships to hold themselves together and an exquisite sensitivity to humiliation. Both of these amplify the tendency toward violence. The excessive dependency should not be thought of as a simple neediness, but rather as a tendency to disorganize if nurturant figures are not around or if humiliation is inflicted on the patient. This propensity toward fragmentation arouses so much shame that almost anything, including life-threatening actions, will be used to cover it up.

Our particular population includes a number of patients with neurologic diagnoses varying from conversion reactions to paroxysmal disorders to unexplained neuromuscular weaknesses (see Examples 1 and 3). This particular group, all transferred from medical-surgical wards to our psychiatric unit, were patients who had clear-cut coexisting personality disorders, profound vocational difficulties, and excessive dependency in relationships, and were extraordinarily prone to humiliation when their characterologic difficulties were exposed. These patients regularly added to the confusion surrounding workup of their neurologic pathology. Their violent activity provoked in physicians an overemphasis on diagnosis in each case; even a positive diagnosis would not have accounted for the violent act. The patients' activities tended to keep physicians off balance whenever the treatment took a turn toward increased responsibility or independence on the patients' part. Violent or intimidating activities also strengthened the patients' ties to the hospital and thus allowed them to avoid the shame that would have resulted if the patient were to be without hospital support.

Frequently, such vulnerabilities can be clarified by observation of both the current family situation and that in the family in which the patient grew up (Lansky, 1982b). It is quite common for the violence-prone patient to have a personality so vulnerable to disorganization by the slightest humiliation that any efforts to work or hold a family together fail in a short time. Shame about this vulnerability and the need to hold on to family members combine to reinforce the control of intimate persons with intimidation. Thus the shame-producing cycle escalates.

It is more effective in the long run for the therapist to be mindful of the vulnerability and shame that underlie the aggressive outbursts rather than to concentrate on the outbursts themselves. The clinician will be wise to consider antidepressant medication, not just neuroleptics, and to consider the disorganizing effects of humiliation in interpersonal processes, not just uncontrolled aggressivity.

In the presence of intimidating interpersonal processes it may seem remote to try to reach the patient's underlying vulnerability. For the therapist who is able to interpret *intimidation as a pathological defense*, reaching and calming the underlying vulnerability may be feasible even in an emergency situation.

Example 5.   A 35-year-old man was admitted on involuntary detention as a danger to others. For three months, he had been drinking heavily and preoccupied both about dying himself and harming other people. Diagnoses of personality and neurologic deficit were considered. The patient talked a great deal about violence. He was a large man who frightened people by sudden, jerky movements, clenching his fists, and flexing his muscles. He gave the impression of one who could easily be out of control. Ward meetings took place when a number of staff felt too afraid of him to question his absences from the ward or his refusal of neuroleptic medication. A treatment conference was convened. He was informed of his intimidating demeanor. He was incredulous that people could be afraid of him. The fear was reaffirmed by various members of the staff. He protested vehemently that those who were afraid had not been direct with him. Several staff members agreed about the indirectness and reaffirmed that he frightened people. He was again mortified and asked various members of the staff, most of whom confirmed their fears. He protested, "How can you treat me if you're afraid of me?" The interviewer replied, "We *are* treating you while we're afraid of you. You imagine that the fear is something that we can't deal with. Perhaps that's the way you feel when you're terrified." He persisted in asking staff again about their fear, and when it became apparent that they could deal with him, he calmed, talked about his own overwhelming fears and how much they disorganized him. Clearcut schizophrenic symptomatology became evident and appropriate treatment took place. He left the hospital calmed and visited family members in another state.

IMPLICATIONS AND USE OF THE FAMILY

Commonly, the therapist can see relationship patterns in the violent patient by examining other close relationships. It is an error to assume that lack of family involvement means an absence of family relationships (Lansky et al., 1983). If significant members of the patient's family are unavailable, this should be taken as presumptive evidence that the patient has either frightened them, exhausted them, or made so many demands on them that they have finally rejected him. Family members may desert the patient after they have been controlled by a chronically intimidating lifestyle (Examples 2 and 3). This degree of precariousness or absence of supportive relationships is the very sort of thing that amplifies already existing vulnerability. It may make the patient feel so furious about being let down and about his vulnerabilities and controlling activities that he becomes violent. That the patient engineers such rejections does not keep their effect from being devastating. In patients with a long-standing history of such lability in supporting relationships, comparatively minor absences or separations often cause a clinical difficulty that escalates rapidly.

In the family of origin of violence-prone patients, one may find combinations of unstable nurturance that predispose to personality disorganization: before the age of 10 the patient may have had frequent changes in caretakers, often because of character pathology in the parents (Lansky, 1980). A violent parent is common, but not ubiquitous, in the history of violent patients. It is also common for a parent of the same sex to have held the patient overtly in contempt and to have used shaming or public debunking to keep the patient in what that parent felt to be his place (Example 4). These traumata may or may not be accompanied by a general emotional unresponsiveness in either parent, which makes the patient ashamed of any kind of emotional expression or neediness by creating an atmosphere of self-consciousness and frustration in the patient's emotional life. These patterns of unstable nurturance were found throughout our sample of violent patients, regardless of diagnosis.

In the current family situation, one may find either the same emotional unresponsiveness in a spouse or overt shaming transactions that disorganize the patient and keep him from accomplishments that might help him overcome some of his sense of shame. Evidence of pathological distance regulation in the current family situation is often found. Impulsive acts in the family generally keep people together or to regulate mood within the family (Example 1). Such acts are not confined to violence; they include binge drinking and suicidal or self-mutilating acts, which can reorganize the family or lift depressed members out of a depression when they can blame the impulsive activity on others.

Often, the therapist's emotional reaction to the patient—whether it is rejecting, frightened, self-righteous, terrified, overregulatory, preachy— may be similar to the reactions of members of the patient's current and parental family. The therapist's strong reaction may be seen in better perspective when compared with reactions of others serving containment functions.

It is crucial to look at what happens to disrupt supportive situations in the family that should buttress the cohesiveness of the patient's personality. If the patient has exhausted both his family of origin and his current family with his job instability, his need for support, and his inability to keep organized long enough to be a productive member of the family, then his shame at seeing himself this way is likely to be overwhelming. Violence and intimidation, by inducing in others the states that the patient finds shameful in himself, may protect the patient in the short run against a sense of shame. This protection from flooding by such a shameful view of himself is attained, however, at the price of inevitable instability in relationships (Examples 2, 3, and 4).

Scrutiny of the family usually sensitizes the therapist to his own comments that might shame the patient, debunk him, and draw attention to shortcomings that are really beyond his control. Without an understanding of the family, the therapist may make comments that may seem appropriate and well meaning but are, in fact, humiliating, disorganizing, and provoking when seen in the context of the family.

The therapeutic endeavor is strongest when a dependable alliance with the patient is obtained. This is more likely to be near the end of treatment than at the beginning. Nonetheless, a major therapeutic focus of attention from the outset should be the quality of the therapeutic alliance and whether or not intimidation, provocation, excessive dependency, disorganization at times of separations, and the like can be investigated in a way that does not shame the patient. Straightforward interpretation of intimidation as a pathological defense points attention to fears that impede the alliance (Example 5). Within a good working alliance much more can be accomplished to deal with the basic vulnerabilities of the violent patient and ensure a lasting result for treatment.

10

Shame and Domestic Violence

In this chapter, I consider domestic violence from the vantage point of the extreme vulnerability to narcissistic injury of the individuals involved and the way in which such vulnerability influences their behaviors within the family. This point of view encompasses both individual dynamics and a family-systems perspective. I approach the problem of domestic violence in terms of tendencies of the personalities involved to disorganize and of the collusive defensive operations that are the family members' attempts to minimize the chaotic effects of their vulnerabilities.

I am assuming that in a marriage characterized by repeated overt violence, both spouses are likely to have considerable vulnerability to personality disorganization. As a result, they have to deal with the shame that floods them when they become aware not only of this lack of cohesion, but also of the maneuvers in close relationship that they use to hide it. People with such vulnerability seek out spouses with similar personality organization who are available for collusive relationships that keep the marital system from being flooded with shame. Within such relationships, complex regulatory maneuvers that I have previously called pathologic distance regulation (see chapter 5) keep the persons within the family from getting too close or too far away and thus risking personality disorganization and the attendant amplification of shame.

NARCISSISTIC VULNERABILITY IN THE FAMILY

I have already delineated the clinical phenomenology of pathologic distance regulation within collusive relations. Seemingly chaotic behaviors or

158

emotional absences usually have complex regulatory effects on the family. Personality disorganization and attendant shame is often minimized, or at least made tolerable, by adjusting distance among intimates to a reasonably comfortable level, one that is neither too close nor too far away, and by restoring control over the situation to the participants in these defensive operations. I will comment briefly on defensive maneuvers typified by blaming (Chapter 4), by pathological preoccupation (Chapter 5), and by impulsive action (Chapter 6).

In marriages dominated by *blaming transactions*, verbal conflict is characteristically at the forefront of the couple's activities. Often some transgression by a spouse serves both as a precipitant to disorganization in the blamer and a provocation to blame. Blaming attacks may be precipitated by major transgressions or by events as small as exclusion from a conversation, or other types of seemingly mild narcissistic injury. Underneath the apparent chaos seen in blaming transactions is a tightly bound, cohesive dyad, guarded by the blaming transactions themselves from too much intimacy on one hand and from too much distance on the other.

The blaming transaction conveys to the blamed person that he or she has hurt, let down, deserted, or abandoned the blamer. Such transactions carry with them the implication that the blamed person could, if he or she only would, be a perfectly satisfactory person. In that sense, despite tumult and hostility, both the blamer and the blamed person may feel a greatly enhanced sense of power during the act of blame; the blamer by the discharge of the self-righteous accusatory attack, and the blamed person by the attribution of near omnipotent power in the attributions of the blamer. This sense of enhanced power is in striking contrast to the overt shaming that takes place in relationships that involve domestic violence.

Overt shaming, as opposed to blaming, has a deviation-amplifying effect on the family system. Defects, instead of being hidden by transactions within the marital system, are exposed by them; and the dyad, instead of being a refuge from humiliation, is the source of it.

Relationships characterized by *pathologic preoccupation* involve some person or persons whose activities are felt by the family system to confer great prestige or promise on the family. These persons are emotionally absent even when physically present, the absence usually rationalized as preoccupation with the prestigious activity. This kind of emotional absence is often found to precipitate a great deal of depression, blaming, and impulsive action in other members of the family. Families so organized often have several members with high vocational attainment and a great deal of responsibility in their relationships outside of the family.

Collusive systems organized around *impulsive action* in one of its members are often found to have a specific regulatory structure. Often, the impulsive actor, that is, an overdoser, binge drinker, slasher, or sexually impulsive person, is found to act impulsively following some sort of change in a relationship. That change is usually some sort of a narcissistic wound, that is to say, an experience of disorganization when intimates either become too close or too far away.

What follows this precipitating experience is some type of dissociation or personality disorganization that may be consciously experienced as an uneasy or paranoid prodromal phase or may not be consciously noticed at all. The prodrome is followed by the impulsive act itself, which often has an organizing effect on people, for example, by spreading fear of suicide or violence or desertion, or loss of control. Often this sort of control over distance is exercised without actual harm being done. Such impulsive acts are often followed by waves of guilt that serve, among other things, to take attention away from disorganization and other sources of shame in the dissociated or prodromal period. Impulsive action often has a regulatory effect on intimates, reorganizing them, sometimes by intimidation, sometimes for other reasons in a protective array around the impulsive actor, so that again they are neither too close nor too far away.

I hope to extend this line of investigation to the family system characterized by domestic violence. I will consider the problem both in terms of extreme narcissistic vulnerability in the spouses themselves, and in terms of the failure of collusive defensive operations which attempt to cope with that narcissistic vulnerability. Domestic violence is here viewed as a type of impulsive action; but unlike the type of impulsive action that merely intimidates and so reorganizes intimates, domestic violence fails either to restore a feeling of control to those in the system or to keep those persons relatively safe. My attempt will be to provide a view of the problem that will be sufficiently perspicuous to be of use no matter what specific treatment strategies are actually employed.

In marital systems characterized by habitual domestic violence, shame dynamics are of central importance. Unlike the collusive operations typified by blame, pathologic preoccupation, and intimidation (as opposed to actually violent) impulsive action, transactions in marriages characterized by domestic violence are typified by maneuvers that sharply increase shame in the system; that is, *overt humiliation* is a typical transactional mode. Such deliberate humiliation usually shows up prominently in the family history of at least one spouse, and disposes that person to a sensitivity to humiliation in the transactions of the spouses as they deal with each other and often in the experience both spouses have of the therapist's comments. The volatility of the system can best be understood in the light of the dynamics of shame.

A CASE IN DETAIL

In this discussion I deal entirely with material drawn from one case. In so doing, I am fully aware of the dangers of overgeneralizing. I do not presume that every case of domestic violence is like the present one. Nonetheless, I think that enough of pertinent dynamic material is in evidence to make the detailed case material valuable. Any attempts to generalize the results are of course risky, unless further studies or extensive clinical experience give independent testimony to the accuracy of such generalizations.

I am presenting a very detailed case for two reasons: (1) because many aspects of the case that portray both individual and systems dynamics have to be appreciated to allow a clear view of the way in which interlocking character pathology is the problem, and not something simpler, such as troublesome behavior or uncontrolled impulse; (2) because treatment of these volatile emergency situations is difficult to conceptualize and involves more than one modality. Containment by hospitalization, medication, protective custody, or shelter usually are short-term measures and may have to accompany more longer term strategic therapy aimed at altering the shame-amplifying transactions that are usually woven into the fabric of the relationship. Any treatment approach, then, will be drawn from a complex array of possibilities. Only a detailed grasp of the interlocking of individual and systems dynamics, together with an appreciation of the extent to which shame dynamics pervades the relationship, is suitable for the formation of overall strategies to address the problem.

The case material consists of four interviews with a husband and wife. The man, Mario, is 32. His wife, Anna, is 46. They were referred on an emergency basis to the Family Treatment Program, after they appeared for consultation. Mario had struck Anna three times in the last week. This was the first violent episode, the first time in their marriage of six months and relationship of a year and a half. Both were horrified; both came to the hospital wanting emergency intervention, and both wanted him hospitalized. The initial interview was to decide on the advisability of hospitalization, and took place in an open staff interview.

Session 1

The couple came in, and both commented on the presence of other staff members with the interviewer. The therapist inquired what the difficulties were. Anna spoke first. She mentioned in a tearful way that she was frightened and spoke of Mario's being out of control. Mario had humiliated her. Driving to church, she had seen him driving the other way with another woman in a car that she had bought for him. He had not been home the previous evening. As she described this beginning of the week that culminated in the violent episodes, she noted flippantly, "He does not work." She went on to speak of some of the marital difficulties and then offered a little about her own background. She had had several previous marriages, one with an older man by whom she had had two children. She emphasized that this man could not satisfy her sexually. Despite the long time since the divorce, he was still supporting her. Then she married a younger man, an alcoholic. "Mario doesn't drink," but she hastened to add, "He doesn't work either. At least Paul worked." Her commentaries on Mario and the other two husbands were peppered with disparaging remarks, about sexual inadequacy, drinking, or lack of working. She described briefly the family in which she was born. Her mother had yelled a lot. Of seven children, Anna was the sixth. Her father regularly avoided facing problems in the marriage. He drank. He let her down all the time. He couldn't face things at home.

Excerpt 1

THERAPIST (to Mario): What's your view of the marriage?
MARIO: Of our present marriage? We don't share, either one of us or the other. I can come out with an idea which is probably a good one, but she looks at it and says it's a pipedream.
THERAPIST: As you say it, the wind gets knocked out of your sails.
MARIO: Yeah. Anna says I don't follow through on things, but she's going to knock it right from the beginning. If she's going to do that, what chance does it have to begin with. It has no chance of succeeding, if she's not going to back me with it. She's got to be able to sit down there and talk to me and say, "It looks like a good idea, but maybe this won't work out of it, or maybe that won't work out of it." We've never had those kinds of discussions over any ideas I've had.
ANNA: Can I interject?

The therapist stops her from interjecting but assures her that she will have her turn later. Mario goes on to speak of his broken line of thinking, and of Anna's disorganizing effect on him.

Excerpt 2

MARIO: We don't communicate as well as we could. It's funny. We've had three physical confrontations, break-down, knock-down, drag-out fights.
THERAPIST: Why with this marriage?

MARIO: Because Anna seems to have a talent for pushing buttons that make me go . . . . Nobody's been able to get to those buttons before because I always protected them very well. With Anna I'm much more open in that area. I'm much more emotional with her than I ever would get with anybody else . . . I know what can set me off. Unfortunately, she does too.

ANNA: I don't realize it.

THERAPIST: Well, if you can tell me, then she'll have a chance to listen. Perhaps we'll have something to work on.

MARIO: Okay. Anna and I, you know, had an affair before my marriage was ended.

ANNA: You were separated and divorcing. (*Mario becomes flushed.*)

THERAPIST: What happened just now?

MARIO: She aggravated me because she stepped in.

THERAPIST: You look furious at her. Do you feel that way?

MARIO: Yes I do. She stepped in. She stepped all over what I was trying to say. She's broken a train of thought.

THERAPIST: Is that at all typical of what goes on between the two of you?

MARIO: Yes. Very much so.

THERAPIST: Let's stick to that for a moment. . . . If Anna doesn't know what she's doing, or you can't put it exactly in words, this way she'll have a chance to hear. When you started to talk, and said you had an affair before the divorce, she spoke up and said that actually you were separated, and you looked furious.

MARIO: I looked furious because I was angry about it. She does this constantly. I mean it's a matter of I can sit there for 3 hours and listen. But I can't speak for about a minute before she steps on me, stomps, and I have to start all over. And she can go, like in the car on the way here today, she kept saying this and saying this and saying this and. . . .

ANNA: Mario, I'm at my end, honey, I've broken down, I've had it.

MARIO: That's what I mean, she can't keep her mouth shut. I say, "Anna please stop! You've made your point, don't repeat it." From the end of that sentence to the time she repeated it you couldn't measure with a stop watch. . . . That's exactly how I feel. I can't make a point with her, but it seems that after every time we have a physical confrontation she's willing to shut up, back off, let me talk and let me say what I've got to say. It's almost like I have to hit her to get her attention . . . I feel like it's every time that something has to be done it has to be done when Anna wants it done. I'd like to see where I go with my own talents and abilities and thoughts.

When the therapist inquires whether this was a lifelong difficulty, Mario goes on straightaway to talk abut his own upbringing. Mario's father was a Marine drill sergeant, a career soldier who had deliberately put him in humiliating situations.

Excerpt 3

MARIO: He'd come in in the middle of the afternoon and say, "Well we're going down to the post." I'd say well, let me change clothes. He'd say, no, no, that's what you're wearing, wear it, go on. He made me feel like an idiot. . . . He didn't know how to handle a kid this high when he was used to handling 18-year-olds on the drill field and using that kind of thing on them. They understood it, why couldn't I? But I wasn't old enough to understand it. Now I'm at the age I'm at, I can look at what he did and say, "He really didn't do that badly, he just picked the wrong age to do it to me."

THERAPIST: What effect do you think it had on you? Has it spilled into your marital problems?

MARIO: I got so that in school I'd take a piece of paper out of a notebook, and if it had a speck of dirt on it I'd throw it away because it wasn't neat enough, and that's ridiculous. Then as I got older I went to just the opposite. I don't really give a damn. Anna will tell me, "You need a haircut." I don't need a haircut. In my estimation, I won't need a haircut for at least three weeks. Maybe four.

THERAPIST: You don't need a drill sergeant to tell you you need a haircut.

The therapist, feeling that the situation was by no means resolved, inquires about hospitalization. Both Anna and Mario want Mario to be hospitalized. He is admitted to the hospital that day.

Session 2

A week later, in private, in the therapist's office, the couple both told the therapist how unsettling it had been to open things up and at the same time leave them unfinished. Anna resented Mario's obtaining therapy on the ward and wanted therapy herself. Anna mentioned that she hadn't told Mario about two other marriages prior to the one with the older man. The first was when she was 15. Mario, then, is her fifth husband.

They began arguing about whether or not he should have friends that were just his and not both of theirs. Anna then brought up the fact that Mario had had six jobs in the preceding year.

Excerpt 4

ANNA: He's had six jobs this year and six jobs last year. There's no reason for it. There are one or two reasons, and it's not all home problems. Either he is not experienced enough, or he's—or his emotional problems have affected his ability to work. He hasn't been easy to get along with. I can't carry everything if he's not working somewhere. I can carry if he's working somewhere and getting, you know, maybe a small salary, but if he's not getting anywhere, or if he's not being educated, he's not getting anywhere either, it would be very nice if he could get into some kind of training where he could draw something or get benefits while he's being trained. I don't think he can hold a job. We've talked about it, we've gone through it. He gets jobs easily and loses them all the time. This has gone til it hurts him, it hurts me, and hurts the marriage.

THERAPIST: I guess you feel that if he doesn't work, you're doing all the work or that he lets you down all the time. You, on the other hand, Mario, might be very upset by all this criticism and feeling very picked on, feeling there is no way out. How can you do something that matters right now? Where are you both now?

MARIO: You pretty well explained where I'm at.

ANNA: You pretty well explained where I was. Mario came to me practically from his other wife and moved into my house and I kept carrying things, and by the time we got married—before we got married—I co-signed a loan because my credit was good and his wasn't. And I'm stuck with that loan. And I'm making payments on cars because Mario's here and not working, and it's getting to be a little more than even I can handle. You know, the house and everything. At least with Mario here, while it doesn't help a heck of a lot economically speaking, it helps. . . .

MARIO: I'd like to be able to contribute. I'd also like to be able to work at something. I worked at retail for six years. I'm good at it. But I don't like it. You get the position where you're in between somebody above wanting something done one way and a customer wanting to do it another way. You get caught in that all the time, and if you're not extremely stable in all other aspects of your life, you're really in a stress pattern, and I'm not very fond of that.

THERAPIST: I'm getting a feeling, Mario, that it's a little more complicated than that you don't like it. You feel really trapped, as I'm hearing it, and you feel you need to produce an income, but then are forced to put up with so many indignities that you won't be able to do anything that matters. That's what I thought I heard.

MARIO: Yeah, you heard it pretty good. You see, as a mechanic everything you do has a purpose. Nobody bothers you, and you do it. They come and say this needs to be done, and you do it. Take the car out, and that's it. Nobody comes and looks over your shoulder, and the customer isn't allowed there. You do it, get it done, and get rid of it.

THERAPIST: So that line of work, rather than a people- centered kind of thing, is much more suited to your personality, because where you deal with the public and deal with a supervisor and everything gangs up on you, I take it, it's just the wrong fit for you.

MARIO: If I feel like telling the brake lining to go to hell, I do that. There's nobody around to worry about whether I said it in front of the wrong person.

In the midst of Mario's beginning to talk about how humiliated he is in the job situation, Anna interrupts to correct him. The therapist intervenes, but she continues.

Excerpt 5

ANNA: What you have heard from Mario and what I have lived with Mario for over a year are two different things. He wants to start at the top. Everybody would like to, but unfortunately everybody doesn't get to. Mario, you know, last week he was talking about his ideas. Every time he has an idea he brings it up, and I squash it. Unfortunately, he doesn't carry these ideas out and so he comes and puts them on me because I've got the credit and I can go on and say hey, I'd like to borrow some more money to put him in business. We'd only been married a very short time and he wanted me to start a business with him but he wouldn't carry through with it. He would just be, you know, because Mario doesn't carry through. He's got a lot to learn. He's got to go out and work and he's got to make a minimum pay for a while, and then go slowly. You just can't reach for it and it's going to be there. It's just not going to be there that fast.

Mario has a wonderful mind, he has ideas, great ideas. But he doesn't know how to put them through without me, and I can't help him. I can't handle that part of the marriage.

MARIO: Okay, let me make a comment on that. First of all, you don't know what the hell I've done for the last 20 years of my life. You don't know what kind of training I have, whether I can handle a job or not. You don't have any idea. (*shouting.*)

THERAPIST: Mario, that really hurt you, when she said that.

MARIO: Yeah, it knocked the shit out of me, as a matter of fact, because she has no idea what kind of training I've got, how I've dealt with people, what business experience I've developed. Hell, I've handled six or seven thousand dollars and come out only a few cents off in the cash register.

ANNA: That's an accountant's job.

MARIO: No it isn't, it's a manager's job to do that. What the hell do you mean, it's an accountant's job. (*shouting*) I've made schedules for people that covered a goddamn month at a time, seven days a week, 24 hours a day, with nine people, and had everybody happy.

THERAPIST: You sound so angry and put down. Do you feel that way?

MARIO: Yes, I feel that way. She still doesn't know what the hell I'm capable of doing. She has no idea what my experience levels are, and she'll sit there and say that I'd better crawl before I can walk, and I've heard my father say that all my goddamn life.

THERAPIST: The drill sergeant again.

MARIO: Yeah.

ANNA: All right, let's go back to the mechanics, okay?

THERAPIST: Is this typical of what you get into in the marriage? You know, he's so hurt that no matter how much truth there is in what you're saying, nothing's going to get done right here unless we understand how you both feel, and work with that for a while. Because I think you're so hurt, Mario, by what she's saying, that the content's going to get lost. (*To Anna*) Do you follow what I'm saying? He's going to hear it like his father telling him he's not good enough.

ANNA: All right. Why should I have to work, wash dirty, greasy clothes because he won't take the time to do them, and put up with this when he's going to think he's too good for the job anyway, and quit it or walk out or fool around and get fired over something silly. I don't really think he's all that incapable. I think a lot of it is his attitude. He walked out on a couple of

bosses and didn't even give notice. You don't do that on a job—
you can't. People can't live with themselves and build up
anything out of life doing things like that and then running.

Anna fulminates about Mario's irresponsibility. The therapist interrupts,
attempting to get the focus onto their anxieties and their method of
communicating them. He asks Mario what he would like from Anna to help
him, even when she disagrees and even when she is very firm in feeling
that he's wrong. Toward the end of the session both Anna and Mario turn
to the therapist for the solution to their difficulties, expressing resentment
that their problems were just thrown back on them. Anna again stated that
she wanted her own therapist. Both are upset and angry with the therapist
for opening up hostilities and leaving them vulnerable when the session
ends. The therapist empathizes with this plight and agrees to make inquiries concerning an individual therapist for Anna.

Session 3

A week later, the therapist began by announcing a two-week absence: the
next session would be in three weeks. Both Mario and Anna reported that
things had gone much better. The therapist tried to enlist their curiosity
about what had made things better. Mario noted that they had come from
different backgrounds. The therapist wondered what effect this has had on
the marriage. Anna talked about Mario's not being at home. There were
fights constantly if he was not there. It would have been better if he had
worked, but as long as he was doing nothing, he could at least help her with
the heavier tasks. They began to argue about the job situation. Should he
continue as a mechanic or go to school? He talked of wanting a better job.
Perhaps he would sell his tools and use that for tuition. She jeeringly noted
that he always wanted to start at the top, but he couldn't handle any
pressure at all. He again became furious.

Excerpt 6

MARIO: I really want to follow through on it. There's nothing I can do
about that particularly without more training, and that takes
time. I've got to work on the time I'm training. It's kind of a rock
over here and a hard place over there.
ANNA: That's right. I think you ought to follow through on that job.
You've never had any kind of pressure.
MARIO: (*to the therapist*) How can we blow off some of this anger
that's building? She gets angry, and I get angry, and she gets

more bitter, and you know it escalates quickly after the anger starts.

THERAPIST: (*to Anna*) You agree?

ANNA: For the first time, Mario's sitting here facing something instead of running out the door and leaving. And he's even asking what we can do. That's the first time he's done that.

MARIO: You present an idea or counteroffer, and if you want to back our idea, she wants to back hers, and we get to a point where it's a dominance fight, and it has been from the beginning. Either one of us, each of us wants to be in the dominant position.

ANNA: I don't.

MARIO: That's a bunch of bull.

ANNA: I would give it to you so easily if you would take it, Mario. I'm so tired of it, I'm so tired of the decisions. I'm so tired.

MARIO: Then why do you fight the decisions I make?

ANNA: If you would make a decision and carry it through on your own without bothering me, without me making the decision. . . .

MARIO: Then why do you produce counterarguments all the time?

ANNA: You ask my opinion. . . . (*Mario interrupts.*)

MARIO: No, no, as a matter of fact, I sometimes don't. I can say I'd like to do this, and you say 'Why don't you do it that way?' All of a sudden I'm saying to myself, well if I do this, then I'll have a fight with her because she doesn't want me to do it that way. There's always a counteroffer.

ANNA: That's a copout.

MARIO: No, it isn't a copout. There's always a counteroffer. Goddammit, the other day I was digging out the garden. You weren't even happy with the way I was digging the garden.

ANNA: You haven't even been in the garden since you came in here.

MARIO: (*flustered*) Okay, a month ago I was digging up the garden and you weren't happy about the way I was digging up the garden. (*furious*) What difference does it make what time frame it was? You still weren't happy with the way I was doing it.

ANNA: Apparently, you weren't doing it right. Apparently—

MARIO: (*interrupting*) Well, who's right? The guy wielding the shovel or the person watching?

ANNA: I don't remember the incident. What were you doing?

MARIO: I was digging up the other half of the garden, where you had the corn planted and the lettuce planted after the tree was chopped down. just before the tree was cut up.

ANNA: I don't remember.

MARIO: Well, that's a copout.

ANNA: Have you ever stopped to think that maybe it was just an off-day for me, or maybe I just—Why are you so sensitive to my criticism anyway?

At this point the therapist interrupts, noting Mario's anger, and asks if this sort of interaction is typical—Anna vehemently pointing to Mario's irresponsibility, and Mario feeling totally disorganized by her so doing. They both agree that it is. The therapist goes on to explore with Mario how Anna can make him feel supported and still have her own opinions, even differing with him. Mario begs to be allowed to make his own mistakes. Anna starts to interrupt, but the therapist instructs her to listen, to get an understanding of him, and to rest assured that her point of view will also be discussed. Mario again talks of his sensitivity and of his humiliation proneness.

Excerpt 7

MARIO: It's sometimes difficult for a person to learn from another person's mistakes. Now, she's assuming that I've been through all these things before and I've made these mistakes and I know how it's going to go and there's no sense in doing it that way because I've done it that way before. . . . What I'm saying, what I would like her to do is shut up and let me make my own mistakes. . .

ANNA: But you haven't. . . .

MARIO: . . . A lot of movement within my framework, the one I'm living in, to have the opportunity either to become what I want, or falling down the tubes, one or the other. . . . I'm not a real easy person to give criticism to.

ANNA: You can say that again.

MARIO: I don't particularly care for it. Number one, because I have succeeded in a number of things that other people have not succeeded in trying the same damn thing. It may not have been a job. It may have been way of doing something that they didn't learn. You know, like everybody all through school told me that if you didn't study, you'll never pass. And I didn't, but I carried a B-plus average all through school, with a 90% comprehension rate. And I have a 95% retention rate of anything I read or hear.

ANNA: So you should be in college, then.

MARIO: (*yelling*) Probably I should, but that's beside the point.

The therapist tries to calm Mario and link the current turmoil in the discussion to Mario's history of debunkings from his father.

THERAPIST: I understand what you don't like about what she does. Tell me what you would like her to do.

MARIO: No, no. What I'm saying, what I would like her to do is shut up and let me make my own mistakes.

THERAPIST: Well, specifically, if you decide you want to go to real estate school. . . .

MARIO: (*interrupting*) . . . and if it turns out to be a mistake, at least I made the decision and it wasn't a compromise on my part.

ANNA: But you haven't.

MARIO: Between what I wanted and what she wanted.

THERAPIST: Let me interrupt. Let Mario and me talk, and then you and I will talk, and that way the two of you will both have a chance to listen without preparing your argument, and you'll each be assured that you'll get a chance to talk, too. I get a sense that it's very difficult to resolve things. You both keep ending up in the same stalemate. So, (*to Mario*) she should appreciate that you need to have your space, so to speak, and to make your own mistakes, or at least to have enough. . . .

MARIO: A lot of movement within my framework, the one I'm living in, to have the opportunity either to become a success or what I want, what my idea is, or falling down the tubes, one or the other.

THERAPIST: And I guess we know from our previous talks, I'm sure she knows better than I, that you are very sensitized to debunking comments from your father and that you are very vulnerable to that. . . .

MARIO: (*interrupting*) You know what the greatest pleasure in my whole life was? My father was a crack shot with a pistol and a rifle, and the greatest pleasure in my whole life was he was firing his pistol and I took the pistol and left-handedly beat him. It was the greatest—that shining hour . . . because every time I had picked up a weapon he said, 'You're handling it wrong, you don't know what you're doing.' The man's an expert no doubt about it. He can take any one of the military makes, take it apart and put it back together, and fire it. But the shining hour of my life was when I beat him left-handedly. (*calms*)

THERAPIST: But you talk very much as though being told what's good for you isn't really advice; it's a method of undermining you and knocking the wind out of your sails, and putting you in your place.

MARIO: Yeah. That can't be done that way or this way, or I don't think anybody's done it. I don't think you can do that, a lot of that.

THERAPIST: Would you agree that you're quite sensitive to every sort of advice given that way.

MARIO: Yeah, I'm very sensitive to it.

THERAPIST: And your wife gets a fair amount of that sensitivity.

The therapist had a chance to draw their attention to the process between them by labeling their mutual reactivity as one major problem between them. They began to talk about their communicating, and in particular about Mario's need to feel heard and finish his line of thinking, especially if this would not endanger Anna's right to disagree with him. Mario was calmed greatly by the process, but Anna, far from having her attention drawn to the process in the marriage and calming her anxieties about losing her point of view, seemed fired to even more criticism about Mario's half-baked ideas. She seemed oblivious to his escalating shame and anger and continued talking about his inability to follow through with anything. The therapist again tried to mediate. Anna talked about her own needs and how much he had let her down. Mario talked more about the process and how it disorganized him.

Near the end of the session, the therapist noted that each of them seemed to be a long way from feeling safe with the other's point of view. Mario talked angrily of her excluding him from a big part of her life. She said that he meant the way she invested and spent her money given to her by her third husband to provide for the children. She had kept the money separately and followed her third husband's advice to keep Mario out of the arrangements. It was not community property. Mario began shouting. The therapist closed with a vain attempt to get them to look at the process and understand the anxieties that motored the escalation of tensions.

Session 4

Three weeks later, the therapist, recently returned, heard for the first time that Mario's demands for more and more passes from the ward were presenting a management problem. Anna began the session angrily, again saying that she had nobody to talk to, that she had called in angrily and was written up as an angry person. Mario said jeeringly that she had been written up as a drunken person. She talked angrily about the hospital pass on which he played bridge with the other woman. Another argument about his refusal to join her at a dance class ensued. Mario said that the level of the class was too advanced for him, and the mutual anger mounted.

The therapist commented that, both in the session and by his behavior on the ward, Mario seemed to be setting himself up to leave angrily. Mario then petulantly challenged the need to be in the hospital. He wasn't getting any medication; he wasn't being helped. The therapist commented that there was less and less structure, more and more passes, more and more anger, more confusion and provocation. Mario asked again why he had to be in the hospital. The therapist noted that the original reasons were for protection and also for therapy, and then he inquired about Mario's anger, wondering if that wasn't what he had felt in other situations, on jobs, and in the marriage. Mario acknowledged being very offended and insulted and humiliated by these limits.

When Mario started to feel calmer talking about this, Anna interrupted, saying that it was her feeling that he should stay in the hospital and get no passes whatsoever. He screamed that she should be locked up in a place for alcoholics. A furor developed between them. Mario turned to the therapist and asked about an application for disability benefits that he had given to the therapist shortly before. The therapist asked if he thought he was disabled. Mario proceeded to blame Anna for his difficulties, and another argument ensued. Mario turned to the therapist and asked what the therapist thought was wrong with him. The therapist ventured tentatively that he saw Mario's personality as such that he became chaotic without structure, that he became very resentful if structure was applied, and that that difficulty caused him difficulties in many areas: jobs, marriages, and now even the hospital.

The therapist continued that the vulnerabilities and lability might suggest a kind of depression. Mario was furious at this and, saying that he was upset at the idea of medication, asked the therapist to justify the diagnosis. The therapist explained that any medication would be optional but might help with his vulnerability and disorganization. Mario vented his fury at Anna, saying that he couldn't have a normal life because of her.

Excerpt 8

MARIO: You know why I'm angry? Because she's using the hospital as a way of keeping me out of a normal life structure right now.

ANNA: That's not true. You life should be here. You should be here. You're a patient.

MARIO: She's telling me I should be in the hospital when I don't really feel I should be, and she's using it as a wedge between us, and I'm not going to allow that. Either we're going to have a marriage or we're not going to have a marriage, but we're not going to have a half-marriage.

ANNA: Well, we had a half-marriage before because you laid all the responsibility on me. You said that you needed structure to get up and go to work. Well, honey, I had to get you up. The responsibility was on me every morning to get you up. That alarm went off for an hour before you'd get out of bed, and with me yelling at you. I was the one at you every morning, yelling, 'Mario, get out of bed.' That was the way every day started. Let's talk about your job.

MARIO: Okay, let's talk about it.

ANNA: Okay, you're going into an unstructured job, you're going to be your own boss. I've seen you in a job. The day we married I started you. Monday, you went into an unstructured salesmanship job and you blew it, babe, because you went down and gambled. You weren't taking care of business, and so instead of quitting you just left. You know, I mean you left on really bad terms. Okay, this is the type of person you are now. All right, we laid out the money which we couldn't afford to give you another chance at another job because you're not making with the mechanics. I'm going to sit by, and I'm going to watch, and see how you do with that, and hope to God you don't blow it.

Anna goes on to talk about how poorly he did at unstructured jobs. Mario returns to the disability. The therapist points out that there seems to be two ideas in his head that didn't go with each other. One, that he is disorganized and upset and very needful of help and disability and relief from responsibility, but also that he is very patronized, manipulated, and humiliated by people telling him that he cannot come and go as he pleases when he is perfectly capable of it. The therapist offered the opinion that Mario has great difficulty figuring out what to do with those notions of himself. Mario becomes defiant on the matter of continued hospitalization. Anna says that she will refuse to have him home if he signs out. Mario becomes more and more furious and asks why he had to be here, and a furor ensues again between Anna and Mario. The therapist hopes that Mario will not feel he must leave just because Anna says that he must stay. An appointment time is set for the following week, and the session ends.

Mario left the hospital on the next day and did not return.

THE STRUCTURE OF DOMESTIC VIOLENCE

Domestic violence, as I have noted, is a kind of impulsive action. But the kind of domestic violence here considered is a type of impulsive action that does not take place within a system that can absorb and minimize the disorganization, impulsivity, and attempts at reorganization that follow narcissistic wounding. With intensely humiliation-prone individuals so constituted that they provoke shame, habitually shame others, and react strongly to being shamed, the collusive marital system amplifies each spouse's vulnerabilities rather than minimizing them. Distance regulation, that is, the reorganization of the system around a *safe* distance among intimates, fails, leaving both spouses ashamed, powerless, and aware, at some level, of their basic destructiveness within relationships. The collusive relationship has basically failed to bind and absorb narcissistic vulnerability within the system in such a way as to minimize the sense of shame.

The features of impulsive action outlined in Chapter 9 come into play in collusive relationships. As we gain perspective on the case material by discussing violence in terms of those features, Mario, the "violent" person, will receive somewhat more emphasis than will Anna; nevertheless, her role in the destructive relationship is evident. I will make some comparisons between the type of violent impulsive action here illustrated and the more cohesive types of collusive relationships, such as blaming transactions.

1. *Vulnerability to personality disorganization*: Beneath his bluster and considerable verbal dexterity, Mario's extreme narcissistic vulnerability, that is, his tendency to disorganize, is evident in a number of areas. The consequences of this tendency are convincing in his history of job losses and marital failures. Another dimension emerges from his vividly recollected history of humiliation by his father. He defends against this humiliation with a kind of characterologic swagger and provocativeness that is evident in Excerpt 6. The neediness and disorganization are evident throughout the case material, but especially at the beginning and at the end of Session 2, which shows in both spouses, a neediness and a shame over it that is not relieved by transactions within the marital system. Anna's vulnerability is also evidenced by a history of five marriages, all of them devalued in some way. Her method of handling her own shame is to disorganize, debunk, and shame the other person. Her demandingness is also apparent throughout.

2. *Precipitant*: The circumstances that cause events to escalate to the point of violence are prominent in both spouses. Mario's provocativeness is first talked about in the episode described in the first session, his being seen by his wife with another woman in the car that Anna had bought for him; later it shows up by his provoking limits on the ward and by his presenting a constant and inconsistent array of plans to his wife. Noteworthy throughout the transcript is Anna's style of expressing her anxieties and criticism (however well founded) in a manner that disorganizes, humiliates, and publicly shames. Mario is able to talk about this time after time in many of the excerpts. When Mario is wounded by some remark, talk about the process and clarification calms him down rather easily; and when he

feels understood talking about the process, he is able to calm down and admit his responsibility in the difficulties and proceed to talk constructively. When he talks to Anna, however, his disorganization is compounded, and his line of thinking and sense of an organized self scarcely last more than a few sentences.

3. The *prodrome*: Mario's ability to talk about his experience of disorganization, and the amplification of this experience in the process between Anna and him gives a good view of the broken line of thought resulting from the overt shaming transaction. This is evident in Excerpts 2, 4, 5, and 6. The degree of overt disorganization is much more than is usually seen, for example, with couples who blame. Blaming couples often imply in their accusatory outbursts that the blamed person *could* do almost anything if only he or she would. However unpleasant they may be, blaming transactions are usually not overtly shaming.

4. *The act itself* is most strongly characterized by the fact that actual harm was done. Both spouses feel frightened, out of control, and weak. This state of affairs is in sharp contrast to blaming transactions, in which the blamer feels self-righteous and powerful and the transgressor who is blamed is also accused in a certain way of being very powerful. The blamed person feels wronged, perhaps, but not frightened, humiliated, and disintegrated in public. The result of the act of actual violence (as opposed to intimidation transactions with the threat of violence) is that both Mario and Anna feel weak, out of control, frightened, and more ashamed.

5. *Reaction to the act*: Very often an impulsive actor, for example, a binge drinker or a pathological gambler, expresses some guilt over what has been done—some genuine concern for the other person. This guilt may be so intense that it overshadows the disorganization and accompanying shame. But Mario's reaction to the act is aimed instead at buttressing his shameful sense of self. He said in a passage shortly after Excerpt 3:

"Well, it's like I never really had a temper that manifested itself in violence. I had a temper where I yelled a lot, but I never am aware of my size. I'm six feet three—I can take a pipe and bend it into a pretzel with my wrist. I can take a can that's closed—a soda can that's closed—I'm right-handed, and with my left hand pop it open. So I know what kind of power I generate with my physique and size and weight, and I hesitate to use this."

Mario's reaction to his loss of control is a certain amount of fright and a wish to exert control, but no real concern, not even temporarily, for Anna. His guilt is voiced in a kind of amazement of his own power, not as a sense of pain for having harmed a love object. He covers over weakness with even more provocativeness. Neither spouse seem to have moments of protectiveness or concern about the other.

6. *Pathologic distance regulation*: The totality of these factors is a

failure of effective defensive operations in the collusive relationship. That is to say, the act itself, far from reorganizing the marital system in the way that blame and intimidating impulsive action do, instead tears the system apart and subverts the spouses' confidence in the protectiveness offered by the marriage itself. This security is a common feature of the other types of defensive operations that I have described: in blaming transactions, the blamer and the blamed are locked in a self-righteous transaction that may have a tremendous emotional cost but actually binds the system securely together. The preoccupied person, who is physically present but emotionally absent, may bind the system together by supplying enormous reliability and prestige to the system even if family members' emotional needs are not met. The impulsive actor may organize rescuers or those intimidated by the impulsive act so that the system persists or even reorganizes. Not so with the case of actual violence. The sense of shame and the vulnerabilities are too intense to be bound by the defensive activities that can be handled by the maneuvers of blame, preoccupation, and impulsive action. The defenses simply are not powerful enough to deal with the overwhelming vulnerability. There is a failure of effective regulation of a safe distance to intimates and a basic failure of restitution, that is, of the way back to objects after the process of detachment that follows personality disorganization.

IMPLICATIONS FOR TREATMENT

In this case, the act of overt violence within the marriage can be seen as a failure of restitution, a failure of people to bind together in a protective collusive system. There is too much vulnerability, too much shame generation, too much reactivity, too much humiliation proneness, too much overt shaming, and too much shameful disorganization and provocation for the system to absorb. Too many shame-producing features are present that must be bound in the system, so the narcissistic vulnerability spills over as provocation on the part of Mario and overt shaming on the part on Anna. These features are underscored in the history of her marital failures and his job failures. The couple as a unit is too busy with internal turmoil to maintain any sort of directed, purposive activity within the marriage or outside of it. This chaos goes far beyond what can be contained even with the high-cost defensive operations that are evident in blaming and preoccupied families and even those with habitual intimidating impulsive action. Shame in the therapeutic process, that is in relation to the therapist, is seen in the beginning and end of Session 2; it mounts in Mario's whole relationship to the ward, evidenced at the end of Session 4.

The presence of so much shame in the system has far-reaching implications for treatment. Drawing attention to shame does not minimize it: this is not true of guilt, which is often based on an exaggerated fantasy of the effects of one's actions or hostilities. The shame when one appears disorganized, defective, and out of control in the presence of the other is not based simply on fantasied aggressions or attack or hurt. Humiliation tends to be about genuine deficits and to feed on itself.

Mario is provocative. He has incompatible views of himself, one as perfectly competent and merely misunderstood, and the other as genuinely damaged and in need of help. His provocativeness and cockiness in relationships where he is dependent put his employers and those in helping relations to him in a position where they must set limits, which humiliate him even further. His unacknowledged shame turns to rage (Lewis, 1971). When Mario's difficulties combine with his wife's pathologic propensity to disorganize and inflict shame, the tension in the system escalates to the point where the system flies apart, fails to offer security or a sense of specialness or power, and eventuates in violence.

This case, with its vulnerable spouses exerting an undermining effect on each other's integrity, demonstrates a type of marital bonding that is both unstable and dangerous. The spouses have a more ominous prognostic status than do those who can bond to form a stable, protective family system, even if that system comes at a high emotional cost. Persons who can become part of families with blame, pathologic preoccupation, or intimidating impulsive action as organizing transactions have a better prognosis than Mario and Anna do. These patients prognostically are closer to those who later in their careers as psychiatric patients present as solitary "borderline" patients with families that refuse to be involved with them (Lansky et al., 1983).

This point of view has enormous significance for an approach to treatment. Such patients have chaotic character pathology that does not in any real sense remit or become dormant. They attract equally chaotic mates to form unions that are both incohesive and dangerous. Interventions must usually be on many levels in this type of domestic violence. Protection of the victim and restraint of the violent spouse are obviously of first priority in the short run, but such measures as confinement in hospital or shelter fall short of addressing the long-term propensity each spouse has for reestablishing or recreating the same situation. These spouses have neither the cohesion of personality nor the ability to control themselves that are the prerequisites for learning from experience.

It is not possible to talk of definitive treatment strategies for these vulnerable and volatile people. Maneuvers designed to restrain the violent person or protect the victim must be combined with long-term nurturant therapeutic experiences that allow such vulnerabilities slowly to heal. Conjoint psychotherapy sessions should focus empathetically on the disorganizing effects of the couple's reactivity to each other. An intergenerational approach is decidedly useful in pointing to patients' reactivity to each other without shaming them (see Excerpt 3). With the degree of vulnerability and chaos present in cases such as these, a clear view of the difficulties and of the central role of shame is necessary for effective treatment strategies of any type.

11

Murder of a Spouse
A Family Systems Viewpoint

The difficulties in attaining a useful understanding of spouse abuse and domestic violence are compounded by the fact that systematic research is often done using methods that ignore or, at least, oversimplify the family systems viewpoint. Here I consider some systems aspects of a case of murder of a spouse in which the couple had been seen in a tape-recorded, brief conjoint interview two months before the husband murdered his wife.

In the hope of working toward a clarification of some systems aspects of the heightened reactivity that transcends the capacities of the marriage to restore a homeostasis that is calm or at least relatively safe, I will present a case report and a condensation of a transcribed brief interview with the couple. I hope to use this tragic illustrative case as an opportunity to think further about the regulation both of disorganization and reequilibration and of shame in narcissistically vulnerable families. The clinical contact was both brief and interrupted, and the case material was assembled retrospectively from documents and not from an evolving clinical involvement. Accordingly, my formulations on the psychological makeup of each of the spouses is quite tentative, and my conclusions more speculative than in discussion of mechanisms regulating emotional distance and shame. I do not presume to provide an "explanation" of the murder from a family systems viewpoint. However, I do hope, in spite of these limitations, that the line of thinking enhances the usefulness of a family systems perspective for the all-too-prevalent problem of spouse abuse and that questions may be raised about systems aspects of the case that are often ignored or passed over.

CASE REPORT

Mr. C, a 30-year-old, black male without prior history of psychiatric treatment, presented to a hospital outpatient clinic with complaints of depression and marital difficulties. He had beaten his wife on several occasions. He suffered from a hot temper, extreme jealousy, anorexia and weight loss, and some early morning awakening. He denied feeling either suicidal or homicidal. For five months, he had been living apart from his wife of one year, though the couple had had frequent contact. A conjoint session was scheduled, but he missed that session. He later admitted that he had picked up his wife, put a gun to her head, and threatened to kill her if she testified against him in an upcoming trial. The couple did attend a conjoint session the following day. Mr. C was hospitalized at that time.

Mr. C was the youngest of two children born to a wealthy, educationally aspiring family. He described his father as a stern disciplinarian and his mother as cold. He had no history of delinquent behavior as a youth. He had a head injury as a child, but did not lose consciousness. His medical history was otherwise unremarkable. He finished two years of college and spent five years in the military service, receiving promotions and an honorable discharge. He had begun a business after leaving the military service and was doing reasonably well. Before he met his wife, he had had no prior relationships with women other than prostitutes. He had become engaged to his wife after a very brief courtship. She impressed the outpatient evaluation team as demanding and sexually provocative. She was well-educated and successful in the business world. She had a 10-year-old son. Mr. C's parents did not like her and refused to attend the wedding. The C's marriage had been chaotic from the start. He had been arrested numerous times during the year for threatening his wife with guns, knives, and blunt weapons and for actual violence. The violence ended in temporary separation. The couple had a four-month-old daughter. Mr. C engaged in episodic heavy drinking on weekends.

The Interview

Shortly after Mr. C was hospitalized, the couple was seen conjointly in an interview that was part of a course in family evaluation for psychiatric residents. The interview took place in a conference room with interviewer and family at one end of the room and about a dozen resident physicians and ward staff onlookers at the other. The interview was about 40 minutes in length. The interviewer and students were told that the interview would be with a hospitalized spouse abuser and his wife; they had never seen Mr. and Mrs. C before. The couple appeared with their baby at the time appointed for the interview. Their appearance, demeanor, and behavior were in striking contrast to the expectations formed during the presentation. Mr. C was calm, soft-spoken, mild-mannered, and considerate. He was of medium size and build. He showed a solicitous, even nurturant attitude toward the baby and his wife and was courteous and thoughtful with the interviewer. Mrs. C exuded dominance and showiness. She was attractive. Her dress and bearing were sexually provocative. Her gestures were flirtatious, even seductive. in contrast to the onlookers' expectations that she would be protective toward the child, she chose a chair near the interviewer and placed the baby carriage next to her husband on the side of the room farthest from the audience. This positioned her between the interviewer and the audience—clearly in the spotlight during the interview. Her behavior, then, was powerful, preemptive, and sexualized; his, diffident, soft-spoken, receptive, and nurturant. These presentations of self seemed in striking contrast to the clinical concerns for safety of mother and child and the content of the interview.

> WIFE: (*looking at the audience*) Is this conference like this every week?
> INTERVIEWER: Yes. We see a family and try to select one that might profit from the interview. Is it all right to proceed? (*Wife nods in assent.*) (*to both*) Do you have any questions about how we proceed?
> HUSBAND: No.
> INTERVIEWER: There are the two of you here and the youngster four months old.

Mrs. C seats herself opposite and facing the therapist; Mr C, with the baby, is on the other side of the therapist.

> INTERVIEWER: Is there agreement between you about what the problems are?
> HUSBAND: I know what it is. It's me. I'm trying to correct it.
> INTERVIEWER: How do you see the problem?
> HUSBAND (*hesitant*): There's a misunderstanding. One side doesn't give in. Then I get physical. But she's abusive with her mouth.
> INTERVIEWER (*to the wife*): What were you thinking when he said that?
> WIFE: Maybe I can change my behavior so we can get along.
> INTERVIEWER: But tell me, from your point of view, what are the difficulties?

WIFE: Well—mistrust.

INTERVIEWER: What actually happened so that he is in the hospital, so that there are troubles in the marriage?

WIFE: He's jealous. He's outraged at a lack of attentiveness from me. If it was just that, it would be okay, but he gets violent.

INTERVIEWER: There has actually been hitting?

WIFE: Yes. He hurts himself and me and his parents. He's outraged. The last time it was over a phone conversation. He demanded to know who it was. We've been separated six months. I said I didn't know the person's address.

INTERVIEWER: What was going on with him?

WIFE: Ask him.

INTERVIEWER: I will, later, but I'd like to get your point of view. What do you imagine?

WIFE: That the man shouldn't have called. Men shouldn't call me.

Her overtly sexualized behavior during the interview at this time provides confirming counterpoint to the dialogue. She shames him by broadcasting sexual attentiveness and availability to others.

INTERVIEWER: You describe your husband as quite a tough customer. (*Looking over at husband with the baby.*) But I'm watching him take care of the baby. He seems to be very good at it, very caring. You describe rage and suspiciousness at your involvements. Am I understanding all of this?

WIFE: Yes.

INTERVIEWER: When did this all start?

WIFE: Oh, in August.

INTERVIEWER: How long had you known each other?

WIFE: Seven months.

HUSBAND (*interrupts*): No, four to five months.

INTERVIEWER: This the first marriage for both of you?

BOTH: Yes.

Interviewer inquires about their ages: wife is 29; husband is 30.

INTERVIEWER (*addressing wife again*): What attracted you to him?

WIFE: His personality. He's ambitious. I liked his personality; I liked making love with him. He wants to be a family man. We have fun. I felt open, like I could share. I liked him. We spent every day together and the nights together.

Mrs. C does not show more than superficial curiosity about why she was attracted to him. This is noteworthy, considering the yearlong history of frequent violent eruptions.

> INTERVIEWER: How long did you live together married?
> HUSBAND: Four to five months.
> INTERVIEWER: Then you separated. What led to that?
> WIFE: He frightened me. I'd leave the house to prevent altercations. I'd leave for a friend's house. He'd look for me. I told him I wasn't coming back. Then he felt depressed, like he had a nervous breakdown. He broke up things.

His violence can be seen as an effort to restore self-respect and prevent loss after such a "nervous breakdown." Mrs. C seems unable to comprehend the vulnerable aspects of her husband's personality and her effect on those vulnerabilities.

> INTERVIEWER: You certainly paint a picture of a rageful, jealous, explosive, volatile man. I don't know if your husband agrees. I'll ask him later. But I wonder if you see any way in which the relationship might have set him off.
> WIFE: No. Well, I shared things about other relationships. There were men in my past. I didn't think he was jealous. I lived with a man. I have a 10-year-old son. He didn't trust me. And after I was pregnant, his mother didn't like me. She didn't come to the wedding. When the daughter was born, she didn't come to the hospital. And then he started asking if I was pregnant by someone else. I'm a better person than that. I'm not just looking to leech onto him. Anyway, he is not in a financial position for that.

She speaks, apparently oblivious to the fact that she is shaming him.

> INTERVIEWER: Before I talk to your husband, let me find out a little bit about what your life was like before you met him.
> WIFE: Oh, I have a natural sibling and two half-sisters. My oldest sister is forty. My mother and father were each married previously. They're still married.
> INTERVIEWER: What was their marriage like?
> WIFE: Well, they were separated for 12 years. My mother and my father are much different. My father is agreeable; my mother's always trying to excel. My father's a comfortable man. He's secure. Didn't want to take chances, but my mother was very

ambitious. I saw changes in my mother when I was fifteen. She got into a career. She has a master's degree. My father's a blue-collar worker. They weren't on the same level.

The parental marriage evinces a discrepancy in capacities and attainments of husband and wife that is similar to that in the Cs' marriage.

INTERVIEWER: She was ashamed of him?

WIFE: Yes, but she was very comfortable with the security, too.

INTERVIEWER: Any idea how that marriage might have affected you?

WIFE: Oh, it would have if I'd have been younger. I wouldn't want to be in the situation with a person who's not of a common growth level. Not just for finances. It really affected my younger sister, though. She didn't do well in school. She's like in a shell. She didn't explore much. She's got a daughter. She's kind of complacent. My parents have recently moved back with each other. [She goes into detail about her college degrees and her subsequent successes in the business world.]

The interview points up Mrs. C's inability to link the impact of her family of origin to difficulties in her later life. She can see these connections in her sister's life.

INTERVIEWER (*to the husband*): You've been listening, and I notice you've been taking care of the baby very skillfully, and the baby is near you and not near your wife. It sort of doesn't match what I've been hearing about you. What had been going on in your mind while your wife was talking?

HUSBAND: Well, I'm listening to her evaluation.

INTERVIEWER: No, I mean, what were you feeling?

HUSBAND: Well, she left out a lot.

INTERVIEWER: So give me your side of it.

HUSBAND: Well, I admit it when I'm wrong, but she left out a lot of things. Why we separated.

INTERVIEWER: What's wrong with the marriage?

HUSBAND: Well, it's my uncontrollable temper, my jealousy. But it's both of us. Nobody backs off in the arguments.

His acknowledgment of rage and jealousy keeps attention on his anger, which makes him feel powerful The focus on his rage also hides the disorganization (fragmentation) and vulnerability (noted by his wife) that are sources of great shame for him. Interviewer asks for details.

HUSBAND: It's horrible. Mostly it ends in violence.
INTERVIEWER: What usually happens?

Wife attempts to interrupt with an objection, but the interviewer stops her and asks Mr. C to continue.

HUSBAND: Well, you want me to tell you a situation?
INTERVIEWER: Yes, something of what gets you going.
HUSBAND: She pushes my buttons.
INTERVIEWER: Can you be specific?
HUSBAND: Uh, yes. I had a court case going on. I assaulted her two months ago. I told her I was going to kill her. She had to go to the hospital.

Interviewer asks for details.

HUSBAND: Well, it's the lack of trust.
INTERVIEWER: You worry about deceit?
HUSBAND: She gives me reason. She doesn't always carry herself respectably.
INTERVIEWER: She comes on to men sexually?

This has been strikingly evident throughout the session itself in Mrs. C's dress, her posturing, and her overt seductiveness while talking to the therapist. These activities were going on at the same time that she talked about herself in the victim role.

HUSBAND: Yes, especially when she drinks. Our first altercation was about that. She had diet pills and alcohol. She was acting loose and flirtatious, going from one person to the other. Then she ended up with one person. First she said she knew him; then she told me she hadn't met him before.
INTERVIEWER: That would anger lots of men, but how about your anger?
HUSBAND: I try to control it.
INTERVIEWER: What do you understand about your anger?
HUSBAND: Well, I'm possessive.

Interviewer asks for details.

HUSBAND: There weren't any problems till we got married, really.

INTERVIEWER: Some people struggle with jealousy and suspiciousness, but do you ever wonder why most other men don't beat their wives?

HUSBAND: Well, they're in different situations. If she says I might take a little situation and blow it up to something really explosive, I might hit her.

INTERVIEWER: Sometimes people are more liable to blow up if the world when they were growing up has been very uncertain for them or if they haven't been able to rely on people. Was it that way with you? What were your early years like?

HUSBAND: Well, I was mischievous like all small boys. My family was pretty supportive.

The interviewer's invitation to consider the sources of his vulnerability frightens Mr. C. He had elsewhere been more frank about dysfunction in his family of origin. Interviewer inquires.

HUSBAND: My parents are still married. I've got a sister thirty-two.

Interviewer asks for details.

HUSBAND: She thought I got all the attention.

INTERVIEWER: Who were you closest to when you were growing up?

HUSBAND: My mother.

INTERVIEWER: What was she like?

HUSBAND: A very kind lady.

The resident physician's presentation preceding the interview noted that Mr. C had described his mother as cold and uncaring and the parental marital tensions as severe.

INTERVIEWER: And your father?

HUSBAND: He disciplined me. I wasn't a battered child, but he hit me in the backyard, hit me pretty hard.

INTERVIEWER: Was he out of control?

HUSBAND: At times.

INTERVIEWER: At all like you?

HUSBAND: No.

INTERVIEWER: What was your parents' marriage like?

HUSBAND: Lots of problems. I remember when I was two or three, they were arguing, they were fussing. I don't really know about what. My father hit my mother a few times. But there weren't policemen or yelling.

His comments suggest, but minimize, abusiveness by his father, and a chronic marital rift often with Mr. C in the middle of marital tensions.

INTERVIEWER: (to wife) What were you thinking when your husband was talking?
WIFE: Boy, I try to avoid pushing his buttons.

She seems unable to empathize with her husband as one who is constantly beset by fearful and disorganizing experiences.

INTERVIEWER: We're near the end of the time we have and I have to move along quickly. Is there anything either of you feel that's been omitted that would give us a better understanding of things? Has this been a safe place to talk?
WIFE: Well, he's had time to rest in the hospital. He's not violent. I'm glad he's here. He's concerned with legal things. (Interviewer inquires.) A rape charge.
INTERVIEWER: That's a serious charge.
WIFE: Well, he didn't do it, but he never knows what his future's like.
INTERVIEWER: Are you tending to minimize how upsetting things are, talking about his treatment as though it were resting up. But you've told us about rape and about guns. Isn't that out of control and frightening?

Wife comments that it's hard to talk in a large group. The interview concludes because of time limitations.

The general impression of those present concurred with the resident physician's concern that the danger of violence was considerable. This concern was conveyed to the couple and to Mr. C's parents.

Mr. C was well liked by the hospital staff; He was consistently calm and polite. His antidepressant medication helped stabilize his sleep. He did leave the hospital for a weekend and got drunk but returned without doing any harm. As his court date approached, he pressed for discharge and finally ran away from the hospital. Continued efforts to reach him were not successful. He was discharged from treatment and did not return.

The subsequent course of events became known in retrospect from Mr. C's court testimony. Mr. and Mrs. C had planned for his leaving the hospital without medical concurrence. They had signed a lease on an apartment together, but, when he left, they did not live together. They fought frequently. Withdrawn and depressed, Mr. C moved back to his parents' home. About six weeks after he left the hospital, he took his daughter away from day care. Mrs. C reported the kidnapping to the police. An emergency team took him into custody near his parents' home. He was released. Planning to kill himself, he bought a gun. The following day, Mrs. C phoned him, and they agreed to try a reconciliation. He drove to her office that day and encountered her leaving accompanied by another man. He shot and killed her and then went to his parents' home and threatened suicide. His parents convinced him to turn himself in.

FAMILY SYSTEMS CONSIDERATIONS

Mr. C's history includes a number of features common in the history of men who batter: alcohol abuse, a history of witnessing violence between his parents, and a history of being abused as a child (Fitch and Papantonio, 1983). He also showed findings compatible with a neurologic injury: headaches, a history of head injury, and computer-tomogram evidence of a two-centimeter deficit lateral to the left ventricle—perhaps a limbic system injury, making him more vulnerable to sustained rage. Nonetheless, his history and organic vulnerabilities do not explain the murder. No psychological or neurological profile of the murderer can obviate the need for an understanding of what factors held the marital system together and what tore it apart. For a truly explanatory account of the murder, the interlocking of the personalities of the two spouses must be considered. The actual case material, pieced together as it was outside of the context of unfolding conjoint treatment, is not complete enough to offer us a satisfactory understanding of the murder. However, the case does provide an opportunity for reflection and inquiry about the systems aspects of escalating domestic violence ending in murder.

Why did the couple continue their tortured relationship after numerous acts of violence and after warnings from Mr. C's parents, from police, and from outpatient and impatient treatment teams? Why did they stay involved or seek out renewed involvement after the separation? Why did he erupt into violence? Why did she provoke him? The data do not allow definite answers, but the systems aspects of this case—the "fit" between the spouses in the system—permeate deeply to the individual psychological makeup of the spouses. The powerful collusive mechanisms that regulate shame, guilt, and sexual excitement so combined as to make the fatal outcome seem predictable if not inevitable at the time the couple were seen together.

Seen from the point of view of *regulatory mechanisms*, the marital system is one in which there was a failure of adequate regulation of hostility, narcissistic vulnerability, and optimal distance between the spouses. As a regulatory system that could not correct itself—even to avoid murder—this marriage had specifically lethal features that are not present in marriages in which other types of pathological regulation of narcissistic equilibrium are predominant.

The regulatory mechanisms in chaotic, dysfunctional family systems, including those with violence and intimidation in the picture, regulate emotional distance and discharge of affect. As noted previously, they include overt verbal conflict (or blame), emotional absence (or pathological preoccupation) that often precipitate outbursts in other family members, and intimidating impulsive action. I have categorized these "mechanisms" by reference to dominant manifest transactions or observable relationship patterns. More than one mechanism may be present in a family. These disrupting features—ones that family members complain about—prove, on scrutiny, to be surface manifestations of highly complex, collusive, defensive operations that preserve the family homeostasis and keep the family, especially the marital system, from being flooded with overwhelming shame. Thus, the surface disruption, especially if it is dramatic and fearful, may conceal the more covert regulatory and conservative function of the entire process.

Blaming transactions are usually a response to a disorganizing narcissistic disturbance (however subtle) in the marital equilibrium. The episode of blaming reestablishes, however unpleasantly, the boundaries of the marital dyad (Chapter 4). These utterances typically attribute great powers and neglectful disregard or persecutory intent to the blamed person, who presumably could have behaved reliably or soothingly for the blamer if only he or she would. Such transactions do not expose the blamed person as being out of control and inadequate or basically defective. Thus, blaming transactions, excoriating though they may seem, are rarely shaming.

Pathological preoccupation typically takes place in a context that accepts the preoccupied person's emotional absence as justified by pursuits vocational or creative that will increase the family's narcissistic completeness and which will diminish, rather than amplify, the family's sense of shame (Chapter 5). Such emotional absences often trigger outbursts in other family members.

Violent or intimidating impulsive action, considered from the standpoint of its interpersonal setting, typically occurs in response to a change in narcissistic equilibrium in the family system that had amplified shame in the person who subsequently became violent. For example, the (subsequently) violent person may feel flooded with shame when he or she loses control or status within the family, either by his or her decline, physically or financially, or through the maturation or independence of other persons in the family system. in such cases, "violence" usually means intimidating and threatening, often indirectly communicated, and serving as an attempt to restore the equilibrium that had been recently lost with the change in family homeostasis (Chapter 6).

In other cases of family violence, more volatile narcissistic equilibrium in the marriage is upset by continual overt shaming on the part of one of the spouses that provokes physical attack from the other (Chapter 10). The equilibrium in this type of marriage is more fragile because the spouses are more fragmentation-prone and filled with shame. The symptomatic disruption does not serve (as it does with blaming, pathological preoccupation, and the milder forms of intimidating impulsive action) to reequilibrate the system and give the violent person some control over loss and humiliation. The shaming transaction regulates the narcissistic equilibrium of the person doing the shaming. it attempts to compensate for the disorganization due to shame, rage, and envy, but it aggravates intrafamilial cycles of impulsive action to a continual, mounting, deviation-amplifying pattern of interaction that has a high likelihood of escalating beyond panic induction, threats, and intimidation to the point where actual harm is done to persons.

The Cs' marriage was of the latter type, that is, overt shaming restoring the narcissistic equilibrium of one spouse (Mrs. C) but capsizing that of the other (Mr. C), who, in turn, reestablished his feeling of narcissistic intactness by violent acts. His unacknowledged shame turned to rage, then to violence (Lewis, 1971). The individual regulatory mechanisms served to amplify shame-violence cycles without reaching a calm equilibrium. The "regulation" accomplished by her shaming and by his violence, then, concerned their individual tensions only and not the overall homeostasis in the family. The marital system was so constituted that marital conflict escalated. Concern for the safety of the spouses and of the child were not effective deterrents to this escalation.

This conceptualization of conflict escalation due to unacknowledged overt shaming in the marital system raises many questions about the system and the individuals that compose it. How did the individual vulnerabilities and defensive needs of the spouses and the reciprocal interaction of their ways of regulating tension and self-esteem contribute to a pattern of repetitive physical violence? Why did they choose each other? Why should a man with such vulnerabilities choose a woman who was so powerful, provocative, and discontented? Why did she, successful in business, a strong, attractive woman with advanced university degrees, choose a man so weak and volatile? What accounts for the failure of regulation in the marriage? As noted earlier, the individual pathology was too profound: his propensity for disorganization, his sense of shame, his relentless attachment to her, her sadism, her sense of guilt and need for punishment. The regulators of intense turbulence—shame, rage, guilt, sexual excitement—were more organized toward managing individual tensions (reduction of displeasure) than toward accommodating to the reality of the ever-mounting danger (modification by reality). Perhaps the system was overburdened by the presence of a small child and the increased risk of each spouse's feeling excluded from a parent-child dyad with the baby and the other spouse. The material provides more opportunity to follow lines of thinking from a systems perspective than it provides answers. Nonetheless, we can question and speculate.

Consider the issue of *mate selection*. Shame was a major source of Mr. C's difficulties. His overriding sense of shame derived from many sources: his history of abuse, his witnessing parental marital violence, his upbringing in a chronic marital rift, constitutional and, perhaps, acquired neurologic vulnerabilities, the legacy of which was a profound and sustained humiliation proneness and a vulnerability to narcissistic disorganization. His violent response to such disorganization was probably related in some way to his abuse at his father's hands and the abusiveness he witnessed in his own parental dyad. His violence was a reaction to that humiliation. But why did he choose and remain attached to a woman who shamed him? The factors operative in mate selection are another enigma that would not be solved with more knowledge of Mr. C's past. Why didn't he marry a calm, nurturant woman who might have helped him deal with his vulnerability to narcissistic injury? Why, instead, did he marry a flamboyant, powerful, overtly shaming woman who "pushed his buttons" and humiliated him sexually? Did he, perhaps, feel the need to be seen with a sexually provocative woman for purposes of buttressing a sense of shame and inferiority about himself as a sexual competitor?

Mrs. C's choice of husband is equally enigmatic. Attractive, accomplished, successful, and seemingly confident, she selected a man with a limited capacity to attain her level of poise or accomplishment. Her marital situation seems, curiously, to repeat significant aspects of her mother's marriage—to a basically nurturant man who could not keep up with her academically, vocationally, or sexually. Whether her choice reflected her fear or guilt at the prospect of surpassing her mother in her marriage, or whether it provided an opportunity for her to project her own sense of shame and to exercise her sadism, castrativeness, and destructiveness, is not clear. Her behavior, certainly on the surface, was that of a woman intent on destroying her husband and inviting, and eventually suffering, destruction of herself. Whatever the role of unconscious guilt and outright sadism in Mrs. C's makeup, those factors certainly combined to make her sexual humiliations relentless, even in the face of clear and repeated danger.

What is the role of *sexual excitement* in the dysfunctional system? The case material is too limited to shed light on the role of sexual excitement in the marital choice. Was aggressive excitement (in both) in some way a condition for sexual excitement? He was a passive, quiet man who was filled with rage. Perhaps her sexually sadistic shamings provided him with an opportunity to reverse and triumph over his basic sense of shame in the act of violence. This opportunity may have created conditions under which sexual excitement could be felt and expressed. Her release of sadism provoked attacks that may have filled her with masochistic excitement (perhaps, in itself, a source of shame) and still left her feeling powerful in the relationship.

Finally, what strain on the marital equilibrium was posed by *the baby*? The degree of Mr. C's pathology was such that any threat to the intactness of the marital dyad caused him disorganization and feelings of rejection, loss, jealousy, and shame. There may have been an element of displacement (from rage at the baby) in his angry jealousy directed at his wife's other involvements with men. Furthermore, her feeling trapped in the mothering role might have stimulated a burst of (displaced) rage and attack and an (also displaced) urge for freedom from the marital dyad. Marital conflict, however chaotic its surface features, is commonly a method of sealing the marriage off from feared interlopers. The continuing struggles may have been aggravated by the couple's response to the intrusion by the new baby.

The couple is hauntingly reminiscent of Don José and Carmen in Bizet's opera. The heretofore obedient soldier is fascinated by the flamboyant and provocative Carmen, who, in turn, excites and provokes men as a toreador does bulls. Don José cannot find delight in his one-time sweetheart, the peasant girl, Micaela, who carries messages from Don José's mother and wants no more than a quiet, settled marriage to Don José. Don José is destined to kill, and Carmen, to give herself up to be killed. In the famous scene in Act III, Carmen looks at the fortune cards and sees death as her fate.

The systems aspects of the C's leave us with the same sense of tragic destiny as does Bizet's opera. The power of the opera revolves around the inevitabilities of the choice. Why does Don José not choose Micaela? Why does Carmen go to meet her death outside the bull ring rather than staying inside to watch her toreador lover, Escamillo? Exactly the same enigma about the couple's bond to each other is raised by considering the systems aspects of the case.

The Cs' marriage was an extreme version of a marriage characterized by deliberate, overt shaming and violent, impulsive action that could not reach an equilibrium based on restored narcissistic balance or on marital breakup. It escalated to the point of murder. Neither Mr. C's overwhelming vulnerability nor Mrs. C's relentless provocativeness, nor the overriding strength of the attachment, could be modified by forces inside or outside the marital system. In cases such as these, specific systems aspects of the regulatory mechanisms and the forces of attraction and destruction that are being regulated must be clarified and must be a central focus in any sustained approach to family violence.

12

Shame and the Problem of Suicide
A Family Systems Perspective

In this chapter I attempt to put forward a treatment philosophy emphasizing the centrality of a family systems perspective in an approach to the suicidal patient. My focus is on the presumption that generative and reciprocal human attachments are essential to a sense of well-being and that the suicidal predicament is often precipitated either by threats to significant attachments or by exposure of the fact that the types of attachment the suicidal patient is capable of sustaining (or has coerced by suicidal activities) are neither generative nor reciprocal. In either case, the suicidal patient becomes flooded with shame. Shame is the emotion that signals either the loss of meaningful bonding or the awareness of the impossibility of bonding in a meaningful, generative way rather than an infantile one. Shame in this sense is both the premonitory danger signal and the catastrophic end-stage of narcissistic wounding.

In retrospect, the suicidal person's initial account of his or her difficulties is often seen to be constituted so as to minimize that person's sense of shame. The suicidal individual speaking in isolation from his or her interpersonal context is motivated, consciously or unconsciously, to portray his or her difficulties in ways that overlook discontinuous, dissociated, or split-off states and unacceptable behaviors accompanying these states, for example, rageful losses of temper; bouts of blaming; states of greed-tinged expressions of entitlement; demandingness; or claims of having been exploited, ill-used or cheated on the one hand or by emotional disconnectedness or withdrawal on the other hand. Many sorts of impulsive action take place in dissociative states. These include self-harming acts such as

195

ingestions, slashing or acts of violence, and behaviors that intimidate or control others under the threat of violence or impending suicide. Dissociative episodes often induce panic and a sense of responsibility in others and thereby serve to hold relationships together. But the nature of this type of relationship is fundamentally infantile and generates overwhelming shame when the patient is made aware of his or her methods of bonding to others (see Examples 1 and 2). Accordingly, patients' styles of holding onto close relationships tend to be underplayed, rationalized, omitted in their accounts of their activities, or covered over by protestations of remorse over transgressions.

The narrative of the patient in isolation undergoes a "secondary revision" (Freud, 1900, p. 489) that may leave the clinician with a symptomatic picture suggesting that the patient's "suicidalness" is a free-standing state, a symptom, or a straightforward manifestation of depression or other kind of psychic pain rather than being an interpersonal event reflective of disruption in the narcissistic equilibrium of family system, past or present. This secondary revision is, of course, a defensive process in the service of avoiding shame. I stress this point because I believe that such "revisions" become potentially disastrous when they dovetail with the widespread failure among clinicians to recognize and appreciate clinical manifestations of shame. When shame is unacknowledged or bypassed, the result is likely to be rage directed inward or out (Lewis, 1971).

The line of thinking put forward here presumes that early experiences with the family of origin of the suicidal patient determines, to a greater extent than most patients acknowledge, the capacity for consistent generative attachment to close persons in adult life. Difficulties dating back to the family of origin and their current manifestations are often rationalized by the suicidal patient, whose narrative is woven so as to deny the significance of the impact of early upbringing on later attachments and to represent the current lack of contact with family as merely circumstantial or due entirely to the family's rejections or neglect.

The final pathway for narcissistic mortifications that precipitate suicidal crises of many, if not most, suicidal persons is *exposure, or fear of exposure, of factors within their psychological makeup that render them, for internal—not external—reasons, unable to have close relationships, or to have them only on fundamentally infantile, rageful, controlling and, hence, shameful terms.* Shame—not guilt, depression, anger, stress, or unspecified psychic pain—is not only the most significant affect for the clinician to consider with the suicidal patient, but also the most difficult to comprehend and the one that tends to be most veiled, masked, or bypassed in both the family process and the therapeutic situation.

Human beings in general experience turbulence if supportive persons are not in an optimal range of closeness but are either too close or too far away. If this turbulence exposes them as too needy or inappropriately dependent on others for cohesion, they will also feel ashamed. Suicidal patients, who are extremely sensitive to both overregulation and abandonment by supportive persons, are flooded with shame if a less than optimal distance is maintained. It is an important clinical characteristic of many suicidal patients that this optimal distance of comfort from supportive persons is both narrow and rigidified.

The treatment approach sketched in what follows is intergenerational and informed by a perspective on shame that I have found underrepresented or outright missing in the literature on suicide, even that comparatively small body of work on suicide and the family (Tabachnick, 1961; Blath, McClure, and Metzel, 1973). The case material is presented to illustrate the nature of the suicidal patient's bond with supportive intimates and the presumption that exposure of the nature of such a bond generates intense shame. I have not attempted to illustrate explicitly either the subjective experience or the verbalization of shame.

SHAME

Suicidal patients from a family systems perspective are people whose significant bonds to intimates have either become acutely jeopardized or exposed as chronically doomed to failure, for example, because of repeated losses of control, overwhelming self-absorption caused by unremitting psychiatric illness, or habitually intimidating styles of relating by threats of suicide or violence. The final common pathway of these predicaments is a *threatened awareness of one's loss of the capacity for intimate bondings due to defects in the self*, that is, due to shame and the exposure of a self whose preexisting sense of shame hitherto been buried in intimate relationships but now is threatened with exposure.

Understanding the suicidal patient from a family systems point of view, and in particular family systems factors favoring both the generation and masking of shame, is the first step toward understanding what the patient is fundamentally ashamed of and why the patient's narrative usually tends to minimize that shame.

Shame is a signal of disruption in relationship bonds set off not only by unempathic or rejecting activities of supportive persons, but also by *endopsychic awareness of one's repeated proclivities to detach from, overreact to, or destroy relationships* by any of a variety of characterological traits. These include neediness, greed or demandingness based on a sense of entitlement (Example 1, to follow), or control of objects through intimidation of violence or suicide (Example 2). Relationships are also imperiled by distancing maneuvers: emotional withdrawal, or intolerance of intimacy or closeness, rationalized or otherwise, burdened both by the inattentiveness and lack of reciprocity due to illness, physical or psychiatric, breakdown in the parental role, or other narcissistic breakdowns, for example, due to aging or bodily illness.

Shame results from actual or threatened exposure of aspects of a person's makeup that make him—he feels—unlovable, destructive, unable to have or tolerate close relationships. To feel shame is to be found out and seen as unworthy, unlovable, dirty, out of control, infantile, hurtful, inadequate. It is the failure that comes from what one *is*, of the self rather than from what one *does* to hurt others (Wurmser, 1981).

Shame in psychoanalytic terms is a superego anxiety, that is, a warning of impending narcissistic danger, signaling the danger of exposure that would risk social bonding. Shame is a public emotion that is easily hidden or masked by other emotions.

The assumption is often made that prominent affects or emotional states other than shame are central to the suicidal predicament. Depression, guilt, psychic pain, and anger have all been considered to be primary sources of suicidal anguish. I submit that these emotional states play a secondary role in the suicidal patient and that the primary emotional mortification is due to shame. Shame, however, is usually masked or hidden behind depression, guilt, psychic pain, anger, or anxiety-ridden states of turbulence.

Depression is the emotional state most commonly and intuitively linked to suicide. But it is unlikely that suicidality results from depression itself as opposed to the patient's shame over his or her depressive preoccupations, disattachments, dysfunctions and being a burden within a supportive relationship. That is, *patients are ashamed about being in a relationship burdened by their depression*, very often because depression could not be tolerated early in life (Stolorow, 1985).

Guilt is an emotion much more easily conceptualized than shame is. Understood as anguish over transgressions, fantasied or real injuries to the other, guilt is less upsetting to confront than is shame. Guilt has to do with real or imagined transgressive *actions* that harm another person. Shame concerns *the self*. It is a public emotion. It results from being exposed as inadequate, destructive, dirty or unlovable (Erikson, 1950). In the therapeutic setting, shame is a constant and real risk.

Many inexplicable bouts of rage and upset result from unacknowledged shaming in the therapeutic process (Lewis 1971). Patients feel guilty about hostility or fantasied (or actual) attack, conscious or unconscious, on their loved ones. They feel *ashamed* of being exposed as dependent on the very persons they attack—so enraged are they about the dependency that they attack their loved ones in order to restore a sense of narcissistic equilibrium. It is implicitly assumed in formulations involving guilt that the patient's concern is for the object rather than for the view of self among others and that the main source of mortification by guilt is *having hurt others*. Mortification by shame concerns *being exposed* as one who is nasty and attacking and at the same time fragmented and dependent. Formulations based solely on guilt tend to attribute more cohesion to the personality of the suicidal patient than is usually warranted (Kohut, 1971).

Psychic pain is often adduced as a major determinant of suicidality (Himmelhoch, 1988). We do not have adequate words to describe the experience of acute schizophrenic or manic-depressive turmoil or other sorts of psychic anguish, and we too often assume that these forms of agony in isolation explain the patient's suicidality. The more common situation is that self-absorption, defective ego strength, or failure to perform a generative family role produces shame that leads to suicidal feelings (Example 1). I argue that the pain of the suicidal patient is quite specific and involves shame, or the futility of meaningful bonding, and not just inchoate agony.

Anger is another emotion commonly regarded to be a source of suicidality. Again, close examination of clinical situations in which anger in the suicidal patient seems to be directed inward usually reveals that the suicidal person is ashamed of dependent attachments and of being revealed and exposed as highly dependent on the person at whom he or she is so angry. That is to say, shame, particularly unacknowledged shame, precedes the rage (Lewis, 1971; Scheff, 1987). This type of rage is at a dominant other who regulates the narcissistic equilibrium or emotional security of the patient, so that the anger serves not just to harm the object, but also to *expose* the patient as both needful of narcissistic supplies and rageful at the source of them.

Suicidal crises, then, reflect a narcissistic breakdown, a collapse and exposure. It is important to realize that clinically we are usually dealing with bypassed shame. The suicidal patient usually relies on bonds that are perpetuated on a basically shameful level. That patient with an already acute sense of shame, derived from either illness or early family upbringing, becomes threatened with exposure and loss of meaningful, albeit infantile attachments that help mask the shame. Bypassed shame was exhaustively studied by Lewis (1971, 1987). Such unacknowledged shame has a great deal to do with generating hostile dependency and envy (Berke, 1987). Theoretical discussions of hostility and envy usually overlook the significance of shame in the clinical picture.

If shame is understood, it becomes easier for the clinician to evolve a picture of the human psyche as much more fluid than the suicidal patient would like to see or to remember. Bypassed shame deriving from early familial developmental defects predisposes the vulnerable person to require coercive and infantile bond formation in adulthood, that is, to form collusive relationships that mask shame but also become a source of shame when the nature of the bond is exposed (Examples 1 and 2). The precariousness of these relationships is often the key to understanding suicidal crises in shame-ridden patients, especially if it is understood that the suicidal patient's *method* of bonding to, or controlling, objects is very often by unacknowledged coercion or panic induction. It may also take the form of dovetailing with neurotic needs of intimate others in collusive relationships. These relationships, which are based on pathological projective identification (Ogden, 1979), are more organized around avoidance of shame than are more mature relationships. Thus when the patient's methods of binding relationships are exposed, shame becomes overwhelming and the bonding becomes much more precarious (Example 1). I am referring here to the kind of situation that one finds in the families of chronically intimidating suicidal or violent patients or in patients with hostile dependent relationships characterized by shame and envy. When the infantile nature of such relationships is exposed, the bonding is often eroded.

These considerations have very important implications for the treatment situation, because suicidal patients will often induce or provoke a type of relationship in the treatment setting that is similar to the unstable bonds found in their families of origin or families of procreation (Lansky, 1982a; Schwartz, 1979). If, in fact, the patient's account of the suicidal predicament is revised in accordance with defensive needs to avoid or minimize shame, the treatment situation is at risk for two serious difficulties. First, what has been repressed in the narrative is likely to be acted out in the treatment situation. And, second, unacknowledged shame generated by the intensely ambivalent dependency within the treatment situation is likely to generate rageful or envious attack on the supportive relationship (see Example 1 for both these features).

The suicidal patient's shame usually comes from either of two sources. The patient suffered early familial trauma that powerfully affects mate selection and predisposes adult familial bonding to collusive dependent bondings that attempt to minimize shame (and of which the patient is additionally ashamed) (Examples 1 and 2); or the suicidal patient has an overt psychotic illness that makes his standing in the family precarious. In the first type, the patient is ashamed of self, and in the second, the family is ashamed of the patient, or at least so the patient fears.

CLINICAL EXAMPLES

A Man without a Family

Example 1. A 32-year-old man was admitted to the Family Treatment Program desperate and voicing suicidal feelings within a general aura of intense emotional turmoil. Despite his ragefulness, his protestations of misery had a vulnerable quality about them that drew caretakers to him. He had no job. He represented himself as unable to work because of his general propensity to become upset or become enraged. He had recently been discharged from another psychiatric hospital. He had spitefully slashed his wrists and forearms on the day of his discharge. He acknowledged that he had gained some benefit from that hospital stay but protested that he was discharged under unfair circumstances.

He described his upbringing in a family that was ridden with chaos. His mother divorced his father when he was three. His father died in an automobile accident. When he was six, his mother married a sadistic and violent man who, in the patient's opinion, eventually drove his mother to suicide. The patient was (for unclear reasons) on poor terms with his siblings and felt that no relationship was possible with his stepfather.

He had been married and divorced twice. The first marriage ended because of his drinking. He had a two-year-old son from his second marriage. The second marriage had ended in tumult, and the patient said he had been denied access to his son because he had been violent and assaultive to his wife in defiance of a court order to stay away from her. In the hospital he voiced the fear of losing his temper in court or when talking to his wife and being put in jail for parole violations. He had the fantasy of going back to the Midwestern city where his in-laws lived and committing suicide in front of them.

He was a nice-looking young man who radiated enough pathos and vulnerability to draw people to him and protect him. He took every opportunity to portray himself as a desperate, suicidal person with no place to go. At first he could not move his attention, even briefly, away from his sense of hurt and rage at injustices done him. Then he began to talk about the extent and volatility of his rage. For instance, if cut off unfairly by a motorist on the freeway, he would follow the motorist off the freeway and start a physical fight. Any insult or lack of respect would ignite in him a blind rage.

He was placed on antidepressant medication, noticeably decreased in his volatility. He developed a strong relationship with his therapist and seemed to have some capacity for self-observation when he was not rageful. He was considered a candidate for a special extension in hospital stay arranged for patients engaged in meaningful psychotherapeutic work. There were mixed feelings about this extension among staff. Some staff members felt that his expressions of suicidal intent rather than his actual involvement in therapy prompted the extension of his stay. Nonetheless, he was allowed to participate in this program, which gave him some freedom from the usual ward activities.

The patient became increasingly arrogant in his relationship to the ward. He showed a grateful, compliant aspect of himself to his therapist, a competent but overprotective person. The patient called his therapist by his first name; got extra sessions and extra time from the therapist, who also intervened when he had difficulty dealing with the ward. He treated the rest of the ward staff in a high-handed and contemptuous fashion. On one occasion when he was away from the ward without permission, he came back in a rage and told one of the staff members that he had just purchased a knife. The therapist saw him privately, and the patient produced the knife and handed it to the therapist. The nursing staff, however, were upset both by the presence of a knife and by the special treatment the patient received. A serious staff split grew (Stanton and Schwartz, 1954). The therapist felt that things were reasonably well in hand because the patient had handed over the knife and calmed down. The nursing staff felt that the patient, high-handed, contemptuous, and manipulative, had engineered one special treatment after another.

Close to the time of his discharge, the patient's high-handed treatment of the ward escalated further. He missed required meetings and came and went as he pleased. The therapist tended to sympathize with his need to organize his life outside the hospital. The rest of the staff became enraged at his irresponsibility and contempt. The problem of splitting was discussed in staff meetings, and a workable, albeit tense, consensus was reached. When he missed a required meeting two days before discharge, the therapist decided that it was best to discharge him a day early rather than either let him be excused or restrict his privileges. The staff concurred, and the patient was discharged to outpatient treatment.

Returning to the ward for outpatient treatment, he did not speak to any of the staff other than his therapist, whom he called by his first name. He frequently asked to leave ward meetings to meet with the therapist.

The staff began to realize that the constellation of relationships that had unfolded on the ward had a great deal to do with why this man was so desperate and alone. His combination of seductiveness and contempt, of neediness and irresponsibility, projected an image of himself as isolated and rageful, prone to fall apart, and extremely suicidal. The staff found itself feeling responsible for his safety. The ward's assumption of responsibility for him seemed to relieve him of all responsibility for his own life. It seemed for a time that it was our worry, not his, that he would kill himself if dismissed from the hospital for misbehavior. At the very time that the staff seemed to have assumed responsibility for his safety, his activities split the staff into protectors and persecutors.

When this type of hostile dependency was viewed in the light of his seductiveness toward the therapist and the contempt for the rest of the staff, it became easy for us to understand why this man had been abandoned by his family and his previous treatment team. We came to appreciate that the divisiveness, protestations of entitlement, and irresponsibility emerging on the ward were probably typical of this man's envious response to caretaking relationships—which he desperately needed but which also filled him with shame that had never been acknowledged.

The exposure of this patient's inevitable tendency to turn every supportive relationship into the sort of tumultuous situation we saw on the ward resulted in unmanageable upsurges of shame, which, in turn, gave rise to his suicidal thoughts and actions. His intense neediness forced him into embracing dependent relationships that amplified his already great sense of shame. That shame generated envious attacks and splitting, which had destroyed relationships in the past and made him even more ashamed of his inevitable destructiveness in close relationships.

We were able to compare our understanding of his hostile dependent relationship to the ward with accounts that he had given on admission of his rejections by family and previous treatment situation. We came to appreciate how his account of his difficulties at the time of admission had repressed awareness of these shame-rage spirals. Since they were not acknowledged, they were not interrupted. The result was further escalation of his hostile dependent actions until his unavoidable rejection. His suicidal impulses followed his awareness of himself as one who inevitably attacked and destroyed relationships on which he desperately depended.

An Emergency Family Therapy Session

Example 2.   An emergency family session was held with Sue, a 25-year-old suicidal woman with a diagnosis of borderline personality; some features of her disorder suggested a Bipolar II Disorder. She had been admitted with a history of two serious overdoses of medication. As the time for her discharge neared, Sue announced to the staff that she had been suicidal the previous weekend but had gone on pass telling nobody at the hospital or at home. A family meeting was called. Ralph, her fiancé, her father, and her mother agreed to come. The parents had been divorced for many years. The mother did not appear for the family session, which was held with several staff members in attendance, including Sue's resident psychiatrist. The resident psychiatrist had recently returned from several weeks' vacation. Sue's discharge had been postponed.

The interviewer began the emergency session by noting the mother's absence. Ralph, Sue's fiancé, an unusually supportive man who seemed to be able to tolerate limitless upset and suicidal regression on Sue's part, noted that mother was probably scared. He was able to see in her what he could not, at that point, acknowledge in himself. Sue's father began by blaming the mother. He was the person with whom Sue lived. He provided material support but was unempathic and utterly unable to acknowledge any of his feelings about Sue's suicidal activities and the demands they made on him.

The therapist wondered if resentments concerning the divorce, now some 15 years in the past, may have had something to do with mother's not appearing. He noted, however, that, if this were true, mother would have put her comfort ahead of Sue's safety and security. He also emphasized his and the entire staff's anxiety about the situation and uncertainty as to what to do about it.

This acknowledgment of anxiety in the role of container was experienced with obvious relief by Ralph and by Sue's father. Ralph's thoughts immediately went to his own anxiety and suicidal thoughts when his parents' marriage was falling apart. Contemplating what to do about Sue, Ralph mused that he was not a professional. The therapist picked up on the remark by commenting that the ward staff were professionals with lots of experience with suicidal patients, but they were nonetheless frightened and uncertain about the situation. Having been through this experience with other patients many times before, the staff and the therapist in particular wanted the family to understand their own anxiety so that they would not become overburdened and wear out.

At this point Sue acknowledged that she was frightened that the family would wear out. Her father burst forth with an idealized view of his ability to provide any sort of care that she needed at any time. He seemed, at that point, not to be in touch with the helplessness, anger, and guilt he felt at bearing all the responsibility for Sue's safety, even though he had to work and obviously could not be on hand to watch her.

The therapist, again using his own feelings, empathized with that part of the containing function of the family that was frightened, worn out, resentful, that is, with feelings that were felt to be shameful and, accordingly, were disowned (and eventually projected) by Sue's familial containing system. The therapist remarked that Sue's needs when she announced that she was "suicidal" seemed quite unclear. What was expected of Ralph? Of her father? Of the hospital? Of herself? He also pointed to the manner in which Sue's communications amplified everybody's anxiety.

When Sue proclaimed that she was responsible for herself, the therapist noted that two impulsive suicide attempts certainly kept the family anxious about her potential for suicide. The second overdose had occurred after her discharge from a hospital when she and Ralph had gone on vacation and she had taken an overdose of medication. In the face of this behavior the family could hardly assign her responsibility for her own safety without considerable anxiety. At this point the father's anxiety, as well as his empathic failure, could be clarified when he made some remarks about how necessary it was that Sue be watched constantly.

The therapist was then able to repeat questions concerning what Sue needed from other people; about what she could be held responsible for; and about how she transmitted panic about the possibility of her suicide. Sue attempted to disown the fact that she spread such panic, but the therapist pointed out the manner in which she controlled people by inducing anxiety. He noted that her communications and actions would greatly raise anxiety about her safety and ensure her being taken care of in the short run but would predispose the family system to wear out sooner or later. Ralph and Sue's father were now able to acknowledge much more anxiety and even to grant that their wearing out eventually was something of a risk. This admission had been made possible only by the therapist's acknowledgement, made frankly and without shame, of the treatment team's similar anxieties with the containing function.

The collaboration could now begin without the pathological controlling defenses by which Sue established a bond to Ralph and her father. Once the family could acknowledge without unmanageable shame the risk of their being overburdened, wearing out, or resenting their obligations to Sue, then the relationship could be reformed on a more realistic basis that took fears and resentments into account.

This emergency treatment session proved to be pivotal. In a long and difficult course, Sue managed to work out a successful treatment collaboration with her father and with Ralph whom she later married. This session helped turn the containing alliance into a workable long-term relationship as opposed to a panic-ridden familial overregulation almost inevitably doomed to wear out. Such a relationship as the latter would be based on a type of control that would generate shame that if unacknowledged, would be likely to generate envious attack. If panic induction and control by intimidation were to continue and cause the relationship to wear thin, Sue would be at high risk to be left deserted, desolate, hopeless about herself, and at higher risk for a completed suicide (Maltsberger and Buie, 1974).

THE FAMILY

The suicidal person cannot be understood except within the context of intimate relationships. Only from a family-systems perspective can the states of mind of the suicidal person be understood as more than isolated phenomena portrayed in accordance with the patients' defensive needs.

In advocating a family-systems perspective, I am not making a simple etiological assertion or psychotherapeutic prescription, for example, that the family of origin always causes difficulties that predispose to suicidal crises, or that conjoint family therapy is always the treatment of choice for the suicidal patient, or that the reason for any one crisis is always to be found in the current familial predicament, or that the family should be contacted any time that the patient is seen to be actively suicidal. None of those propositions has universal validity, yet each should be considered and explored by the clinician faced with any suicidal patient, just as an internist seeing any gravely ill person will embark on a radiographic and laboratory workup and not just a physical examination before assuming that the clinical situation is clear.

I have come to adopt an intergenerational "container" model in viewing the suicidal patient (Lansky, 1981b). This simple model frames both the patient's needs and the role of the treating system such that *they can be usefully compared with other containing systems, past, present and future.* The container model, by realigning the clinical situation of the suicidal patient within a family-systems perspective, has proved enormously helpful in illuminating the origins of the patient's difficulties; in obtaining a clear appreciation of the extent and nature of the actual dysfunction; in preparing for psychotherapeutic exploration; and in managing acute, subacute, and chronic suicidal problems.

The family perspective also clarifies the determinants of the patient's sense of shame. Indeed, a major benefit of discussing the suicidal patient's containment needs from an intergenerational perspective is that such an approach mitigates the patient's immediate sense of shame in the therapy situation. The patient is better able to view himself or herself as the product of unfolding developmental processes over generations, thus as understandable and comprehensible, rather than as unacceptable, unlovable, and out of control. This approach minimizes the blame and contempt that often surround examination of the patient's chaotic affects and controlling maneuvers and does so without abrogating the patient's responsibility for his or her actions (Example 2).

Areas for family focus include the following:

1. *The family of origin as determinant of adult attachment behavior.* Accordingly, difficulties in the family of origin must be understood in order to understand these difficulties in later life. A close relative's suicide, especially that of a parent or having a parent, particularly a parent of the same sex, who was held in contempt is an important factor. Gross defects in nurturance, physical or sexual abuse, or involvement in pathological marital difficulties are powerful determinants of adult attachment behavior. Overtly preoccupied (emotionally distant) families or gross failures of empathy in the family system may be harder to detect on initial workup. Often the difficulties of a characterologically impaired suicidal patient can be understood as a response to being parentified or scapegoated or becoming the object of blame in the family of origin. Such pathological involvement in the parental marriage serves both to exploit a marital rift and also to gain some feeling of control over pathology in a parent or in the marriage. These patterns tend not only to endure but also to recreate themselves in choice of mate. Pathological involvements in the family of

origin limit the future patient's capacity to form adult bonds based on mutual generativity and reciprocity. These limitations are a significant source of shame. If this shame is unacknowledged, rage or envious attack of the shame producing bond frequently occurs.

2. *Dysfunction in the current family* arises from residual deficits from family of origin that often manifest themselves in self-absorption, blaming sprees, an inability to attend to or be empathic with others, emotional detachment, intimidating impulsive actions, hostile dependency, or envy. Adult relationships are frequently characterized by control of others by inducing guilt or by entering into collusive relationships that draw children into their wake. This type of family relationship is extraordinarily difficult to modify because of the enormous amount of protection against shame afforded by collusion.

When pathological forms of distance regulation have gotten out of control, the patient may be expelled from the family system, either the family of origin or the current family, or both. The patient may rationalize the rejection as unprovoked or, less commonly, as emanating from a malignantly intermeshed family process for which he or she carries a substantial responsibility. Such patients may say that they are ashamed to be seen by their children because they cannot control drinking, or that they are unwelcome after a long period of intimidating family with suicide threats or threats of violence, or that they are preoccupied, so self-absorbed with drug abuse that they cannot contribute to the family's emotional or material support.

Failure in a spousal, or especially in a parental role, is much more devastating than patients' testimonies might, at first, lead us to believe (Examples 1 and 2). So is retardation of the potential for individuation or separation from family posed by physical or psychiatric illness of any type (Example 1). In each of these types of infantile adult bonding or failures of bonding, exposure of the infantile nature of the bond floods the patient with shame.

3. *Even very brief contact may provide an estimate of the containing availability of the family of origin or the current family.* A phone call concerning the patient's predicament may reveal that the family containing system is solid and supportive; overeager and at risk of burn-out; or exhausted by the patient's excessive demands or exploitative or irresponsible behavior. Such rejection from the family often presages completed suicide (Straker, 1958; Rosenbaum and Richman, 1970).

Family psychopathology may be in evidence. For example, the family may be split, the divorced parents refusing to confer in the same room, even to discuss the patient's safety (Example 2). Or they may have become dispassionate or burned out, finally ignoring the patient's attempts at object control by intimations of suicidality.

4. Finally, the container model allows us to look at *erosive behavior in the treatment setting* and other social systems, such as previous marriages or jobs, that can be understood as isomorphic with situations that occur in current family systems or derivatives of predicaments in family of origin (Examples 1 and 2). The treatment team has, by these comparisons, the opportunity to scrutinize itself for countertransference derived reactivity to the patient—overregulation, withdrawal, blaming, overprotectiveness or failure to address intimidation by the patient (Maltsberger and Buie, 1974).

This family systems perspective assumes that there is within everyone a much more highly developed set of social emotions than is generally acknowledged. Failure to become a bonded, generative, giving, mature member of a family is narcissistically mortifying—much more so than suicidal patients usually admit, because of the shame those patients have at failing in these roles (Retzinger, 1991).

No schema or set of family therapy techniques can be put forward as sufficient to deal with the plight of the suicidal patient unless it provides an avenue for understanding the patient's basic experience of disruption, the emotions and states of mind accompanying turbulence in close past and present relationships. A family systems approach must be complemented by an appreciation of the suicidal patient's emotions and subjective experiences. Central to this appreciation is an understanding of shame and its relation to other emotions and to the vicissitudes of the intimate relations of the suicidal patient.

CONCLUSION

I have attempted to outline an attitude toward suicidal patients that places central importance on the disruption of meaningful, mature bonding. In so doing, I am emphasizing the predisposition to precarious or infantile bonding that results from serious psychiatric illness or from the effects of traumatic nurturance in the family of origin.

Shame, as both the *signal of danger* to meaningful bonding and the *end product of the breakdown of the capacity to bond*, is the most significant emotion in the clinical picture. Shame is frequently masked by other, more visible emotions or by revisions in the patient's accounts of the suicidal predicament. The clinician who understands the unique properties of shame will also appreciate that the interpersonal world both in the family and in the treatment situation is highly fluid. Suicidal patients are struggling with deficits that make meaningful bonding precarious; consequently, shame is a very real risk accompanying the inevitable exposure that takes place within the therapeutic setting. The therapist who understands shame will be better able to minimize the narcissistic wounding that results from the exploration of the sequelae of traumatic nurturance or major psychiatric illness on the suicidal patient's current abilities to form meaningful and enduring bonds, both in the family and in the treatment situation.

13

Escalation of Trauma in the Family of the Patient with Organic Brain Disease

"I'm humiliated beyond my understanding."
—Brain-injured Vietnam War veteran

A therapist or caregiver may, at first surmise, be drawn to think that to the family of a person who has organic brain disease trauma is a simple consequence of the neurologic deficit, that is to say, of the dysfunction caused by the brain lesion itself. Such a view, of course, would lead the therapist to be psychotherapeutically pessimistic inasmuch as the cause of the trauma is not dynamic and not reversible by psychotherapeutic or other means. Viewing the "trauma" as caused by the brain lesion, then, would leave the therapist with a scant arsenal of therapeutic techniques basically aimed at support and reassurance.

Another line of thinking, however, is that the traumatic situation in many such families is psychotherapeutically workable. This line of thinking derives from a conceptualization that emphasizes the centrality of unacknowledged shame in the escalation of conflict. This perspective also sees a significant portion of the therapist's task as surmounting his or her own feelings of futility and pessimism and making a thorough estimate of the dynamic factors involved in each case. These factors do not reside in the patient alone but, rather, in the interplay of the patient's defensive processes with those of the family.

Psychopathology in such cases is best viewed from a family systems, rather than a strictly neurological, perspective (Pasnau, Fawzy, and Lansky, 1981; Lansky, 1984b). The overall traumatic impact of psychopathology, as distinguished from simple neurologic deficit, is the result of the interaction of the patient's defenses—especially defenses against the shame of exposure of loss of cognitive integrity—with rigid and inflexible role assignments within the family. These combine into a familial collusion that escalates the traumatic effect of the deficit in two significant ways. First, the collusion, in opposing acknowledgment that a change has occurred in the family because of dysfunction in one of its members, makes the family's realistic adaptation to that change difficult or outright impossible. Second, the patient's shame when his or her deficits are exposed remains unacknowledged and undergoes transformations specific to bypassed shame. That is to say, it is manifested as anger, obstinacy, uncooperativeness, spite, or willful destructiveness, rather than as a manifestation of what has been called a "catastrophic reaction" to exposure of deficit (Goldstein, 1940).

My central thesis revolves around situations in which the family fails to recognize a catastrophic reaction as a reaction to exposure of deficit. The rigidity of family role assignments (that is, specific, preexisting family psychopathology) impedes the acknowledgment of shame; the actual disruption seen in the family of the patient with organic brain disease can be understood as a manifestation of escalated turbulence due to unacknowledged shame, not simply to neurologic deficit.

CATASTROPHIC REACTIONS AND SHAME

Goldstein's (1940) observations of patients suffering head injuries during combat in World War I convinced him that above and beyond deficits posed by the specific injury was the patient's vulnerability to a catastrophic response to exposure of deficit:

> Let us begin with the observation of the behavior of one of our patients in a task which seems simple. We give him a problem in simple arithmetic which before his sickness he would without any doubt have been able to solve. Now he is unable to solve it. . . . By simply looking at him we discover a great deal more than his arithmetical failure. He looks dazed, changes color, becomes agitated and anxious, starts to fumble. A moment before he was amiable; now he is sullen and evasive or exhibits temper. He presents a picture of a very much distressed, frightened person, a person in a state of anxiety. It takes time to restore him to a state which will permit the examination to continue. In the presence of a task which he can perform, the same patient behaves in exactly the opposite manner. He looks animated and calm, and appears to be in a good mood; he is well-poised and collected, interested, cooperative; he is "all there." We may call this state of the patient in the situation of success *ordered behavior*; his state in the situation of failure, *disordered or catastrophic behavior* [1940, pp. 85-86].

These catastrophic reactions, Goldstein observed, were gross and obviously disorganized at first; they later acquired more finesse and subtlety as the patient learned to avoid exposure of the deficit, for example, by avoiding certain experiences or by ever more subtle confabulations. Typical and florid manifestations of catastrophic response are an abrupt and fragmenting loss of self, integrity, and continuity, followed by embarrassment, anxiety, visible disruption, and, later, depression. Sequelae of these breakdown experiences are maneuvers designed to regain face, cover up the deficit, withdraw from social contact, or change the type of social bonding.

Initially, Goldstein's discoveries were acknowledged as having great significance for our general understanding of psychopathology. In recent years, however, neurologic and psychiatric thinking about disturbances in brain functioning has become reductionistic and technologically based to the point where the phenomena that Goldstein emphasized, along with most other interpersonal phenomena associated with organic brain syndrome, have been overlooked or relegated to the realm of epiphenomenon or artifact. Theorists who have attempted to localize the lesion for the catastrophic reaction have sometimes tended to miss the point that catastrophic reactions are a function of exposure and of a loss of integrity, not of a specific area of deficit (Heilman, Watson, and Bowers, 1983). They concern the self-before-others, not strictly a cognitive deficit.

Furthermore, Goldstein's groundbreaking discoveries were made before the mainstream of psychodynamic thinking began to conceptualize and integrate into theory the disorganizing experience of exposure before the other (or the internal image of the other) as deficient or defective. It was not until 1971 that Kohut and Lewis—working independently—published major works identifying such disorganized experiences as variants of narcissistic fragmentation or shame. Goldstein's observations stop short of linking these episodes and defenses against them with experiences of shame, and the more visible symptomatology as attempts to prevent, compensate, or readjust after disorganizing, shaming experiences. Nonetheless, what Goldstein actually described was the experience of and reaction to exposure of deficit or lack of integrity before-the-other. This conceptual advance draws our attention to the patient's reaction to specifically interpersonal trauma, not simply to neurologic trauma. The patient appears before-the-other as damaged, dysfunctional, and lacking in cognitive integrity.

Catastrophic reactions do not happen in the absence of the other. They are manifestations of trauma to the sense of self-before-others in situations involving sudden exposure of one's deficiencies. This reaction is more global, less specific, and more bound to interpersonal context rather than a simple reaction of frustration or embarrassment to cognitive deficit.

Catastrophic reactions, then, are reactions to the sudden loss of integrity of self as such; they are akin to what Kohut (1971, 1972) called fragmentation experiences and, more generally, acute shame reactions. As such, catastrophic reactions partake of the affective and interpersonal vicissitudes of shame in general.

Example 1. A 67-year-old retired military officer was admitted to a psychiatric inpatient service for workup of dementia and depression. His wife had requested numerous evaluations previously. Although each of these had shown pronounced dementia, she persisted in treating his condition as though it were uncertain.

On the ward, he was found to be a pleasant gentleman who spent his days watching television, especially the news, and reading the newspapers. His cognitive deficits were pronounced, but not global: he had a good fund of general knowledge; his remote memory was largely intact; he could retain much of what he read in the newspaper; but he could not perform calculations or reason abstractly. He was compliant and cordial, albeit slowed and somewhat muted in responsiveness.

The staff noticed flareups when his wife and son visited. He became stubborn and adamant in dealing with his provocative and disrespectful adolescent son, who seemed to have no compassion for his father's plight. His wife did nothing to make matters smoother between father and son. When his wife discussed problems about their substantial and complicated financial dealings, the patient became upset and angry, and then sullen and withdrawn. She reacted to this behavior as if it were stubbornness and rejection that confirmed his unreasonableness. Marital quarrels ensued and quickly developed into intense, angry, emotionally charged stalemates. These upset states had been one of the major reasons for the patient's admission to the hospital. (See ROLE OF THE FAMILY [p. 219] for a continuation of this case.)

SHAME

Working with detailed transcripts of psychotherapeutic sessions, Lewis (1971, 1987) noted not only a high prevalence of shaming transactions in therapist-patient transactions, but also the specific impact of shaming experiences that are not acknowledged. She noted, further, that shame acknowledged by the therapist tended to subside. Unacknowledged shame, on the other hand, was evidenced not only by the acute disturbance in the interaction, but also by the patient's anger and alienation, manifested as conflict, uncooperativeness, spite, or hostility. Lewis's pioneering work demonstrated convincingly that, although such hostile and uncooperative behaviors gave the superficial appearance of residing exclusively in the patient, they actually were markers of an interpersonal event, that is, shaming in the therapist-patient relationship that was unacknowledged and visible only in the manifestations of sequelae of unacknowledged shame.

The following case illustrates the therapist's handling of previously unacknowledged shame in an initial family interview with a patient referred for behavioral disruption, rage attacks, and depression.

Example 2. A 35-year-old, married, Latin-American combat veteran was referred from a neurologic ward after an evaluation of his seizure disorder and memory loss, which resulted from a head injury sustained in combat 14 years previously. The psychiatric referral was for depression and disruptive outbursts in the home. The patient turned repeatedly to his wife for help with the therapist's initial questions.

THERAPIST: I see you're looking at your wife.

PATIENT: Yes.

THERAPIST: She is a help to you. Now, I wondered what it is like for you and for the family for you to have this difficulty in your memory and to have seizures.

PATIENT: My friends make jokes, make fun of it. They don't understand. It's hard for me to carry on a conversation because I keep forgetting the words and my wife helps me a lot. It's been real bad.

THERAPIST: Do you feel that you have to rely on her too much?

PATIENT: I feel that I sometimes do, especially after a seizure. There's one day, two days, some time where I'm not myself I'm completely a different person and I do end up relying on her a lot.

THERAPIST: Well, is that okay, or do you feel upset or do you feel uncomfortable?

PATIENT: I feel ashamed, very ashamed.

THERAPIST: To have to rely on Dolores' help.

PATIENT: Well, it's from being from a Mexican background. The way I was brought up. I mean, making a living. You have to be the man of the house and that's that. The woman doesn't have too much to say. But with us it's a reverse role.

THERAPIST: So she does a lot?

PATIENT: She takes care of all of us. She takes care of the bills. She takes care of all the important things we have to do.

THERAPIST: Well, on one hand, you could say she's a very good wife, but then that doesn't make you feel much like a man.

PATIENT: Right. It makes me feel embarrassed.

THERAPIST: Embarrassed and not confident, maybe even ashamed. Does that have something to do with why you get depressed?

PATIENT: I think it does.

THERAPIST: Can you say something about that?

PATIENT: Well, I just think that somehow what happened to me should never have happened. I was wounded in Vietnam. Ever since then I've seen nothing but people letting us down, even when we have approached them for help. They told me I was an alcoholic. They told me because of my—I had one psychiatrist say to me—it was because of my Mexican background. I was having a hard time keeping up in the middle class because I struggled so hard. I used to get depressed.

THERAPIST: That was an upsetting thing to hear.

PATIENT: (laughingly) I'll never go see him again. (laughter) That's typical, though, of what we've been going through.

THERAPIST: So you felt criticized.

PATIENT: (faintly) Right. (louder) So throughout the years we have tried to support our family and maintain some kind of family respect.

THERAPIST: Have you been able to work?

PATIENT: No. Dolores helps me at work. The last job I had, for example, I used to work for the post office. She would push me and direct me, tell me which way I was supposed to walk and deliver the mail.

THERAPIST: So you had a route but you couldn't remember the route?

PATIENT: You're right. I would be walking and I would black out and I'd just keep walking straight ahead. She would get me by the back and push me to go where I was supposed to go.

THERAPIST: So you had to rely on her (patient nods) for a great deal, just to keep up with the household and pay the bills.

PATIENT: Not only that, but she has to . . . we have two kids.

THERAPIST: Two kids? How old?

WIFE: (after a long pause during which husband is silent) Twelve.

PATIENT: Twelve and fourteen.

THERAPIST: Now, when I ask you questions like that and you have to rely on Dolores for the memory, that's upsetting, isn't it?

PATIENT: Yes sir, it is.

THERAPIST: You looked as though your spirits really sank.

PATIENT: (very low voice) Yes sir. (long pause)

THERAPIST: And when you get depressed after a seizure, is it sort of like that, too?

PATIENT: Yes sir.

THERAPIST: So I guess you're pretty angry that you're not as whole as you once were.

PATIENT: I feel that. There's a lot of anger in me. I feel I've been given all the wrong breaks in life.

THERAPIST: What else?

PATIENT: My kids. My kids have not known me other than what I am. All their lives they've known me as a person that's had something wrong with him.

THERAPIST: They know their father with something wrong.

PATIENT: Right. And they know that *she* is the boss of the house, not me. She has to take care of everything. They know me at the times when I don't feel good. And let's say we're at a shopping center, somebody has to stay with me because now they think I'll walk off and get lost. That's how they know me.

THERAPIST: So they know a kind of father who is helpless.

PATIENT: Right, and yet people see me and say, "Well, hey, there's nothing wrong with you." But they don't know how I feel or what I think.

THERAPIST: Because you look okay and talk okay.

PATIENT: Right.

THERAPIST: And it doesn't look as though there's something wrong, but it's a humiliation, I take it, to be in your family.

PATIENT: It is. That's the word. I'm humiliated beyond my understanding.

THERAPIST: What do you do when you get humiliated? How do you act?

PATIENT: Sometimes I turn around and take it out on them.

THERAPIST: Like what?

PATIENT: Yell, scream, lock myself in a room and just lay down.

THERAPIST: Anything else?

PATIENT: Well, I start then thinking of taking my knife. (long pause)

THERAPIST: You mean committing suicide?

PATIENT: (very low voice) Yes.

THERAPIST: Have you just thought about it or have you made an attempt?

PATIENT: I attempted once, a long time ago. But the thought is always there, you know.

THERAPIST: Do you feel that they would like to be rid of you?

PATIENT: That's right. I feel if they didn't have me, they'd be a lot better off.

THERAPIST: That's a terrible feeling.

PATIENT: I honestly feel that.

The therapist turns now to the patient's wife and asks her what her experience has been like.

WIFE: Ever since he came out of the service, there have been bad times. The latest moods have changed him. He was a different person and everything. Before he went to Vietnam, he was so different.

THERAPIST: And you had been married only two years when this thing happened?

WIFE: Less than that. I knew him pretty well, you know. I'd known him since we were very young. Eleven. When he came back, he had changed a lot.

THERAPIST: What was the difference?

WIFE: Well, it depends on what. I mean, he got meaner. He was rougher, you know. Before he was so nice and calm and kind, and he came back and he'd just changed. At that time, I didn't know what was going on.

THERAPIST: You're not talking about just the seizures?

WIFE: No.

THERAPIST: Nor just the trouble with his memory. You're talking about his moods.

WIFE: Yes.

THERAPIST: And that's sort of what he said, too. But is there more than he's saying?

WIFE: No, it's everything he's saying, but it just sort of started developing. But I didn't know what it was at the time. They called it seizures and I didn't know what it was.

THERAPIST: He says he has to rely on you and he doesn't feel like the man of the house.

WIFE: He's been feeling like that more and more lately, you know.

THERAPIST: He feels that the children don't see him as a strong father who takes care of his own house. [Wife agrees.] And then he gets angry.

WIFE: He does a lot of yelling when he's so depressed.

THERAPIST: Is drinking in the picture too?

WIFE: It used to be, but not anymore.

THERAPIST: How did he stop?

WIFE: He just stopped, but he gets angry and yells. That scares me. For a while he stopped doing that, but now he won't, so he's started in again. And he just jumps out and (emphatically) *yells*. You know, to me, my body just reacts, you know. I just get frightened and I don't know what's going to happen next.

THERAPIST: The children have been with this all their lives?

WIFE: Yeah, but they don't understand. When they were small, something would happen to them and he would start yelling or something. I tried to take them and hide them or push them away, or put them in a room or some place where they don't see him. So they don't remember too much from when they were small.

THERAPIST: But they must wonder if their daddy is not like other daddies.

WIFE: They do. We try to explain, you know, but . . .

PATIENT: (interrupts) They're very helpful. They really help us a lot.

WIFE: But they don't understand.

PATIENT: They don't. They don't ask too many questions. They know we're not just laying down in bed. They know there's something wrong when we're in the bedroom.

WIFE: He's sick. I say, "Your daddy's sick."

PATIENT: And they know that. They know that Vietnam did it too.

THERAPIST: But can they understand why it is you don't remember things some of the time?

WIFE: Sometimes a little, but not very much.

PATIENT: We sort of accepted it now. Then I started and I started to stutter, and stuttered real bad, and they started calling me Porky Pig.

THERAPIST: Who?

PATIENT: My kids. They were just playing around.

THERAPIST: They thought you were just fooling around?

WIFE: No, it just started developing. It started developing and he started doing more and more. The kids just gave him a nickname, you know, and called him Porky Pig when he stutters.

THERAPIST: So how does it go for the marriage? The memory problems, the seizures, the way he feels about them, the way you feel about them. Doesn't it make for some difficulties in the marriage?

WIFE: Now.

PATIENT: Yeah. I accuse her. I hate to accept it, but sometimes I wonder if she could find something better than I am, you know when I start accusing her of doing things.

THERAPIST: You get frightened?

PATIENT: Right.

THERAPIST: That she won't be interested in you?

PATIENT: Right.

THERAPIST: Do you think she is hanging around with other men?

PATIENT: Right.

THERAPIST: Do you think she does?

PATIENT: No, but sometimes I just can't help but think about it. (falls silent)

THERAPIST: This is upsetting.

WIFE: It's just it upsets me a lot at times. I've known him for so long, I'm not about to give up on him now.

THERAPIST: It's taken a lot for you to be helpful all these years. (long silence)

WIFE: Well, it's very hurting when he starts accusing me of all this. My whole day, you know, is surrounded with him and coming up with taking care of the house and making dinner.

THERAPIST: So you can't get away from it. (Wife nods.) Does that affect your life together? Lovemaking, things like that?

WIFE: No, not really.

THERAPIST: How do things go sexually?

WIFE: Well, for a year and a half it wasn't. He was getting so depressed and everything, so much pressure at work, that there wasn't anything going on.

THERAPIST: While he was trying to hold onto the job, you mean he was too depressed to be interested in sex? (Wife nods in assent.) Is it okay to talk about this?

PATIENT: Yes sir.

THERAPIST: But things are different now?

WIFE: Well, a little bit.

PATIENT: Ever since I've getting this help, I've been feeling a more reassured. You know that.

THERAPIST: Have they been helpful to you a little more?

PATIENT: Yes, they have.

THERAPIST: So that's one of the reasons you wanted to come here to the family treatment program?

PATIENT: That's right.

This couple's ability to acknowledge and discuss painful sources of the patient's shame and the relative absence of pathologically rigid role assignments were important factors in the family's ability to adjust to the patient's deficits.

ROLE OF THE FAMILY

To understand adequately the escalation of neurologic trauma, in addition to considering the experience of *self* in the patient whose organic deficits are exposed, it is necessary to consider the other or others before whom this experience of sudden exposure takes place. The others are not only those in the therapeutic situation, of course, but also those in the family and in the community. If the manifest, traumatic familial disruption is understood to be in some part the result of shame or *exposure that is not acknowledged by the other*, it becomes apparent that factors in the family system that oppose recognition and acknowledgment of the sources of the patient's acute sense of shame will bypass shame, thereby greatly amplifying the traumatic impact of the original deficit.

Enumeration of the kinds of role rigidity in families would carry us beyond the scope of this discussion. For present purposes, it suffices to note that rigidity and inflexibility of role assignments per se pose opposition to the family's adaptive tasks and are indicators of family psychopathology. Furthermore, any such role assignment that dovetails with the patient's manifestations of bypassed shame—for example, being stubborn, tyrannical, imperious, arbitrary—will result in a collusion between the OBS patient and the family that continually bypasses acknowledgment of the sources of the patient's sense of shame, thereby locking the family system into an escalating state of magnified trauma.

Example 1 (continued).   The discrepancy between the patient's behavior with ward staff and with his family prompted a family evaluation. The patient's marriage, his second, was to a woman considerably his junior. He had been a self-sufficient and highly achieving young officer and, when World War II broke out, had achieved great distinction and rapid promotion because of his leadership and bravery in the Pacific theater. He rose to a high rank in the military and also distinguished himself in financial and political matters. He preferred to be occupied with work and had little interest or energy for his wife's emotional needs.

His wife had been raised to be terrified at the prospect of being independent. She very much wanted a strong man, and the early years of marriage had been satisfying and relatively happy for the both of them— she, the pretty young wife who served him well socially, and he, the powerful commander, who could make decisions competently and rapidly, never troubling her with anxiety about the course of their life. They had one son, currently in high school.

In family sessions, it was noticed that the patient's son was floridly disrespectful of him to the point of being contemptuous of and provocative. The boy seemed to regard his father as tyrannical, bullheaded, and imperious, rather than as seriously compromised in intellectual functioning and at the brink of humiliation when his deficits were exposed. The patient's wife did nothing to mollify the situation and, in fact, passively sided with her son. In the face of this coalition, the patient became more stubborn, autocratic, emotionally removed, and almost belligerent. As had happened previously, his wife brought matters of business to the patient for solution, apparently without realization of his markedly diminished cognitive capacities. Although the patient could carry on a conversation and even read the newspapers with comprehension, he could not function at the level of abstract reasoning necessary to conduct the family business. His sullenness and cantankerousness looked, and indeed was treated, as though it were a kind of characterologic crustiness rather than a response to the exposure of his deficits.

As these misestimations were pointed out to the patient's wife, she became irate with the staff. She contacted the hospital administration and high-ranking military officers who were friends of her husband. (This method of coping was in keeping, again, with her turning to a strong man to deal with her difficulties, rather than to take them on herself.) Fortunately, the person contacted made direct inquiries to the treatment team rather than the hospital and, apprising himself of the situation, made himself available for a family session. He convinced the patient's wife to continue in treatment.

Only then, and with a great amount of support, could the patient's wife deal with the panic and depression of being thrown back for the first time in her life on her own capacities and adapt to the realities posed by her husband's deficits. The patient's angry outbursts ceased concurrently with the wife's relying on her own resources and not challenging him beyond his capacities.

The psychotherapeutic possibilities for the patient with OBS hinge, therefore, on the capacities of the family and of the therapist to alter situations in which shame has been generated but not acknowledged in the familial process.

EMOTIONAL REACTIVITY OF THERAPISTS

Professionals, in the presence of manifest tumult and overreactivity or unmanageable tension in the family of the OBS patient, should be alert to the processes involved in the *escalation of conflict* that arises from organic deficit. An understanding of these processes is crucial for the adoption of a family-systems perspective that will enable the therapist to maximize every opportunity to emancipate the family from rigidified responses to the patient's catastrophic reactions and to acknowledge rather than bypass episodes of shame. That acknowledgment paves the way for whatever working through and genuine adaptive change in the family system the specific circumstances reasonably allow.

When the involved professional misestimates this state of escalated family tension, there is a high risk of seeing the therapeutic situation as more hopeless than it is. Such misestimation on the part of the therapist springs from inner sources that should be understood and mastered if the therapist is to function effectively. Premature closure may come from despair or guilt in reaction to the OBS patient's plight, from unresolved conflicts regarding aging and declining parents (if the patient is elderly), or from any unresolved conflict in the grip of which the therapist overestimates the patient's burdensomeness, overlooks his or her shame, or adopts the family's inflexible role assignments. A catalogue of specific countertransferential reactions is beyond the scope of the present discussion. Countertransference responses are likely to be overlooked in the treatment of OBS patients because they usually do not force themselves into awareness as obvious overprotectiveness or attack. The most serious countertransference in the treatment of OBS patients and their families appears as a sense of futility and, hence, premature closure in assessing the amenability of the particular case to change.

The therapist's ability to recognize countertransferential futility and premature closure is frequently of decisive importance. In the sway of such reactions, the therapist risks collusion with the combined effects of the patient's defenses against catastrophic reactions and the family's pathological rigidity of role assignments, thereby exerting a self-fulfilling, pessimistic force on the clinical situation. Such countertransference, then, constitutes a further unconscious collusion that works against therapeutic progress.

The therapist who is able to move beyond the initial countertransferential reactions can better assist the family as a whole to deal with the sources of conflict escalation, that is, the patient's catastrophic reactions and the family's rigid role assignments. It is with these psychopathological phenomena, which result in the escalation of traumatic effect of the original deficit, that the family psychotherapy of the OBS patient is concerned.

14

Posttraumatic Nightmares and the Family
(with Judith E. Karger)

THE PROBLEM

On the surface, there does not seem to be a connection between trauma and its sequelae, including nightmares, and the family of the patient who has experienced trauma. Such traumata as combat, rape, car accidents, or other skirmishes with near annihilation are usually viewed apart from the family process. Posttraumatic nightmares are usually taken to be "replays" of traumatic events that left the individual close to annihilation, overwhelmed, and helpless.

Where, if at all, does the family system enter? Much of the family therapy and family theory literature has been dominated by those who emphasize the family system and minimize, or even devalue, either the significance of dreams or that of extrafamilial pathogenic "events," including trauma on patients' dysfunction. Most investigators of nightmares ignore the issue of family (Hersen, 1971; Van der Kolk et al., 1984). Even Hartmann (1984), an investigator very attuned to psychotherapeutic and psychoanalytic possibilities in treatment, asserted that familial background was of no real significance for nightmare sufferers. We were able to locate only one report (Lidz, 1946) pointing to family dysfunction as almost ubiquitous in acute posttraumatic (combat) nightmare sufferers.

Here we draw attention to the complex and intimate relationship between chronic posttraumatic nightmares and the family system of the nightmare sufferer. Our sample was taken from serial admissions to an inpatient psychiatric unit over a six-month period. Most, but not all, of our

223

posttraumatic nightmare sufferers were admitted many years after the occurrence of the trauma represented in the nightmare. Our findings cannot be generalized either to nightmare sufferers in general or even to posttraumatic nightmare sufferers who do not have psychiatric disorders of sufficient severity to warrant admission to a psychiatric hospital.

SETTING AND CLINICAL CONTEXT

Again, our clinical setting is the Family Treatment Program at the Brentwood Division, West Los Angeles Veteran's Administration Medical Center. In a sustained clinical effort to deal with problems of adult patients who in childhood had suffered sexual and physical abuse, we found that many of these survivors of abuse were combat veterans and that a disproportionately high percentage suffered chronic nightmares. Furthermore, it was difficult and painful for these men to keep a focus either on the experience of abuse in their families of origin or on the dysfunction in their current familial situation. It seemed less distressing for them to discuss the battlefield than the family. Their discourse tended to avoid family turbulence and to gravitate toward the focus on the battlefield. At night they had dreams of the same battlefield trauma that they discussed in treatment. This clinical constellation—patients with massive adult trauma and unsolicited complaints of nightmares, massive sustained trauma in family of origin, gross problems in current familial functioning, and major difficulties keeping the treatment focus on the families—suggested to us that a major defensive function was deflecting attention away from decades of familial dysfunction and onto the trauma in waking life as well as in dreams. This clinical picture prompted us to think that the many layers of familial dysfunction were much less separate from the nightmare experience than the literature on nightmares reflects or that the patients themselves were experiencing.

A SYSTEMATIC INVESTIGATION

For a six-month period, every newly admitted patient was questioned about nightmares. Those who suffered nightmares were asked to cooperate in the study, which involved filling out a questionnaire concerning nightmares and participating in a taped interview of 30 to 60 minutes, recapitulating and expanding on data from the questionnaire. This chapter is devoted only to that portion of the entire group of nightmare sufferers who identified their nightmares as relating to specific traumatic situations that had actually occurred.

The questionnaire was designed so that many questions were open ended, ambiguous, and repetitious enough to allow the patient's personal line of thinking to emerge. The questionnaire dealt with the emotional and bodily experience of nightmares and the meanings attached to them by the patient; and with the history of nightmare disturbance and whether or not it had arisen concurrently with a psychiatric disturbance or changed over time. Patients were asked for details of their current familial functioning; about their family of origin; and, finally, about their late-adolescent and young-adult functioning, immediately prior to and including military service.

By posttraumatic nightmares, we refer to those in which the patients themselves identified the scene of the nightmare as belonging to a specific traumatic situation that had actually occurred. We adhered to this criterion even if further scrutiny revealed that the dream scene did not seem to coincide with the situation that the patient had designated as traumatic.

In the tape-recorded interview, the patient was asked to elaborate on questionnaire responses. This interview was not entirely for research purposes. We felt free to discuss clinical or historical material known to us through participation in the treatment process and used this material to tie some of the questionnaire data into a meaningful whole. The interlocking of our systematic and clinical endeavors became more pronounced as we discovered that patients were not only willing to talk about nightmare experiences, but wanted to talk repeatedly or have the taped material available for their psychotherapy sessions. In the six months of the study, not one patient refused to be part of the project, nor did anyone request that the tapes or questionnaires be destroyed (when they agreed to participate, patients were told that they had this right).

In a six-month period, 41 patients were admitted who had nightmares. One left the hospital against advice before we could interview him. All the others cooperated and consented to the taped interviews. The effect of the interviews went far beyond our initial goal of learning more about nightmares. Patients got in touch with aspects of infantile trauma and current familial dysfunction that they had previously been unable to acknowledge, much less to integrate. When we returned from discussion of family to the dream text, it became clear that these nightmares, even those very close in time (12 days) to the trauma represented in them, were seldom simple, unmodified replays of the traumatic event.

What unfolded for both us and the patients was a view of the dreamer as having more complete psychical continuity than had ever before been experienced. Many elements of familial dysfunction, unmanageable states of mind, early fears, wishes for punishment, outlets for rage, rationalizations for terror, punishment for current familial abusiveness—all these found representation on the "stage" of the traumatic dream scene. Although we were convinced that the designated traumatic event (usually, but not always, battlefield trauma) was itself truly devastating, the reenactments of those scenes in the nightmare were more than simple replays.

They were true dreams, not intrusive nighttime memories, and the staging of the nightmare scenario served also to screen familial trauma. Such traumata included the patient's helpless fear at witnessing parental violence; suicidal wishes after abusing his own children; the terror that seemed to result from the patient's hate or even physical attack on the same-sex parent. In addition, the nightmare scenario provided a concrete setting for expression of basically paranoid states of mind and intense, fearful self-absorption.

We attained an understanding of the patients as psychically continuous persons that aided us in integrating our entire treatment effort. The patients, often at the cost of great pain, were able to use the investigatory experience somewhat as one uses a well-analyzed dream, that is, to reestablish a sense of their psychic continuity (Freud, 1900). This enhanced sense of integration proved clinically useful in allowing us to keep the focus on the family, that is, on the sequelae of early familial trauma, and on overwhelming current familial dysfunction, in cases in which emotional cutoff from family of origin and massive dysfunction or alienation from current family were prevalent.

A CONTINUUM OF FAMILIAL STRESSES

Of the 40 patients who participated in the study, 15 (37.5%) suffered from posttraumatic nightmares. We counted as posttraumatic any nightmare *identified by the patient* as being *about* traumatic experiences that they could specifically identify. We did not include familial trauma unless the patient identified the trauma as replayed in the dream. Only one patient, a woman, identified forced sexual contact with her stepfather in adolescence as a persistent source of nightmares. Of the 15 posttraumatic cases, 11 (73.3%) identified battlefield trauma; 1 (6.7%) sexual attack by her stepfather; 1 (6.7%) a recent assault; and 1 (6.7%) a recent experience of having a companion shot to death while in his presence.

Diagnostically, two of our patients (13.3%) were schizophrenic, one bipolar (6.7%), and the remaining 12 (80%) mixtures of characterological and depressive disorders.

In the vast majority of our patients suffering from posttraumatic nightmares, we found a continuum of familial stress points related to lifelong familial dysfunction. At each of these stress points, the dysfunction constituted a separate and enduring trauma with devastating sequelae. This global familial dysfunction often gained expression in the nightmares. We divided this continuum of stress points, somewhat arbitrarily, into six phases.

1. Early familial dysfunction was found in almost every patient with posttraumatic nightmares (13 of 15 [86.6%]). Gross familial dysfunction

identified by the patient included violence, alcoholism, sexual abuse, splits in the family. In most cases (10 of 15 [66.6%]) there was overt and conscious hatred of the same-sex parent. In addition to hatred, there was contempt felt for that parent and evidences of an identification with this parent that gave rise to a crippling sense of shame and a struggle against that identification (Greenson, 1954).

2. There was evidence in many of these patients of adolescent turbulence (5 of 6 [83.3%] of those questioned). This was an area in our investigation of which we had not been cognizant at the beginning of the study, so our data are less complete than they are for the rest of the life history. Often, patients with postcombat trauma had felt in adolescence that their lives were going nowhere, that they were stuck in difficult familial or vocational situations. They were frequently filled with rage. Most, but not all, of the patients volunteered not only for military service, but specifically for combat (10 of 11, or 90.9%), many with the conscious and explicit wish to kill or to be killed. They were frequently cut off or alienated from their families of origin.

3. Narcissistic wounding coexisting with battlefield trauma was often present (all six questioned). Other investigators (Hartmann, 1984; Lidz, 1946) have noted that posttraumatic combat sufferers tend to be young and often have had coexisting trauma or narcissistic wounding, such as seeing close buddies killed in combat or receiving rejection letters from girlfriends. Our data confirmed the young age, a high prevalence of buddies being killed, and receipt of "Dear John" letters. Emerging psychosis was clearcut or likely in several posttraumatic combat veterans.

4. The traumatic event itself seemed to be the patients' preferred focus, not just in the dream but in the patients' waking thoughts as well. The patients inclined strongly to talk about the damage done them on the battlefield and not the familial traumas or other dysfunctional areas in their lives. Patients tended to focus on the traumatic events with the presumption that they had been seriously damaged by the traumatic events, but the same patients often had great difficulty specifying how sequelae of these traumata showed up in current family life. The traumatic event then served as a focus for externalization, as well as for expression of a state of mind with a dominant affect, often rageful, paranoid, guilty, or self-exculpating. The patient's discourse, shifting from responsibility for current dysfunctioning onto the trauma, closely mirrored the dream-staging that placed the scene of the patient's upset as though that person were a passive sufferer of trauma rather than an active part of chaos within the family system.

5. Current familial functioning revealed that virtually every case (14 of 15 [93.3%]) was cut off from or was grossly dysfunctional in family of procreation immediately prior to admission. These data are hard to assess

since our sample was limited to newly admitted psychiatric patients, who may be presumed to have been currently dysfunctional.

6. We also noticed, in some patients' attitudes toward the staff, evidence of a split self-representation, identity diffusion (Kernberg, 1984). For example, a patient would present a view of self as damaged, entitled to compensation, deserving of justice, ruined, or chronically suicidal as a result of trauma; but, shortly thereafter, the same patient would become enraged or evasive if the focus was placed on difficulties that were presumably a result of these traumata in which they were dysfunctional. That is, they wished to dwell on the source to which they attributed their psychic damage but were flooded with fear, shame, or despair when we encouraged them to scrutinize their current familial dysfunction. Dysfunction in the patient's relationship to the hospital staff frequently prompted our investigation of similar dysfunction in current family relationships.

These familial stress points added up in the majority of our nightmare sufferers to a profile of global lifelong familial dysfunction. While not every patient in our sample was impaired at every stage, the majority were grossly dysfunctional in almost every one of these areas.

There is more than a correlation between the occurrence of nightmares and the presence of familial dysfunction. Our data point to the need to explore the role of predisposing familial factors in the overall and lasting impact of a traumatic situation and the role of such factors in offsetting integrative and reparative mechanisms that might have carried the trauma sufferer at least part way toward self healing.

We present some illustrative cases to point to areas of familial dysfunction that find actual expression in the nightmares themselves, considered as true dreams, not simply as replays of traumatic events.

Even though the patients at first identified their nightmares as simple repeats of traumatic situations, detailed attention to the dream text and to the trauma actually revealed a far more complex relationship. The dream text and the patient's report of the actual traumatic experience differed significantly in most cases. In virtually every case, a full understanding of the discrepancy between dream text and described trauma could be attained only by understanding the full spectrum of past familial dysfunction that the patient had suffered and the specific manifestations of current dysfunction in familial interactions.

Many of the nightmares could be understood as the patient's attempt to rework issues from many points along a lifelong continuum of family difficulties.

CASE EXAMPLES

Example 1. A 38-year-old man, depressed and suicidal, was admitted for his first psychiatric hospitalization, after an affair with a coworker was discovered, endangering both his marriage and his job. His wife of 16 years threatened to leave. His three children sided with the wife. His boss, a friend who had previously been a combat buddy in Vietnam, had been so horrified that he told the patient that he doubted the job would be available after his discharge from the hospital. In addition, his best friend had recently committed suicide.

The patient was the second child born to alcoholic parents. His sister was five years older. His mother was chronically suicidal. The parents' marriage had ended in divorce when he was 12, and he was coerced to testify against his father—the parent to whom he felt closest— because of worry that his mother might abandon him or deteriorate into uncontrolled drinking or suicide. His father died when he was 16. After his father's death, he felt responsible for protecting his mother. Toward the end of high school, he felt trapped and enlisted in the military service with the conscious, albeit guilt-ridden intent of getting away from his mother. He volunteered not only for military service but also for combat. When he was 19, he was called home from Vietnam because of his mother's desperate state. She committed suicide while he was home on leave. He returned to combat, sustained a permanent leg injury and married the nurse who had taken care of him. They were now married for 16 years, had sons, age 13 and 9, and a daughter age 12.

The patient felt that before the affair was discovered, his life had been going well, with job security and a thriving family. His friend had committed suicide after many years of suicidal thoughts and attempts. He had called the patient, desperately asking for help on the night of his suicide, but the patient had refused to see him.

The patient complained of nightmares, which, despite various combinations of psychoactive medication, continued to disturb his sleep every night. He attributed the nightmares to his wartime experiences entirely, despite the fact that he had had no nightmares in the 18 years since he saw combat, until the affair was discovered.

A recent nightmare:

I am walking through the jungle with my dog and I come across a fellow soldier, a friend, who has been hung up on a tree by his wrists and decapitated, with his head being put inside his cut-open stomach, with his penis cut off and put in his mouth. I returned to my patrol unit to inform them but they are all gone and I am alone in the burnt-out village.

The patient added as an afterthought: "This is a true experience with the exception that when I went back to my patrol they were there, and we advanced to the village together."

Another recent nightmare:

This starts out in Vietnam in a village. A plane takes me back to the United States. I went to see my father dying of cancer. My father is lying in bed. There are bottles of blood by his bed. My son is giving his blood to my dad. He's all shriveled up and dying. My father's already dead.

The patient's first thoughts about the second nightmare were: "My son is afraid of me. He keeps thinking I'm going to hurt him or something. He thinks I'm going to die."

This patient at first considered his nightmares to be exclusively about his wartime experiences. Only later could he come to see scenes of his family of origin and his current interpersonal situation as being dealt with in the first nightmare: After the discovery of the dead and mutilated comrade, he returned to find his patrol missing. The terror and aloneness after the death of the man related clearly to his feelings of fear for himself and of responsibility for his mother after his father's death—the same feelings that had prompted his enlistment in the military. The dead comrade also represented the friend who had recently committed suicide—a man whom he saw as all-too like himself—and, of course, his dead mother. The dream work located him back on the battlefield and in conflict situations in which anger came, without the struggles that were only with males. The dream thus pointed to, but also concealed, the rageful dependency on women that had characterized his past relationship with his mother and his current relationships with his wife, his lover, and his female therapist.

In the second nightmare, the patient's horror at the younger man dying in the act of giving blood to the already dead older man represented one layer of his feelings of having been bled and depleted by his father, a poor male model whom he resented bitterly, but also his own harmful effect on his own sons. To his surprise and horror, in his current marital situation his own children sided with their mother against him, just as he had against his own father. As in the first nightmare, the anxiety about death was displaced from himself and his mother onto his son and his father. It is because of father, not mother, that he is called home from Vietnam.

In both dreams, the hostile and anxious dependency on women was displaced into an all-male scenario. The nightmares, however terrifying, kept him away from the painful feeling of being trapped and enraged in dependent relationships with women in which he feared that his own psychic survival and theirs would be endangered if he left.

Only after lengthy, painful family treatment and individual psychotherapy could he begin to relate the nightmares to his familial predicaments, past and present.

Example 2.   A 48-year-old man, admitted depressed and suicidal after a long history of failed close relationships and vocational failures, reported the following nightmare:

> . . . one about Vietnam, I shot a guy off a house. He was on patrol. We got ambushed. When he fell, I felt terrible. He kept blinking his eyes. He could not breathe. I shot him, not because I hated him, but because he was suffering. It was my brother that I shot. First it was a Vietnamese, and then when I looked, it was my brother Roosevelt. I prefer the defusing bomb nightmare over the other one [referring to another nightmare].

Despite the fact that extensive neurological evaluation had failed to disclose a cognitive deficit, this man had persisted in attributing his lifelong difficulties in relationships to a head injury sustained in Vietnam. His early upbringing was replete with abandonment and abuses. There was psychosis, violence, public disgrace. His mother was pregnant with him while married to a man other than his father. Both father and mother rejected him as well. His father was violent toward his mother and him. In addition, his mother was intermittently psychotic, had numerous unconcealed affairs, and beat the patient constantly.

In adult life his difficulties were marked. His wife had left him several years previously because of his abusiveness and coldness. The patient, despite being intelligent and reflective, was loathe to attribute his difficulties to anything other than his wartime head injury (although there was little demonstrable residue). The nightmare, however, disturbed him not just because it reawakened his war experiences, but because it pointed so unmistakably to difficulties in his family of origin and to the state of mind that these early experiences had in common with his battlefield experiences.

In another case, very recent trauma had already become mingled with early familial issues.

Example 3[1].   A 32-year-old man was admitted 12 days after the murder of a friend who was sitting next to him in a car. The patient gave a somewhat evasive account of his connection with the deceased. He referred to him alternatively as "my partner" and "my friend" and described in a confusing way his efforts to locate this man in the weeks preceding the murder. His "partner" had lived well but apparently was not regularly employed. The patient had recently been discharged from an alcohol

---

[1]This case is a condensed version of a case previously published in the *British Journal of Psychotherapy* (Lansky, 1990. Reprinted with permission).

rehabilitation program and was without funds or a place to stay. It seemed to the interviewers not unlikely that he was a drug dealer.

The patient's account of the events was as follows: He and his friend were in a car parked near a liquor store when a car pulled up. He heard three or four shots. His friend, killed instantly, slumped toward the patient, who opened the door and fled. The patient described what appeared to be a fugue state. He awoke in a psychiatric hospital, where he stayed a few days. Shortly after his discharge, he was readmitted to another hospital.

He said his nightmares were exact repetitions of the killing. These nightmares had occurred every night since the shooting 12 days previously. He gave two versions. In the first, he was in his friend's car. A woman came *up with a gun and called him by his first name* (a very unusual one) and shot his friend.

In the second version, he was in the friend's car. There were three or four shots. The friend slumped over. The patient got out of the car and ran (the actual event). He *stumbled*. He ran and fell. It was dark. He ran off a cliff or onto a body of water. The fear of falling woke him.

He had had nightmares since early adolescence, when his baby half-brother died. When the baby was in his terminal illness, the baby's father, running to phone the doctor, *stumbled*. The infant was dead by the time the doctor arrived. The patient recalled his conscious resentment of the new child, who was the only child of his mother's and stepfather's union. He felt that his half-brother had supplanted him. He recalled self-defeating behaviors aimed at getting attention, especially from his mother. He felt that his parents were angry at him. The interviewer noted that the woman in the dream called him by his (quite unusual) first name when she shot his friend. The patient realized that only his mother calls him by that name. The interviewer noted that in both the recent traumatic situation and in the earliest nightmares he was with a more favored male who had died, and there was a recollection of someone running away. The patient then had reminiscences of his family: his mother was unfair; she blamed him for everything. He recalled having harbored conscious rage at her since he was four. He had resented his half-brother's birth. He lived in fear that he would be blamed for those angry feelings.

The nightmare, then, commingled the traumatic situation, the death of his prosperous accomplice, with the earlier death of his more favored half-brother. The latter's death occurred very near to the time his nightmares began. The dream work, by substituting the mother for the unknown recent assailants, brought his fear into the more predictable family situation. It was his mother's wrath over the feelings about his half-brother's death that was to be dealt with rather than the more uncontrollable and incomprehensible assassination of his accomplice.

DISCUSSION

The apparent lack of connection between posttraumatic nightmares and the family system seems the greater because of the lack of overlap in the emphasis, expertise, and methodology of those professionals who treat persons suffering residual effects of trauma, persons willing or wanting to use dreams in their psychotherapeutic work, and persons identifying the family system, past or present, as intimately concerned with their present difficulties in functioning. Indeed, investigators of trauma and nightmares often do not investigate either dreams as such or the family system of the person suffering from nightmares. Those who work with dreams usually do so in the context of long-term therapy (rather than crisis) and individual (rather than family) therapy. They place a decided emphasis on working within an intrapsychic framework, which tends to minimize the need to study external impingement specifically. Those using family-systems approaches tend, of course, to focus on the family system in ways that minimize or ignore dreams or trauma as central features of psychic life or factors that affect peoples' intimate attachments.

"Posttraumatic nightmare" suggests that *the trauma*—an encounter with near-annihilation in the face of which the victim was overwhelmed and helpless—is not only a necessary, but a *sufficient*, condition to account for the presence of nightmares. Indeed, in much of the literature, nightmares following traumas are described more like intrusive memories than true dreams, the latter being woven by dream work, containing manifest and latent levels of meaning, involving imaginings of tension reduction (fulfilled wishes) and usually understood on the levels of both manifest and latent meaning, operations of protection that reveal intrapsychic conflict and how it is handled and, above all, as restoring a sense of continuity to psychic life when they are properly understood.

Posttraumatic nightmares are often not seen as true dreams for two reasons; first, if it is assumed that the nightmare is an exact replay of the scene of the trauma, then there is no latent content and hence no dream work that connects latent dream thoughts into the manifest dream. Second, since the generation of anxiety is, in fact, a defining feature of nightmares, then the nightmare itself poses fundamental difficulties for the theory of dreams, which represent struggles in an affect-dampening and tension-reducing way.

In the posttraumatic nightmares of our sample of hospitalized psychiatric inpatients, the discrepancy between the text of the nightmare and the patient's account of the traumatic situation points clearly to evidence of both dream work and latent content. We have seen a clear relationship between this latent content and a continuum of lifelong familial stresses, the residue of which continue to be experienced as ongoing trauma. Furthermore, the affect arising from the dream can often be better understood when thought of as deriving both from the manifest content and the familial issues expressed in the latent content.

Conclusions based on this patient sample, an unselected inpatient population, cannot be generalized to include all posttraumatic nightmare sufferers or even all psychiatric inpatients who suffer from posttraumatic nightmares. It remains for fully systematic and controlled research to clarify many of the issues raised: the extent to which posttraumatic nightmares reflect both familial trauma and the effects of events designated by the dreamer as traumatic; comparison of familial factors in patients who have nightmares that follow different types of trauma (combat, rape, auto accident, concentration camp survival); comparison of posttraumatic nightmare sufferers with those who experienced similar traumatic stress without the same sequelae. Nonetheless, our sample was large enough and the results striking enough to allow us to conclude that a strong relationship exists between posttraumatic nightmares and lifelong familial trauma and dysfunction.

— V —

Treatment Difficulties

For all that has gone wrong may still be healed,
And surely the worst is passed!
Why are you silent?
Speak to me, father! Don't turn away from me!
Will you not answer me at all? Will you
Send me away without a word?
    Not even
Tell me why you are enraged against me?

Sophocles
Oedipus at Colonus (1269-1274)

15

Conflict and Resistance in the Treatment of Psychiatrically Hospitalized Fathers
(with Ellen A. Simenstad)

THE PROBLEM

Recognition of the treatment needs of severely disturbed fathers has scarcely begun. Clinically, one finds surprising difficulties in focusing on treatment issues dealing with the paternal role of the hospitalized father. In this chapter, we attempt to understand the failure of these patients and the staff treating them to form a working collaboration that addresses central issues in paternity.

We have already noted patients' difficulties facing their problems as fathers (Chapters 2, 7, 8; Lansky and Simenstad, 1986). In the Family Treatment Program we attempted to survey the plight of the psychiatrically hospitalized father preparatory to specific hospital-based treatment strategies. We were able to locate and describe some of the massive deficits found in these men and the difficulties they had in acknowledging that the paternal role was an area for treatment focus.

We hope to pave the way for efforts aimed at treating these men as fathers. Our investigations pointed to overwhelming and generalized residual psychopathology in virtually all these men even at times of presumed remission. We saw few areas in which simple intervention would be of help and little symptomatic remission that took place as a result of sustained therapeutic focus on the problem or therapeutic zeal. These clinical predicaments that were peppered with enormous difficulties, despair, and futility arising from dysfunction in the paternal role. We hope, in this chapter, to heighten sensitivity to the fact that treatment staff are not merely observers of the damage in these chronically impaired men; they are also vulnerable to a reactive futility that may reflect a collusion with the patient, buttressing rather than lessening the patient's own resistance to treatment. By *collusion*, we refer to the unconscious dovetailing of defensive processes of persons in families or in other close collaborative relationships. This dovetailing serves, without a conscious agreement to do so, to regulate either expression or avoidance of certain situations of central dynamic significance to all parties concerned. These latent expressive and protective operations are concealed within the manifest, consciously agreed-upon activities of the collaboration. Collusion is a ubiquitous phenomenon in close relationships and should be considered pathological only if the latent issues are split off and disowned by all parties and exert a force that sabotages (rather than complementing) the manifest basis of the collaboration. Such collusions, if they are discovered, are usually dynamically overdetermined. They amplify deviation and carry the risk of premature dismissal of the clinical situation as hopeless. These collusions, then, pose serious hazards to the entire treatment enterprise and demand the fullest psychoanalytical understanding, preparatory to speculating about possibilities for such patient-staff collusive resistances.

SETTING AND METHODOLOGY

Our interest in the problem of fathers hospitalized on our family-oriented inpatient unit stemmed from many sources. The Family Treatment Program itself provided an especially favorable environment for scrutiny of the problem. In the years of the Family Treatment Program's existence, we have come to appreciate the role in the family system of collusion that creates resistance to therapy in the hospital and to change in life outside the hospital. As we have learn to recognize collusive-defensive patterns and to appreciate impulsive symptoms in the family context as the patient's attempt to control distance to intimates—that is, to prevent them from getting too close or too far away—we have come to appreciate the role of narcissistic vulnerability and other characterologic limitations posed by propensities of the personality to disorganize—and of resultant shame and defenses against it.

Our psychoanalytic orientation and our commitment to family involvement provided a synergistic impetus to the study of fathers. Understanding of the key role of father in facilitating the separation process in individual development (Abelin, 1971, 1975, 1980), and of the multiple roles of father in development, not just as oedipal overlord but in a more complex way, has acquired enough recent momentum (Ross, 1979; Cath, Gurwitt, and Ross, 1982) to be considered a substantial body of knowledge available to enter the mainstream of psychoanalytic development thinking. Family therapy has progressed far beyond the presumption that the mother-child dyad is itself pathogenic and has focused on the entire family system in the genesis and momentum of psychopathology (Bowen, 1966). Our increasing sophistication in viewing psychopathology in crisis and our growing understanding of family systems have drawn our attention to absence as well as presence as significant phenomena. Furthermore, we came to see the absence of family in hospitalized patients as a sign with a great deal of prognostic and therapeutic significance (Lansky et al., 1983) in patients who proved to be demanding, rageful, and intimidating with the ward staff in the hospital.

Consolidation of these areas of emphasis enabled us to remain curious about the familial, and especially paternal, role in psychiatrically hospitalized men who made every effort to minimize or even deny their contact with family during their hospitalizations. We uncovered a distinct reluctance to acknowledge problems in the paternal role. The more we tried to understand this role, the more the overdetermined nature of this reluctance to focus became clear. Patients tended either to externalize their problems or to overfocus on specific symptoms or turbulent circumstances. Staff felt reluctant to press these men to face their problems with their children or felt themselves overcome with the patients' depression when such an effort was made. A similar absence was noted in the clinical literature; a computerized literature search revealed no literature on the psychiatrically hospitalized father.

This absence of focus in patients, therapy teams, and the literature aroused our suspicions that we were dealing with yet another species of defensively overdetermined absence. Such a possibility alerted us to question resistances to straightforward collaboration in therapeutic tasks that might be contained within the patient-staff matrix in ways that might recapitulate similarly futile stalemates in the patient's current family situation or in the one in which he grew up.

Our appreciation of these resistances to treatment collaboration aimed at difficulties in the paternal role led to systematic efforts to explore the problem. Three different avenues were employed. *Clinical scrutiny* of psychiatrically hospitalized fathers included circumstances of admission, ward behavior, hospital course, and follow-up. The clinical treatment setting was the matrix in which other activities occurred. These included taped and transcribed *intergenerational interviews with* each father admitted to the service for an entire year (N = 75, only four fathers refused). These three-generational interviews covered patients' recollections of their fathers as father; of their mothers as supporter of father's paternal role or in undercutting it; of their wives' support or lack of it for the patients' own paternal function; and finally of their own view of themselves as father to their children. Questions were deliberately open ended and general. Finally, *groups for hospitalized fathers* (continuing into the posthospital period) were begun. The groups were established primarily to explore the problems of these men and only secondarily for the purpose of treatment.

OVERVIEW OF FINDINGS

Clinical observation (Lansky, 1984a) highlighted the patients' tendencies to represent their problems as illness (manic depressive, schizophrenic, alcoholic), as resulting solely from turmoil in circumstances (usually familial), or as isolated symptoms (drinking, voices). Even with staff emphasis on fathering, patients continued to resist focusing on obvious and even overwhelming crises in the paternal role. Observations in a series of groups for fathers highlighted some of these difficulties (Lansky and Simenstad, 1986). Most of our recently admitted fathers welcomed the offer of such a group, but few attended and even fewer stayed. The groups tried to be supportive of members and to use common predicaments of the fathers as a basis for supportive group identifications. Groups homogeneous for predicament have been highly successful in our program for other difficulties, yet therapists and patients alike experienced these groups as overwhelming and depressing. The patients that profited from these groups were those few fathers who had years before been cast out of their families but who had contact with their children thrust upon them recently by circumstances; that is, they had no choice but to deal with their children. In these few, a history of extreme narcissistic vulnerability with an inability to relate and constant preoccupation emerged as memories of their experiences of father when their children were young. More visible pathology (drunkenness, abusiveness, marital strife, desertion, violence) covered up these basic narcissistic defects, which were often compounded by frightening identifications with similar vulnerabilities and methods of handling them in the father's own father (Chapter 8 above).

Intergenerational interviews showed ubiquitous and overwhelming damage in the fathers' capacities to fulfill the paternal role. These defects were experienced by the patients in ways that were characteristic of their particular diagnoses. For example, borderline patients consistently blamed their own fathers for abusing them and leaving them poorly prepared for the paternal role. They carried a conscious sense of being damaged and cheated; they felt rage and a sense of entitlement, along with an unconscious sense of being doomed to identify with their own fathers. They evidenced split views of women. Their mothers at first were idealized and seen as victims of their fathers, but later as much more like their wives—divisive and tending to pair off with children in coalitions, excluding and even provoking their husbands. The borderline fathers all felt that they were inadequate fathers themselves; even those who blamed their wives for divisiveness painfully acknowledged their inadequacies. Those borderline patients who identified themselves as uncontrollable alcoholics always viewed their lack of control with a conscious and pervasive sense of shame. These men, to avoid more shame and to protect their families from themselves, often voluntarily absented themselves from their children.

Schizophrenics seldom blamed either parents or spouses for their difficulties but tended to have an all-too-painful awareness of the devastating limitations imposed by their condition. Manic-depressive fathers usually combined the characteristics of borderlines and schizophrenics. Their histories showed severe familial trauma. None of our manic-depressive patients reported a satisfactory relationship with his own father. Almost everyone made a conscious effort to be a better father than his own father had been. Several of these men gave themselves good marks in achieving these goals, despite their pathology, and expressed gratitude toward their wives. Our small sample of manic-depressive fathers had a greater proportion of men for whom treatment had a positive effect on their role as fathers than did any other diagnostic group. Manic-depressive fathers' talk was full of manicky affect and denial of emotional reality. Written transcripts of what they said, in contradistinction to the impression left by their personal discourse, revealed an overwhelming sensitivity to psychic reality and great pain at their developmental deficits and current limitations. These transcripts seemed strikingly incongruent with their affect while they spoke to the interviewers.

Our investigative activity illuminated the global underlying psychopathology in these men and the complex mechanisms that hospitalized fathers of any diagnosis used to compensate for narcissistic vulnerability and lack of authority and status in the family. These mechanisms frequently consisted of impulsive actions such as violence, threats of violence, communication of suicidal intent, self-harm, binge drinking, and generally intimidating lifestyles that served for a time to control intimates in the family. These men were not bound to their intimates by the providing, protecting, and leadership function from which a father's authority is usually felt to be derived.

The matter of therapy remained problematic. Simple scrutiny of the problem and investigatory zeal were not enough. Most of our sample came and left with massive deficiencies and real as well as fantasied failures in the paternal role. This lack of initial therapeutic success was not due to denial that problems existed; there was usually a mutual sense of enormity of the therapeutic tasks ahead of us. Yet many of the staff in our programs shared the patients' sense of depression and futility. Our staff is highly sophisticated and thoroughly seasoned in dealing with the same population from which our sample of fathers was drawn. Their response might have been due quite simply to the realization by both themselves and the patients that the limitations imposed by the patients' global incapacities were indeed overwhelming, chronic, and utterly devastating. That is to say, the pervasive sense of futility might, purely and simply, have arisen from a genuine perception of bedrock pathology.

Alternatively, however, there is the possibility that their futility arose from a view of reality that appeared more grim than seemed to be the case to our staff during our efforts in studying these men. The issue is a crucial one, for if the futility felt by all concerned is seen to have arisen simply from appreciation of the clinical facts, then the situation can be presumed to be virtually hopeless. On the other hand, if the futility itself is a result of dynamically overdetermined collusion between patient and staff, the situation might be more hopeful. We feel, then, that an exploration of potential treatment obstacles, amplified by covert collusion in the patient-staff relationship—a situation homologous to transference resistance and transference-countertransference stalemates in the strictly analytic situation—should be considered. Accordingly, we view our findings with some sensitivity to the fact that unrecognized and unresolved conflict and resistance involving patients and staff may have contributed to the pessimism resulting from our focus on fatherhood and may have undermined specific treatment efforts aimed at the problems uncovered.

CONFLICT AND RESISTANCE

We turn to a consideration of the sources of conflict and resistance in patients and staff on a hospital ward. We do so neither to explain retrospectively our treatment difficulties nor to imply that the outcome might have been better with improved awareness and handling of transference and countertransference. These fathers were severely impaired, and our staff were seasoned in the recognition and management of countertransference phenomena. Our intent here is to provide a perspective on the range of obstacles to treatment that we saw over the years and to foster a sensitivity to the dynamics of such obstacles as they occur in a hospital setting.

Resistances and conflicts arise from many sources. Some obstacles are not resistances in the true dynamic sense but stem from the disorder and realistic reactions to it. Such disorders as manic-depressive illness, schizophrenia, alcoholism, or crisis manifestations of borderline pathology are overwhelming when they are in exacerbation. Patients and staff alike may be overwhelmed either by the florid, acute disorder or by the restitutive or controlling maneuvers of reactions against shame that pose symptomatic crises. Sophisticated staff may get beyond these more manifest features of the clinical situation to a view of the chronic deficits faced by the psychiatrically impaired father. Many of our staff, accustomed to working with this population, saw treatment difficulties as arising from the florid illness, compensatory defense mechanisms, and bedrock residual pathology. Realistically based as any of these difficulties are, they may feed into deeper transferential issues and dovetail with countertransference problems. Whatever the patient's basic disorder is, there is some endopsychic perception of a basic defectiveness that resonates with the hospitalized father's overall personality organization and becomes accentuated in the caretaking situation in the hospital. All these hospitalized men responded to a basic neediness by seeking out caretakers for help and for soothing. This regressively reactivated neediness, related as it was to the inability to function and the designation as defective, produced a great deal of shame and envy and intensified defenses against these feelings. Any tendency on the part of patients toward dyadic fixation—that is, the formation of close dyads perpetrating the omnipotent illusion of self-sufficiency—became amplified in the hospital. Such patient-staff dyads often antagonized other staff factions, thus resulting in staff splitting. Accordingly, pressure on factions of staff members to form protective dyads increased the risk either of staff splitting if patients were gratified or of rageful acting out by the patient if they were not. Many of these patients tended to split off their need for caretaking and to disavow their dependent relationship to the hospital. Such splitting was, in part, a defense against the shame and envy that would accompany the patients' awareness of their dependent state and in part a manifestation of envy in his hostile-dependent relationship to the hospital staff.

The patients who did not provoke staff splits were often the most impaired. Those patients who saw their global limitations and their neediness clearly and who made no apparent attempt to take their hurt out on the staff did so at a fearful price. The fathers who were most collaborative carried with them very little sense of self-worth and were almost constantly suicidal.

In virtually all the fathers, the feelings of authority, worth, and status that come from having a truly generative, giving relationship with spouse and child were absent entirely. These men were powerless, helpless, and defeated. Many overt symptoms could be understood as attempts to deal with these feelings of powerlessness and helplessness. Intimidation, violence, and suicidal episodes gave these men a certain control by intimidation. Several fathers in our sample have been admitted in crisis involving suicide threats, wrist-slashing, or threats of violence. Such crises had served to control wives or children by inducing in them of a sense of panic or a feeling of responsibility for the chaos in the patient, who at the same time seemed alarmingly indifferent to the consequences of such acts. Self-soothing from drugs or alcohol frequently added to the intimidating scenario and provided transient chemical relief from their tensions and lowered their awareness of their humiliated plight. Such maneuvers tended either to repel spouses immediately or to draw spouses into pathologic involvement with the disorder. Consequently, the very sort of pathologic distance regulation that compensates for the basic weakness, disorganization, and helplessness these men felt made it unlikely that they could have continued relationships with caring and supportive spouses who had no emotional stake in the continuance of these pathological patterns.

We began to appreciate these same forces as countertransference pressures. Staff may, and usually do, react to pathologic distance regulation on the part of patients who control supportive persons by indirectly communicated violence, self-harm, or loss of control. As we acquired experience, we realized that the same phenomena were occurring in the current family, or ex-family, on the ward (with the patient as perpetrator) and, often, in the family of origin (with the patient as victim). Nonetheless, the impact of pathologic distance regulation, or pathologic projective identification is such as to create the constant danger of keeping the staff anxious, off balance, and feeling that matters of crisis are more their worry than the patient's. Risk is high that the staff will become overinvolved, split, and exhausted and that they ultimately will reject the patient.

A problem clearly noticed in our staff was their infection by the patient's affects of futility, depression, hopelessness, and shame. The similarities between these staff responses and those of patients who, in the intergenerational interviews, portrayed parents as unable to tolerate their darker and more negative feelings made us suspect that staff may to some extent have been drawn into a dramatization that replayed the patient's archaic conflicts with parents (and later spouses) who could not tolerate him and ultimately left him emotionally abandoned. What portion of the futility was realistically based, and what portion induced by the caretaking staff's participation in these archaic collusions, cannot be ascertained a priori.

Some conflicts can be presumed to have been posed by the structure of the ward and the gender of the patients involved. The ward is directed by a male physician. The patients are predominantly male, and the staff of psychotherapists, predominantly female and professional. Such an organization presents what the patients may see as a highly sexualized organization to the treatment scene. A dominant male is seen to be in charge of competent, caretaking females administering to a very damaged male population. Even outside the limits of professional propriety, very few of the men would consider themselves appropriate suitors for the staff women, yet all had intimate psychotherapeutic relationships with the women. The effect of this sort of intimacy on both sexes remains, of course, speculative but cannot be presumed to be negligible. For many of the men, control by strong women who made them feel ashamed and dominated was a significant theme both in family of origin and family of procreation; such themes dominated the intergenerational interviews of many of the men. An intimate relationship with women who served solely as caretakers could only be expected to reactivate conflict in these areas. Unresolved neurotic conflicts in the staff—fears of sexuality, excessive voyeurism, sadism, or outright castrativeness—of course, only intensify these issues (Ferholt and Gurwitt, 1982).

Related to, but not identical with, these issues are both staff's and patients' fantasies about the paternal role. Unresolved oedipal awe (usually sustained by fear of father or a remote relationship with their own fathers) may leave as a residue an idealized view of what a father should be: always masterful, powerful, sexual, providing, protecting, guiding, and fearless. The shame, guilt, and anxiety of patients with these residual fantasies superimposed as goals on the treatment situation may dovetail with staff fantasies to make the psychiatrically hospitalized father's plight seem unduly hopeless and efforts to treat him unduly futile.

Any of these potential difficulties may exist as low-key, commonplace fantasies or may reflect neurotic conflicts of severe magnitude (that is, countertransference in the classical sense). Any may combine with the patient's difficulties with the resultant collusive agreement that the psychiatrically hospitalized fathers' affects, deficits, and problems cannot be usefully acknowledged and addressed and in some cases are minimized. Such collusions then intensify very real problems to the point that these seem unmanageable or hopeless.

TREATMENT IMPLICATIONS

We cannot estimate the extent to which psychoanalytically enlightened approaches to conflict and resistance in the therapy of these men can alter the treatment situation. Such uncertainty is part of any approach that is truly psychoanalytic. That is to say, a major part of the problem with unconscious resistance is that significant dynamically determined resistances usually preclude either the analyst's or the patient's accurately assessing the magnitude of "reality" problems and developing appropriate strategies to cope with them. Many covert sources of resistance are apparent behind the overwhelming affect and failure of focus in these cases. These abound in the clinical field and undermine the collaborative therapeutic alliance around issues in paternity. These sources of resistance must be understood if straightforward treatment strategies are to succeed.

Realization of this by the hospital staff is vital if they are to take leadership in clarifying the self-sabotage that is always the cost of collusive resistance.

The task of therapy, then, can best proceed if conflict and resistance are considered dynamically and are seen either as forces that flare up and obstruct the treatment or as forces that clarify and abate in the context of treatment by a staff that is willing to acknowledge and accept chaos and shortcomings both in themselves and in the fathers who are in treatment and still remain confident and caring. All too often, this is the kind of caretaking that the psychiatrically hospitalized father has never received and that he cannot provide for his offspring. The hospital staff's ability to scrutinize and tolerate awareness of conflict and dynamically determine resistance to collaboration not only paves the way for straightforward strategy and problem solving, it also provides the potential for a *process of caretaking*. Such a process has the potential to interrupt cycles in collusion and self-defeat and provides the basis for modifying and correcting internalizations that may be the foundations for useful treatment approaches.

References

Abelin E. (1971), The role of the father in the separation-individual process. In: *Separation-Individuation*, ed. S.B. McDevitt & C.F. Settlage. New York: International Universities Press, pp. 229-253.

_____ (1975), Some further observations and comments on the earliest role of the father. *Internat. J. Psycho-Anal.*, 56:293-302.

_____ (1980), Triangulation: The role of the father and the origins of core gender identity during the rapprochement subphase. In: *Rapprochement*, ed. R. Lax, S. Bach & J. Barland. New York: Aronson, pp. 151-170.

American Psychiatric Association (1980), *Diagnostic and Statistical Manual of Mental Disorders* (DSM III). Washington, DC: American Psychiatric Association.

Atkins, R. (1982), Discovering daddy: The mother's role. In: *Father and Child*, ed. S. Cath, A. Gurwitt & J.M. Ross. Boston: Little Brown, pp. 139-149.

_____ (1984), Transitive vitalization and its impact on father-representation. *Contemp. Psychoanal.*, 20:663-676.

Berke, J. (1987), Shame and envy. In: *The Many Faces of Shame*, ed. D. Nathanson. New York: Guilford, pp. 318-334.

Bion, W.R. (1954), Notes on the theory of schizophrenia. *Internat. J. Psycho-Anal.*, 35:113-118.

_____ (1957), Differentiation of psychotic from the non-psychotic personalities. *Internat. J. Psycho-Anal.*, 38:266-275.

_____ (1977), *Seven Servants*. New York: Aronson.

Blath, R., McClure, V. & Metzel, R. (1973), Familial factors in Suicide. *Dis. Nerv. Syst.*, 34:90-93.

Blos, P. (1974), The genealogy of the ego ideal. *The Psychoanalytic Study of the Child*, 29:43-88. New Haven, CT: Yale University Press.

Bosormenyi-Nogy, I. & Spark, G. (1973), *Invisible Loyalties*. New York: Harper & Row.

Bowen, M. (1966), The use of family theory in clinical practice. *Compar. Psychiat.*, 7:345-374.

Brenner, C. (1959), The masochistic character: genesis and treatment. *J. Amer. Psychoanal. Assn.*, 7:197-225.

247

Breuer, J. & Freud, S. (1893-1895), *Studies On Hysteria. Standard Edition*, 2. London: Hogarth Press, 1955.

Brown, G.W., Birley, J.L.T. & Wing, J.K. (1972), Influence of family life on the course of schizophrenic disorders: A replication. *Brit. J. Psychiat.*, 121:241-258.

Bursten, B. (1972), *The Manipulator*. New Haven, CT: Yale University Press.

Cath, S., Gurwitt, A. & Gunsberg, L. (1989), *Fathers and Their Families*. Hillsdale, NJ: The Analytic Press.

_____ Gurwitt, A. & Ross, J.M. (ed.) (1982), *Father and Child*. Boston: Little Brown.

Darwin, C. (1872), *The Expression of the Emotions in Man and Animals*. Chicago: University of Chicago Press, 1965.

Delgado-Escueta, A.V. (1981), The nature of aggression during epileptic seizures. *New Eng. J. Med.*, 305: 711-716.

Dicks, H. (1963), Object relations theory and marital studies. *Brit. J. Med. Psychol.*, 36:125-129.

_____ (1967), *Marital Tensions*. New York: Basic Books.

Ekstein, R. (1965), A general treatment philosophy concerning acting out. In: *Acting Out*, ed. L. Abt & S. Weisman. New York: Grune & Stratton, pp. 162–172.

Erickson, S. (1970), *Language and Being*. New Haven, CT: Yale University Press.

Erikson, E. (1950), *Childhood and Society*. New York: Norton.

Fairbairn, W. (1952), *Psychoanalytic Studies of the Personality*. London: Tavistock.

Ferholt, J. & Gurwitt, A. (1982), Involving fathers in treatment. In *Father and Child*, ed. S. Cath, A. Gurwitt & J.W. Ross. Boston: Little Brown, pp. 557-568.

Fitch, E.V. & Papantonio, A. (1983), Men who batter: Some pertinent characteristics. *J. Nerv. Ment. Dis.*, 171:190-192.

Freud, A. (1936), *The Ego and the Mechanisms of Defense*. New York: International Universities Press, 1946.

_____ (1968), Acting out. *Internat. J. Psycho-Anal.*, 49:165-170.

Freud, S. (1894), The neuro-psychoses of defense. *Standard Edition*, 3:45-61. London: Hogarth Press, 1962.

_____ (1899), Screen memories. *Standard Edition*, 13:303-322. London: Hogarth Press, 1962.

_____ (1900), *The Interpretation of Dreams. Standard Edition*, 4 & 5. London: Hogarth Press, 1953.

_____ (1905a), *Three Essays on the Theory of Sexuality. Standard Edition*, 7:125-243. London: Hogarth Press, 1953.

_____ (1905b), *Fragment of an Analysis of a Case of Hysteria. Standard Edition*, 7:7-122. London: Hogarth Press, 1953.

_____ (1914), Remembering, repeating, and working through. *Standard Edition*, 12:145-156. London: Hogarth Press, 1958.

_____ (1917), Instincts and their vicissitudes. *Standard Edition*, 14:109-140. London: Hogarth Press, 1957.

_____ (1920), *Beyond the Pleasure Principle. Standard Edition*, 18:7-64. London: Hogarth Press, 1955.

_____ (1921), *Group Psychology and the Analysis of the Ego. Standard Edition*, 18:67-143. London: Hogarth Press, 1955.

_____ (1923), *The Ego and the Id. Standard Edition*, 19:3-66. London: Hogarth Press, 1961.

_____ (1937), Constructions in psycho-analysis. *Standard Edition*, 23:255-269. London: Hogarth Press, 1964.

Frosch, J. (1970), Psychoanalytic considerations of the psychotic character. *J. Amer. Psychoanal. Assn.*, 18:24-50.

Giovacchini, P. (1973), Character disorder: with special reference to the borderline state. *Internat. J. Psycho-Anal.*, 2:7-36.

Glover, E. (1931), The therapeutic effect of inexact interpretation. *Internat. J. Psycho-Anal.*, 12:397-411.

Goffman, E. (1959), *The Presentation of Self in Everyday Life*. Garden City, NY: Doubleday Anchor.

Goldstein, K. (1940), *Human Nature in the Light of Psychopathology*. New York: Schocken.

Greenacre, P. (1963), Problems of acting out in the transference relationship. In: *The Capacity for Emotional Growth, Vol. 2*, pp. 695-712.

Greenson, R. (1954), The struggle against identification. *J. Amer. Psychoanal. Assn.*, 2:200-217.

Hartmann, E. (1984), *The Nightmare*. New York: Basic Books.

Hartmann, H. & Lowenstein, R. (1962), Notes on the superego. *The Psychoanalytic Study of the Child*, 17:42-81. New York: International Universities Press.

Hegel, G.W.F. (1807), *The Phenomenology of Spirit*, transl. A.V. Miller. Oxford: Oxford University Press, 1977.

Heilman, K.M., Watson, R.T. & Bowers, D. (1983), Affective disorders associated with hemispheric disease. In: *Neuropsychology of Human Emotion*, ed. K.M. Heilman & P. Satz. New York: Guilford.

Hersen, M. (1971), Personality characteristics of nightmare sufferers. *J. Nerv. Ment. Dis.*, 153:27-31.

Himmelhoch, J. (1988), What destroys our restraints against suicide? *J. Clin. Psychiat.*, 49(suppl):46-52.

Howells, J.G. (1970), Fallacies in child care, II: That fathering is unimportant. *Acta Paedopsychiat.*, 36:47-55.

Jacobson, E. (1964), *The Self and the Object World*. New York: International Universities Press.

Johnson, A. & Szurek, S. (1952), The genesis of antisocial acting out in children and adults. *Psychoanal. Quart.*, 21:323-343.

Katz, J. (1988), *Seductions of Crime*. New York: Basic Books.

Kernberg, O. (1967), Borderline personality organization. *J. Amer. Psychoanal. Assn.*, 15:641-685.

_____ (1975), *Borderline Conditions and Pathological Narcissism*. New York: Aronson.

_____ (1976), *Object Relations Theory and Clinical Psychoanalysis*. New York: Aronson.

_____ (1984), *Severe Personality Disorders*. New Haven, CT: Yale University Press.

Klein, M. (1934), On the early development of conscience in the child. In: *Contributions to Psychoanalysis*. London: Hogarth Press, 1968.

_____ (1946), Notes on some schizoid mechanisms. In: *Developments in Psychoanalysis*, ed. M. Klein, P. Heimann & S. Isaacs. London: Hogarth Press, 1952.

Knight, R. (1940), Projection, introjection and identification. *Psychoanal. Quart.*, 9:334-341.

Kohut, H. (1971), *The Analysis of the Self*. New York: International Universities Press.

_____ (1972), Thoughts on narcissism and narcissistic rage. *The Psychoanalytic Study of the Child*, 27:360-400. New Haven, CT: Yale University Press.

_____ (1977), *The Restoration of the Self*. New York: International Universities Press.

Lamb, M.E., (ed.) (1976), *The Role of the Father in Child Development*. New York: Wiley.

_____ (ed.) (1981), *The Role of the Father in Child Development*, 2nd ed. New York: Wiley.

_____ (ed.) (1986), *The Father's Role*. New York: Wiley.

Langs, R. (1976), *The Bipersonal Field*. New York: Aronson.

Lansky, M.R. (1977a), Establishing a family-oriented inpatient unit. *J. Operational Psychiat.*, 8:66-74.

_____ (1977b), Schizophrenic delusional phenomena. *Compr. Psychiat.*, 18:157-168.

_____ (1980), On the idea of a termination phase for family therapy in the hospital. In:

Group and Family Therapy 1980, ed. L. Wolberg & M. Aronson. New York: Brunner/ Mazel, pp. 323-334.

_____ (1981a), Treatment of the narcissistically vulnerable couple. In: *Family Therapy and Major Psychopathology*, ed. M. Lansky. New York: Grune & Stratton.

_____ (1981b), Family Psychotherapy in the hospital. In: *Family Therapy and Major Psychopathology*, ed. M.R. Lansky. New York: Grune & Stratton, pp. 395-414.

_____ (1982a). The role of the family in the evaluation of suicidality. *Internat. J. Fam. Psychiat.*, 3:105-118.

_____ (1982b). Masks of the narcissistically vulnerable marriage. *Internat. J. Fam. Psychiat.*, 3:439-449.

_____ (1984a), The family treatment program of the Brentwood VA Medical Center. *Fam. Systems Med*, 2:102-106.

_____ (1984b), Family psychotherapy of the patient with chronic organic brain syndrome. *Psychiat. Annals*, 14:121-129.

_____ (1990), The screening function of posttraumatic nightmares. *Brit. J. Psychother.*, 7:384-400.

_____ (1991), Shame and fragmentation in the marital dyad. *Contemp. Fam. Ther.*, 13:17-31.

_____ Bley, C.R., Simenstad, E., West, K. & McVey, G.G. (1983), The absent family of the hospitalized borderline patient. *Internat. J. Fam Psychiat.*, 4:155-171.

_____ & Simenstad, E.A. (1986), Narcissistic vulnerability in a group for psychiatrically hospitalized fathers. *Group*, 10:149-159.

Laplanche, J. & Pontalis, J.B. (1973), *The Language of Psychoanalysis*, trans. D. Nicholson-Smith. New York: Norton.

Lax, R. (1975), Some comments on the narcissistic aspects of self-righteousness: Defensive and structural aspects. *Internat. J. Psycho-Anal.*, 56:283-292.

Lewis, H.R. (1971), *Shame and Guilt in Neurosis*. New York: International Universities Press.

_____ (ed.) (1987), *The Role of Shame in Symptom Formation*. Hillsdale, NJ: The Analytic Press.

Lidz, T. (1946), Nightmares and the combat neurosis. *Psychiat.*, 9:37-49.

Loewald, H. (1951), Ego and reality. *Internat. J. Psycho-Anal.*, 32:10-18.

_____ (1971), Some considerations on repetition and the repetition compulsion. In: *Papers on Psychoanalysis*. New Haven, CT: Yale University Press, 1979.

Mahler, M. (1971), A study of the separation-individuation process and its possible application to borderline phenomena in the psychoanalytic situation. *The Psychoanalytic Study of the Child*, 26:403-424. New Haven, CT: Yale University Press.

Malin, A. & Grotstein, J. (1966), Projective identification in the therapeutic process. *Internat. J. Psycho-Anal.*, 47:26-31.

Maltsberger, J.T. & Buie, D. (1974), Countertransference hate in the treatment of suicidal patients. *Arch. Gen. Psychiat.*, 30:625-633.

Morrison, A. (1989), *Shame: The Underside of Narcissism*. Hillsdale, NJ: The Analytic Press.

Murray, J. (1964), Narcissism and the ego ideal. *J. Amer. Psychoanal. Assn.*, 12:477-511.

Odier, C. (1956), *Anxiety and Magic Thinking*. New York: International Universities Press.

Ogden, T. (1979), On projective identification. *Internat. J. Psycho-Anal.*, 60:357-373.

Pasnau, R., Fawzy, F. & Lansky, M. (1981), Organic brain syndrome and the family. In: *Family Therapy and Major Psychopathology*, ed. M.R. Lansky. New York: Grune & Stratton.

Retzinger, S. (1987), Resentment and laughter: Video studies of the shame-rage spiral. In: *The Role of Shame in Symptom Formation*, ed.H.B. Lewis. Hillsdale, NJ: Lawrence Erlbaum Associates, pp. 151-181.

_____ (1991), *Violent Emotions*. Newbury Pk., CA: Sage.

Rosenbaum, M. & Richman, J. (1970), Suicide: The role of hostility and death wishes from the family and significant others. *Amer. J. Psychiat.*, 126:128-131.

Rosenfeld, H. (1964), *Psychotic States*. New York: International Universities Press.

Rosenthal, R., Rinzler, C., Wallsh, R. et al. (1972), Wrist cutting syndrome: The meaning of a gesture. *Amer. J. Psychiat.*, 128:1363-68.

Ross, J.M. (1979), Fathering: A review of some psychoanalytic considerations. *Internat. J. Psycho-Anal.*, 60:317-328.

Sandler, J., Dare, C. & Holder, A. (1973), Acting out. In: *The Patient and the Analyst*. New York: International Universities Press.

Sartre, J.P. (1945), *Being and Nothingness*, trans. N. Barnes. New York: Washington Square Press, 1966.

Scheff, T. (1987), The shame-rage spiral: A case study of an interminable quarrel. In: *The Role of Shame in Symptom Formation*, ed. H.B. Lewis. Hillsdale, NJ: Lawrence Erlbaum Associates, pp. 109-149.

_____ (1990), *Microsociology*. Chicago: University of Chicago Press.

Schneider, C. (1977), *Shame, Exposure, and Privacy*. Boston: Beacon Press.

Schwartz, D. (1979), The suicidal character. *Psychiat. Quart.*, 5:64-70.

Searles, H. (1965), *Collected Papers on Schizophrenia and Related Subjects*. New York: International Universities Press.

Slipp, S. (1984), *Object Relations: A Dynamic Bridge Between Individual and Family Treatment*. New York: Aronson.

Sperling, M. (1974), A contribution to the psychoanalytic treatment of character disorders with acting out behavior. *The Annual of Psychoanalysis*, 2:249-267. New York: International Universities Press.

Stanton, S.H. & Schwartz, M. (1954), *The Mental Hospital*. New York: Basic Books.

Stolorow, R. (1985), Toward a pure psychology of inner conflict. In: *Progress in Self Psychology, Vol. 1*, ed. A. Goldberg. New York: Guilford, pp. 193-201.

Straker, M. (1958), Clinical observations on suicide. *Canad. Med. Assn. J.*, 19:473.

Tabachnick, N. (1961), Interpersonal relations in suicide attempts. *Arch. Gen. Psychiat.*, 4:16-21.

Tyson, P. (1982), The role of the father in gender identity: Urethral erotism and phallic narcissism. In: *Father and Child*, ed. S. Cath, A. Gurwitt & J.M. Ross. Boston: Little Brown, pp. 175-188.

Van der Kolk, B. et al. (1984), Nightmares and trauma: A comparison of nightmares after combat with lifelong nightmares. *Amer. J. Psychiat.*, 141:187.

Vogel, E. & Bell, N. (1967), The emotionally disturbed child as the family scapegoat. In: *The Psychosocial Interior of the Family*, ed. G. Handel. Chicago: Aldine.

Winnicott, D.W. (1956), The antisocial tendency. In: *Through Paediatrics to Psychoanalysis*. New York: Basic Books, 1975, pp. 306-315.

_____ (1963). Psychotherapy of character disorders. In: *The Maturational Processes and the Facilitating Environment*. New York: International Universities Press, 1965, pp. 203-216.

Wurmser, L. (1981), *The Mask of Shame*. Baltimore. MD: Johns Hopkins University Press.

Wynne, L. (1961), The study of intrafamilial alignments and splits in family therapy. In: *Exploring the Base for Family Therapy*, ed. N. Ackerman. New York: Family Service Assn. of America, pp. 95-115.

Yogman, M.W. (1982), Observations on the father-infant relationship. In: *Father and Child*, ed. S. Cath, A. Gurwitt & J.M. Ross. Boston: Little Brown, pp. 101-122.

Index

Blath, R., 197
Bley, C.R., x, 7, 89, 115, 127, 134, 156, 178, 239
Blos, P., 113
Borderline *See sub* Personality
Bosormenyi-Nagy, I., 100
Bowen, M., 8, 70, 116, 124, 239
Bowers, D., 212
Brenner, C., 58
Breuer, J., 38, 61, 95
Buie, D., 205, 208
Bursten, B., 89, 106

C

Castration complex, 4
Cath, S., x, 3, 4, 7, 131, 238
Character *See* Personality; *sub* Defense
Collusion
  familial, 8, 32, 42–43, 46–48, 80, 88, 154, 211
  marital, 9, 60–73, 81, 85, 114, 124–125, 158, 175, 177, 189–190
  transference-countertransference, 75–76, 96, 111–112, 147, 154, 238, 242, 245–246
Compromise formation, 72, 76
Conflict
  escalation of, ix, 6–7, 10–11, 141–142, 191, 210, 221
  intrapsychic, 10, 12, 30, 52, 244–245
Containment model, 134, 146, 148, 206–208
Conversion, 28
Countertransference, 48–49, 62, 75, 109–111, 133, 142, 208, 222, 242, 244, 245
  See also sub Collusion

D

Dare, C., 95
Darwin, C., 38
Defense
  character, 105–106
  intrafamilial, ix, 6, 31–32, 37, 210–211
  primitive, 52–53, 61, 62, 65, 75
  transpersonal, 8, 32, 38, 43, 62, 78–80, 83, 88–89, 124
  unconscious, 102
  See also Collusion; *sub* Shame

Delgado-Escueta, A.V., 146
Dependency, 151, 153–154, 157
  hostile, 11, 56, 60, 64–67, 199–200, 207, 243
Depression
  affect of, 6, 37, 39, 42, 83, 98, 114, 127, 157, 159, 198, 212, 244
  clinical, 8, 60–61, 68, 71–72, 78, 81, 133, 141, 142, 226,
  parental, 19, 100, 111
  See also Bipolar illness
Devaluation, 18, 42–44, 53, 89
Dicks, H., 63, 116
Disengagement, 89, 195
Disorganization *See sub* Personality
Displacement, 31, 32, 82–83
Dissociation, 6, 52, 72, 76, 97, 100, 115, 125, 149, 160, 196–196
Distance, regulation of, 12,
  borderlines and, 42–46, 49–50, 115
  impulsive action and, 94, 97–98, 104, 108–110
  marriage and, 63, 67, 70
  pathologic, 43, 46, 77–92, 141, 144, 150, 156, 158–159, 176–177, 207, 244
  suicide and, 196–197
  violence and, 149, 152, 175, 189–190
  See also sub Therapy
Divorce, 53, 70, 98, 135, 207
Dreams, 32, 96, 226, 233
  See also Nightmares
Drive theory, 94

E

Ego
  development, 29
  function, 38, 39, 88–89, 111–112, 147, 199
  integrity 90–91
  See also sub Splitting
Ekstein, R., 85
Empathy
  analytic, 48, 109, 111–112, 145, 206
  need for, 9–11, 69, 111
Emptiness, sense of, 40–42, 44, 71, 73, 101, 104, 112, 114
Entitlement, sense of, 49, 65–66, 71–72, 122, 195, 240
Envy, 9, 11, 42, 59, 125, 134, 191, 199
Equilibrium, narcissistic, 137, 198–199